# STATUTORY SUPPLEMENT TO
# LABOR AND EMPLOYMENT LAW
## PROBLEMS, CASES AND MATERIALS IN THE LAW OF WORK

### Second Edition

By

**Robert J. Rabin**
*Professor*
*Syracuse University College of Law*

**Eileen Silverstein**
*Professor*
*University of Connecticut School of Law*

**George Schatzki**
*Professor*
*University of Connecticut School of Law*

for
**THE LABOR LAW GROUP**

**AMERICAN CASEBOOK SERIES®**

**WEST PUBLISHING CO.**
ST. PAUL, MINN., 1995

*TEXT IS PRINTED ON 10% POST
CONSUMER RECYCLED PAPER*

# Table of Contents

# STATUTORY SUPPLEMENT TO
# LABOR AND EMPLOYMENT LAW

## Second Edition

\*

# CONSTITUTION OF THE UNITED STATES OF AMERICA

**Article 1, Section 8.** [1] The Congress shall have Power To lay and collect Taxes, Duties, Imposts and Excises, to pay the Debts and provide for the common Defence and general Welfare of the United States; but all Duties, Imposts and Excises shall be uniform throughout the United States;

[2] To borrow money on the credit of the United States;

[3] To regulate Commerce with foreign Nations, and among the several States, and with the Indian Tribes; * * *

ARTICLES IN ADDITION TO, AND AMENDMENT OF, THE CONSTITUTION OF THE UNITED STATES OF AMERICA, PROPOSED BY CONGRESS, AND RATIFIED BY THE LEGISLATURES OF THE SEVERAL STATES PURSUANT TO THE FIFTH ARTICLE OF THE ORIGINAL CONSTITUTION.

## AMENDMENT I [1791]

Congress shall make no law respecting an establishment of religion, or prohibiting the free exercise thereof; or abridging the freedom of speech, or of the press; or the right of the people peaceably to assemble, and to petition the Government for a redress of grievances.

## AMENDMENT II [1791]

A well regulated Militia, being necessary to the security of a free State, the right of the people to keep and bear Arms, shall not be infringed.

## AMENDMENT III [1791]

No Soldier shall, in time of peace be quartered in any house, without the consent of the Owner, nor in time of war, but in a manner to be prescribed by law.

## AMENDMENT IV [1791]

The right of the people to be secure in their persons, houses, papers, and effects, against unreasonable searches and seizures, shall not be violated, and no Warrants shall issue, but upon probable cause, supported by Oath or affirmation, and particularly describing the place to be searched, and the persons or things to be seized.

## AMENDMENT V [1791]

No person shall be held to answer for a capital, or otherwise infamous crime, unless on a presentment or indictment of a Grand Jury, except in cases arising in the land or naval forces, or in the Militia, when in actual service in time of War or public danger; nor shall any person be subject for the same offence to be twice put in jeopardy of life or limb; nor shall be compelled in any criminal case to be a witness against himself, nor be deprived of life, liberty, or property, without due process of law; nor shall private property be taken for public use, without just compensation.

### AMENDMENT VI [1791]

In all criminal prosecutions, the accused shall enjoy the right to a speedy and public trial, by an impartial jury of the State and district wherein the crime shall have been committed, which district shall have been previously ascertained by law, and to be informed of the nature and cause of the accusation; to be confronted with the witnesses against him; to have compulsory process for obtaining witnesses in his favor, and to have the Assistance of Counsel for his defence.

### AMENDMENT VII [1791]

In Suits at common law, where the value in controversy shall exceed twenty dollars, the right of trial by jury shall be preserved, and no fact tried by jury, shall be otherwise re-examined in any Court of the United States, than according to the rules of the common law.

### AMENDMENT VIII [1791]

Excessive bail shall not be required, nor excessive fines imposed, nor cruel and unusual punishments inflicted.

### AMENDMENT IX [1791]

The enumeration in the Constitution, of certain rights, shall not be construed to deny or disparage others retained by the people.

### AMENDMENT X [1791]

The powers not delegated to the United States by the Constitution, nor prohibited by it to the States, are reserved to the States respectively, or to the people.

### AMENDMENT XI [1798]

The Judicial power of the United States shall not be construed to extend to any suit in law or equity, commenced or prosecuted against one of the United States by Citizens of another State, or by Citizens or Subjects of any Foreign State.

### AMENDMENT XII [1804] [OMITTED]
### AMENDMENT XIII [1865]

Section 1. Neither slavery nor involuntary servitude, except as a punishment for crime whereof the party shall have been duly convicted, shall exist within the United States, or any place subject to their jurisdiction.

Section 2. Congress shall have power to enforce this article by appropriate legislation.

### AMENDMENT **XIV** [1868]

Section 1. All persons born or naturalized in the United States, and subject to the jurisdiction thereof, are citizens of the United States and of the State wherein they reside. No State shall make or enforce any law which shall abridge the privileges or immunities of citizens of the United States; nor shall any State deprive any person of life, liberty, or property, without due process of law; nor deny to any person within its jurisdiction the equal protection of the laws. * * *

Section 5. The Congress shall have power to enforce, by appropriate legislation, the provisions of this article.

### AMENDMENT **XV** [1870]

Section 1. The right of citizens of the United States to vote shall not be denied or abridged by the United States or by any State on account of race, color, or previous condition of servitude.

Section 2. The Congress shall have power to enforce this article by appropriate legislation.

# FEDERAL LAWS RELATING TO CIVIL RIGHTS

## CIVIL RIGHTS ACT OF 1866
### (42 U.S.C. SEC. 1981)

#### Equal rights under the law

All persons within the jurisdiction of the United States shall have the same right in every State and Territory to make and enforce contracts, to sue, be parties, give evidence, and to the full and equal benefit of all laws and proceedings for the security of persons and property as is enjoyed by white citizens, and shall be subject to like punishment, pains, penalties, taxes, licenses, and exactions of every kind, and to no other.

## CIVIL RIGHTS ACT OF 1870
### (42 U.S.C. SEC. 1982)

#### Property rights of citizens

All citizens of the United States shall have the same right, in every State and Territory, as is enjoyed by white citizens thereof to inherit, purchase, lease, sell, hold, and convey real and personal property.

## CIVIL RIGHTS ACT OF 1871
### (42 U.S.C. SEC. 1983)

#### Civil action for deprivation of rights

Every person who, under color of any statute, ordinance, regulation, custom, or usage, of any State or Territory, subjects, or causes to be subjected, any citizen of the United States or other person within the jurisdiction thereof to the deprivation of any rights, privileges, or immunities secured by the Constitution and laws, shall be liable to the party injured in an action at law, suit in equity, or other proper proceeding for redress. * * *

# CIVIL RIGHTS ATTORNEY'S FEES AWARD OF 1976 (42 U.S.C. SEC. 1988)

## § 1988. Proceedings in vindication of civil rights; attorney's fees

The jurisdiction in civil and criminal matters conferred on the district courts by the provisions of this Title, and of Title "CIVIL RIGHTS," and of Title "CRIMES," for the protection of all persons in the United States in their civil rights, and for their vindication, shall be exercised and enforced in conformity with the laws of the United States, so far as such laws are suitable to carry the same into effect; but in all cases where they are not adapted to the object, or are deficient in the provisions necessary to furnish suitable remedies and punish offenses against law, the common law, as modified and changed by the constitution and statutes of the State wherein the court having jurisdiction of such civil or criminal cause is held, so far as the same is not inconsistent with the Constitution and laws of the United States, shall be extended to and govern the said courts in the trial and disposition of the cause, and, if it is of a criminal nature, in the infliction of punishment on the party found guilty. In any action or proceeding to enforce a provision of sections 1981, 1982, 1983, 1985, and 1986 of this title, title IX of Public Law 92–318 [20 U.S.C. 1681 et seq.], or title VI of the Civil Rights Act of 1964 [42 U.S.C. 2000d et seq.], the court, in its discretion, may allow the prevailing party, other than the United States, a reasonable attorney's fee as part of the costs.

---

# EQUAL PAY ACT OF 1963

## 29 U.S.C. Section 206(d)*

### DECLARATION OF PURPOSE

**Sec. 2.** (a) The Congress hereby finds that the existence in industries engaged in commerce or in the production of goods for commerce of wage differentials based on sex—

(1) depresses wages and living standards for employees necessary for their health and efficiency;

(2) prevents the maximum utilization of the available labor resources;

(3) tends to cause labor disputes, thereby burdening, affecting, and obstructing commerce;

(4) burdens commerce and the free flow of goods in commerce; and

---

* 29 U.S.C. § 206(d) is a 1963 amendment to the Fair Labor Standards Act, 29 U.S.C. §§ 201–19. The procedural, jurisdictional and penalty provisions of the FLSA, not reproduced here, apply in claims based on section 206(d).

(5) constitutes an unfair method of competition.

(b) It is hereby declared to be the policy of this Act, through exercise by Congress of its power to regulate commerce among the several States and with foreign nations, to correct the conditions above referred to in such industries.

**Sec. 3.** Section 6 of the Fair Labor Standards Act of 1938, as amended [29 U.S.C. § 206] is amended by adding thereto a new subsection (d) as follows:

"(d)(1) No employer having employees subject to any provisions of this section shall discriminate, within any establishment in which such employees are employed, between employees on the basis of sex by paying wages to employees in such establishment at a rate less than the rate at which he pays wages to employees of the opposite sex in such establishment for equal work on jobs the performance of which requires equal skill, effort, and responsibility, and which are performed under similar working conditions, except where such payment is made pursuant to (i) a seniority system; (ii) a merit system; (iii) a system which measures earnings by quantity or quality of production; or (iv) a differential based on any other factor other than sex: *Provided,* That an employer who is paying a wage rate differential in violation of this subsection shall not, in order to comply with the provisions of this subsection, reduce the wage rate of any employee.

"(2) No labor organization, or its agents, representing employees of an employer having employees subject to any provisions of this section shall cause or attempt to cause such an employer to discriminate against an employee in violation of paragraph (1) of this subsection.

"(3) For purposes of administration and enforcement, any amounts owing to any employee which have been withheld in violation of this subsection shall be deemed to be unpaid minimum wages or unpaid overtime compensation under this Act.

"(4) As used in this subsection, the term 'labor organization' means any organization of any kind, or any agency or employee representation committee or plan, in which employees participate and which exists for the purpose, in whole or in part, of dealing with employers concerning grievances, labor disputes, wages, rates of pay, hours of employment, or conditions of work."

**Sec. 4.** The amendments made by this Act shall take effect upon the expiration of one year from the date of its enactment: *Provided,* That in the case of employees covered by a bona fide collective bargaining agreement in effect at least thirty days prior to the date of enactment of this Act, entered into by a labor organization (as defined in section 6(d)(4) of the Fair Labor Standards Act of 1938, as amended), the amendments made by this Act shall take effect upon the termination of such collective bargaining agreement or upon the expiration of two years from the date of enactment of this Act, whichever shall first occur.

———

# TITLE VII OF THE CIVIL RIGHTS ACT OF 1964

42 U.S.C. Sec. 2000e to 2000e–17

With amendments made by the Civil Rights Act of 1991,
Pub. L. No. 102–166, 105 Stat. 1071 (1991)
(Shown in italics).

### Sec. 701 [§ 2000e]. Definitions

For the purposes of this subchapter—

(a) The term "person" includes one or more individuals, governments, governmental agencies, political subdivisions, labor unions, partnerships, associations, corporations, legal representatives, mutual companies, joint-stock companies, trusts, unincorporated organizations, trustees, trustees in cases under Title 11, or receivers.

(b) The term "employer" means a person engaged in an industry affecting commerce who has fifteen or more employees for each working day in each of twenty or more calendar weeks in the current or preceding calendar year, and any agent of such a person, but such term does not include (1) the United States, a corporation wholly owned by the Government of the United States, an Indian tribe, or any department or agency of the District of Columbia subject by statute to procedures of the competitive service (as defined in section 2102 of Title 5), or (2) a bona fide private membership club (other than a labor organization) which is exempt from taxation under section 501(c) of Title 26, except that during the first year after March 24, 1972, persons having fewer than twenty-five employees (and their agents) shall not be considered employers.

(c) The term "employment agency" means any person regularly undertaking with or without compensation to procure employees for an employer or to procure for employees opportunities to work for an employer and includes an agent of such a person.

(d) The term "labor organization" means a labor organization engaged in an industry affecting commerce, and any agent of such an organization, and includes any organization of any kind, any agency, or employee representation committee, group, association, or plan so engaged in which employees participate and which exists for the purpose, in whole or in part, of dealing with employers concerning grievances, labor disputes, wages, rates of pay, hours, or other terms or conditions of employment, and any conference, general committee, joint or system board, or joint council so engaged which is subordinate to a national or international labor organization.

(e) A labor organization shall be deemed to be engaged in an industry affecting commerce if (1) it maintains or operates a hiring hall or hiring office which procures employees for an employer or procures for employees opportunities to work for an employer, or (2) the number of its members (or, where it is a labor organization composed of other labor organizations or their representatives, if the aggregate number of the members of such other labor organization) is (A) twenty-five or more during the first year after March 24, 1972, or (B) fifteen or more thereafter, and such labor organization—

(1) is the certified representative of employees under the provisions of the National Labor Relations Act, as amended [29 U.S.C.A. § 151 et seq.], or the Railway Labor Act, as amended [45 U.S.C.A. § 151 et seq.];

(2) although not certified, is a national or international labor organization or a local labor organization recognized or acting as the representative of employees of an employer or employers engaged in an industry affecting commerce....

(f) The term "employee" means an individual employed by an employer, except that the term "employee" shall not include any person elected to public office in any State or political subdivision of any State by the qualified voters thereof, or any person chosen by such officer to be on such officer's personal staff, or an appointee on the policy making level or an immediate adviser with respect to the exercise of the constitutional or legal powers of the office. The exemption set forth in the preceding sentence shall not include employees subject to the civil service laws of a State government, governmental agency or political subdivision. *With respect to employment in a foreign country, such term includes an individual who is a citizen of the United States....*

(j) The term "religion" includes all aspects of religious observance and practice, as well as belief, unless an employer demonstrates that he is unable to reasonably accommodate to an employee's or prospective employee's religious observance or practice without undue hardship on the conduct of the employer's business.

(k) The terms "because of sex" or "on the basis of sex" include, but are not limited to, because of or on the basis of pregnancy, childbirth, or related medical conditions; and women affected by pregnancy, childbirth, or related medical conditions shall be treated the same for all employment-related purposes, including receipt of benefits under fringe benefit programs, as other persons not so affected but similar in their ability or inability to work, and nothing in section 2000e–2(h) of this title shall be interpreted to permit otherwise. This subsection shall not require an employer to pay for health insurance benefits for abortion, except where the life of the mother would be endangered if the fetus were carried to term, or except where medical complications have arisen from an abortion: Provided, That nothing herein shall preclude an employer from providing abortion benefits or otherwise affect bargaining agreements in regard to abortion.

*(l) The term "complaining party" means the Commission, the Attorney General, or a person who may bring an action or proceeding under this subchapter.*

*(m) The term "demonstrates" means meets the burdens of production and persuasion.*

*(n) The term "respondent" means an employer, employment agency, labor organization, joint labor-management committee controlling apprenticeship or other training or retraining program, including an on-the-job training program, or Federal entity subject to section 2000e–16 of this title.*

### Sec. 702    [§ 2000e–1].    Applicability to foreign and religious employment

(a) This subchapter shall not apply to an employer with respect to the employment of aliens outside any State, or to a religious corporation, association, educational institution, or society with respect to the employment of individuals of a particular religion to perform work connected with the carrying on by such corporation, association, educational institution, or society of its activities.

(b) *It shall not be unlawful under section 2000e–2 or 2000e–3 of this title for an employer (or a corporation controlled by an employer), labor organization, employment agency, or joint labor-management committee controlling apprenticeship or other training or retraining (including on-the-job training programs) to take any action otherwise prohibited by such section, with respect to an employee in a workplace in a foreign country if compliance with such section would cause such employer (or such corporation), such organization, such agency, or such committee to violate the law of the foreign country in which such workplace is located.*

*(c)(1) If an employer controls a corporation whose place of incorporation is a foreign country, any practice prohibited by section 2000e–2 or 2000e–3 of this title engaged in by such corporation shall be presumed to be engaged in by such employer.*

*(2) Sections 2000e–2 and 2000e–3 of this title shall not apply with respect to the foreign operations of an employer that is a foreign person not controlled by an American employer.*

*(3) For purposes of this subsection, the determination of whether an employer controls a corporation shall be based on—*

*(A) the interrelation of operations;*

*(B) the common management;*

*(C) the centralized control of labor relations; and*

*(D) the common ownership or financial control,*

*of the employer and the corporation.*

### Sec. 703    [§ 2000e–2].    Unlawful employment practices

(a) It shall be an unlawful employment practice for an employer—

(1) to fail or refuse to hire or to discharge any individual, or otherwise to discriminate against any individual with respect to his compensation, terms, conditions, or privileges of employment, because of such individual's race, color, religion, sex, or national origin; or

(2) to limit, segregate, or classify his employees or applicants for employment in any way which would deprive or tend to deprive any individual of employment opportunities or otherwise adversely affect his status as an employee, because of such individual's race, color, religion, sex, or national origin.

(b) It shall be an unlawful employment practice for an employment agency to fail or refuse to refer for employment, or otherwise to discriminate against, any individual because of his race, color, religion, sex, or national origin, or to classify or refer for employment any individual on the basis of his race, color, religion, sex, or national origin.

(c) It shall be an unlawful employment practice for a labor organization—

(1) to exclude or to expel from its membership, or otherwise to discriminate against, any individual because of his race, color, religion, sex, or national origin;

(2) to limit, segregate, or classify its membership or applicants for membership, or to classify or fail or refuse to refer for employment any individual, in any way which would deprive or tend to deprive any individual of employment opportunities, or would limit such employment opportunities or otherwise adversely affect his status as an employee or as an applicant for employment, because of such individual's race, color, religion, sex, or national origin; or

(3) to cause or attempt to cause an employer to discriminate against an individual in violation of this section.

(d) It shall be an unlawful employment practice for any employer, labor organization, or joint labor-management committee controlling apprenticeship or other training or retraining, including on-the-job training programs to discriminate against any individual because of his race, color, religion, sex, or national origin in admission to, or employment in, any program established to provide apprenticeship or other training.

(e) Notwithstanding any other provision of this subchapter, (1) it shall not be an unlawful employment practice for an employer to hire and employ employees, for an employment agency to classify, or refer for employment any individual, for a labor organization to classify its membership or to classify or refer for employment any individual, or for an employer, labor organization, or joint labor-management committee controlling apprenticeship or other training or retraining programs to admit or employ any individual in any such program, on the basis of his religion, sex, or national origin in those certain instances where religion, sex, or national origin is a bona fide occupational qualification reasonably necessary to the normal operation of that particular business or enterprise, and (2) it shall not be an unlawful employment practice for a school, college, university, or other educational institution or institution of learning to hire and employ employees of a particular religion if such school, college, university, or other educational institution or institution of learning is, in whole or in substantial part, owned, supported, controlled, or managed by a particular religion or by a particular religious corporation, association, or society, or if the curriculum of such school, college, university, or other educational institution or institution of learning is directed toward the propagation of a particular religion. . . .

(h) Notwithstanding any other provision of this subchapter, it shall not be an unlawful employment practice for an employer to apply different standards of compensation, or different terms, conditions, or privileges of employment pursuant to a bona fide seniority or merit system, or a system which measures earnings by quantity or quality of production or to employees who work in different locations, provided that such differences are not the result of an intention to discriminate because of race, color, religion, sex, or national origin, nor shall it be an unlawful employment practice for an employer to give and to act upon the results of any professionally developed ability test provided that such test, its administration or action upon the results is not designed, intended or used to discriminate because of race, color, religion, sex or national origin. It shall not be an unlawful employment practice under this subchapter for any employer to differentiate upon the basis of sex in determining the amount of the wages or compensation paid or to be paid to employees of such employer if such differentiation is authorized by the provisions of section 206(d) of Title 29 [the Equal Pay Act]. . . .

(j) Nothing contained in this subchapter shall be interpreted to require any employer, employment agency, labor organization, or joint labor-management committee subject to this subchapter to grant preferential treatment to any individual or to any group because of the race, color, religion, sex, or national origin of such individual or group on account of an imbalance which may exist with respect to the total number or percentage of persons of any race, color, religion, sex, or national origin employed by any employer, referred or classified for employment by any employment agency or labor organization, admitted to membership or classified by any labor organization, or admitted to, or employed in, any apprenticeship or other training program, in comparison with the total number or percentage of persons of such race, color, religion, sex, or national origin in any community, State, section, or other area, or in the available work force in any community, State, section, or other area.

(k)*(1)(A) An unlawful employment practice based on disparate impact is established under this subchapter only if—*

> *(i) a complaining party demonstrates that a respondent uses a particular employment practice that causes a disparate impact on the basis of race, color, religion, sex, or national origin and the respondent fails to demonstrate that the challenged practice is job related for the position in question and consistent with business necessity; or*

> *(ii) the complaining party makes the demonstration described in subparagraph (C) with respect to an alternative em-*

*ployment practice and the respondent refuses to adopt such alternative employment practice.*

*(B)(i) With respect to demonstrating that a particular employment practice causes a disparate impact as described in subparagraph (A)(i), the complaining party shall demonstrate that each particular challenged employment practice causes a disparate impact, except that if the complaining party can demonstrate to the court that the elements of a respondent's decisionmaking process are not capable of separation for analysis, the decisionmaking process may be analyzed as one employment practice.*

*(ii) If the respondent demonstrates that a specific employment practice does not cause the disparate impact, the respondent shall not be required to demonstrate that such practice is required by business necessity.*

*(C) The demonstration referred to by subparagraph (A)(ii) shall be in accordance with the law as it existed on June 4, 1989, with respect to the concept of "alternative employment practice".*

*(2) A demonstration that an employment practice is required by business necessity may not be used as a defense against a claim of intentional discrimination under this subchapter.*

*(3) Notwithstanding any other provision of this subchapter, a rule barring the employment of an individual who currently and knowingly uses or possesses a controlled substance, as defined in schedules I and II of section 102(6) of the Controlled Substances Act (21 U.S.C. § 802(6)), other than the use or possession of a drug taken under the supervision of a licensed health care professional, or any other use or possession authorized by the Controlled Substances Act [21 U.S.C.A. § 801 et seq.] or any other provision of Federal law, shall be considered an unlawful employment practice under this subchapter only if such rule is adopted or applied with an intent to discriminate because of race, color, religion, sex, or national origin.*

*(l) It shall be an unlawful employment practice for a respondent, in connection with the selection or referral of applicants or candidates for employment or promotion, to adjust the scores of, use different cutoff scores for, or otherwise alter the results of, employment related tests on the basis of race, color, religion, sex, or national origin.*

*(m) Except as otherwise provided in this subchapter, an unlawful employment practice is established when the complaining party demonstrates that race, color, religion, sex, or national origin was a motivating factor for any employment practice, even though other factors also motivated the practice.*

*(n)(1)(A) Notwithstanding any other provision of law, and except as provided in paragraph (2), an employment practice that implements and is within the scope of a litigated or consent judgment or order that resolves a claim of employment discrimination under the Constitution or*

*Federal civil rights laws may not be challenged under the circumstances described in subparagraph (B).*

*(B) A practice described in subparagraph (A) may not be challenged in a claim under the Constitution or Federal civil rights laws—*

*(i) by a person who, prior to the entry of the judgment or order described in subparagraph (A), had—*

*(I) actual notice of the proposed judgment or order sufficient to apprise such person that such judgment or order might adversely affect the interests and legal rights of such person and that an opportunity was available to present objections to such judgment or order by a future date certain; and*

*(II) a reasonable opportunity to present objections to such judgment or order; or*

*(ii) by a person whose interests were adequately represented by another person who had previously challenged the judgment or order on the same legal grounds and with a similar factual situation, unless there has been an intervening change in law or fact.*

*(2) Nothing in this subsection shall be construed to—*

*(A) alter the standards for intervention under rule 24 of the Federal Rules of Civil Procedure or apply to the rights of parties who have successfully intervened pursuant to such rule in the proceeding in which the parties intervened;*

*(B) apply to the rights of parties to the action in which a litigated or consent judgment or order was entered, or of members of a class represented or sought to be represented in such action, or of members of a group on whose behalf relief was sought in such action by the Federal Government;*

*(C) prevent challenges to a litigated or consent judgment or order on the ground that such judgment or order was obtained through collusion or fraud, or is transparently invalid or was entered by a court lacking subject matter jurisdiction; or*

*(D) authorize or permit the denial to any person of the due process of law required by the Constitution.*

*(3) Any action not precluded under this subsection that challenges an employment consent judgment or order described in paragraph (1) shall be brought in the court, and if possible before the judge, that entered such judgment or order. Nothing in this subsection shall preclude a transfer of such action pursuant to section 1404 of Title 28.*

## Sec. 704 [§ 2000e–3]. Other unlawful employment practices

(a) It shall be an unlawful employment practice for an employer to discriminate against any of his employees or applicants for employment, for an employment agency, or joint labor-management committee controlling apprenticeship or other training or retraining, including on-the-job training programs, to discriminate against any individual, or for a labor organization to discriminate against any member thereof or applicant for membership, because he has opposed any practice made an unlawful employment practice by this subchapter, or because he has made a charge, testified, assisted, or participated in any manner in an investigation, proceeding, or hearing under this subchapter.

(b) It shall be an unlawful employment practice for an employer, labor organization, employment agency, or joint labor-management committee controlling apprenticeship or other training or retraining, including on-the-job training programs, to print or publish or cause to be printed or published any notice or advertisement relating to employment by such an employer or membership in or any classification or referral for employment by such a labor organization, or relating to any classification or referral for employment by such an employment agency, or relating to admission to, or employment in, any program established to provide apprenticeship or other training by such a joint labor-management committee, indicating any preference, limitation, specification, or discrimination, based on race, color, religion, sex, or national origin, except that such a notice or advertisement may indicate a preference, limitation, specification, or discrimination based on religion, sex, or national origin when religion, sex, or national origin is a bona fide occupational qualification for employment.

## Sec. 705 [§ 2000e–4]. Equal Employment Opportunity Commission

(a) There is hereby created a Commission to be known as the Equal Employment Opportunity Commission, which shall be composed of five members, not more than three of whom shall be members of the same political party....

(b)(1) There shall be a General Counsel of the Commission appointed by the President, by and with the advice and consent of the Senate, for a term of four years. The General Counsel shall have responsibility for the conduct of litigation as provided in sections 2000e–5 and 2000e–6 of this title. The General Counsel shall have such other duties as the Commission may prescribe or as may be provided by law and shall concur with the Chairman of the Commission on the appointment and supervision of regional attorneys....

(c) The Commission shall have power—

(1) to cooperate with and, with their consent, utilize regional, State, local, and other agencies, both public and private, and individuals;

(2) to pay to witnesses whose depositions are taken or who are summoned before the Commission or any of its agents the same witness and mileage fees as are paid to witnesses in the courts of the United States;

(3) to furnish to persons subject to this subchapter such technical assistance as they may request to further their compliance with this subchapter or an order issued thereunder;

(4) upon the request of (i) any employer, whose employees or some of them, or (ii) any labor organization, whose members or some of them, refuse or threaten to refuse to cooperate in effectuating the provisions of this subchapter, to assist in such effectuation by conciliation or such other remedial action as is provided by this subchapter;

(5) to make such technical studies as are appropriate to effectuate the purposes and policies of this subchapter and to make the results of such studies available to the public;

(6) to intervene in a civil action brought under section 2000e-5 of this title by an aggrieved party against a respondent other than a government, governmental agency or political subdivision. . . .

## Sec. 706 [§ 2000e-5]. Enforcement provisions

(a) The Commission is empowered, as hereinafter provided, to prevent any person from engaging in any unlawful employment practice as set forth in section 2000e-2 or 2000e-3 of this title.

(b) Whenever a charge is filed by or on behalf of a person claiming to be aggrieved, or by a member of the Commission, alleging that an employer, employment agency, labor organization, or joint labor-management committee controlling apprenticeship or other training or retraining, including on-the-job training programs, has engaged in an unlawful employment practice, the Commission shall serve a notice of the charge (including the date, place and circumstances of the alleged unlawful employment practice) on such employer, employment agency, labor organization, or joint labor-management committee (hereinafter referred to as the "respondent") within ten days, and shall make an investigation thereof. Charges shall be in writing under oath or affirmation and shall contain such information and be in such form as the Commission requires. Charges shall not be made public by the Commission. If the Commission determines after such investigation that there is not reasonable cause to believe that the charge is true, it shall dismiss the charge and promptly notify the person claiming to be aggrieved and the respondent of its action. In determining whether reasonable cause exists, the Commission shall accord substantial weight to final findings and orders made by State or local authorities in proceedings commenced under State or local law pursuant to the requirements of subsections (c) and (d) of this section. If the Commission determines after such investigation that there is reasonable cause to believe that the charge is true, the Commission shall endeavor to eliminate any such alleged unlawful employment practice by informal methods of conference, conciliation, and persuasion. Nothing said or done during and as a part of such informal endeavors may be made public by the Commission, its officers or employees, or used as evidence in a subsequent proceeding without the written consent of the persons concerned. Any person who makes public information in violation of this subsection shall be fined not more than $1,000 or imprisoned for not more than one year, or both. The Commission shall make its determination on reasonable cause as promptly as possible and, so far as practicable, not later than one hundred and twenty days from the filing of the charge or, where applicable under subsection (c) or (d) of this section, from the date upon which the Commission is authorized to take action with respect to the charge.

(c) In the case of an alleged unlawful employment practice occurring in a State, or political subdivision of a State, which has a State or local law prohibiting the unlawful employment practice alleged and establishing or authorizing a State or local authority to grant or seek relief from such practice or to institute criminal proceedings with respect thereto upon receiving notice thereof, no charge may be filed under subsection (a) [ ] of this section by the person aggrieved before the expiration of sixty days after proceedings have been commenced under the State or local law, unless such proceedings have been earlier terminated, provided that such sixty-day period shall be extended to one hundred and twenty days during the first year after the effective date of such State or local law. If any requirement for the commencement of such proceedings is imposed by a State or local authority other than a requirement of the filing of a written and signed statement of the facts upon which the proceeding is based, the proceeding shall be deemed to have been commenced for the purposes of this subsection at the time such statement is sent by registered mail to the appropriate State or local authority.

(d) In the case of any charge filed by a member of the Commission alleging an unlawful employment practice occurring in a State or political subdivision of a State which has a State or local law prohibiting the practice alleged and establishing or authorizing a State or local authority to grant or seek relief from such practice or to institute criminal proceedings with respect thereto upon receiving notice thereof, the Commission shall, before taking any action with respect to such charge, notify the appropriate State or local officials and, upon request, afford them a reasonable time, but not less than sixty days (provided that such sixty-day period shall be extended to one hundred and twenty days during the first year after the effective day of such State or local law), unless a shorter period is requested, to act under such State or local law to remedy the practice alleged.

(e)(1) A charge under this section shall be filed within one hundred and eighty days after the alleged unlawful employment practice occurred and notice of the charge (including the date, place and circumstances of the alleged unlawful employment practice) shall be served upon the person against whom such charge is made within ten days thereafter, except that in a case of an unlawful employment practice with respect to which the person aggrieved has initially instituted proceedings with a State or local agency with authority to grant or seek relief from such practice or to institute criminal proceedings with respect thereto upon receiving notice thereof, such charge shall be filed by or on behalf of the person aggrieved within three hundred days after the alleged unlawful employment practice occurred, or within thirty days after receiving notice that the State or local agency has terminated the proceedings under the State or local law, whichever is earlier, and a copy of such charge shall be filed by the Commission with the State or local agency.

*(2) For purposes of this section, an unlawful employment practice occurs, with respect to a seniority system that has been adopted for an intentionally discriminatory purpose in violation of this subchapter (whether or not that discriminatory purpose is apparent on the face of the seniority provision), when the seniority system is adopted, when an individual becomes subject to the seniority system, or when a person aggrieved is injured by the application of the seniority system or provision of the system.*

(f)(1) If within thirty days after a charge is filed with the Commission or within thirty days after expiration of any period of reference under subsection (c) or (d) of this section, the Commission has been unable to secure from the respondent a conciliation agreement acceptable to the Commission, the Commission may bring a civil action against any respondent not a government, governmental agency, or political subdivision named in the charge. In the case of a respondent which is a government, governmental agency, or political subdivision, if the Commission has been unable to secure from the respondent a conciliation agreement acceptable to the Commission, the Commission shall take no further action and shall refer the case to the Attorney General who may bring a civil action against such respondent in the appropriate United States district court. The person or persons aggrieved shall have the right to intervene in a civil action brought by the Commission or the Attorney General in a case involving a government, governmental agency, or political subdivision. If a charge filed with the Commission pursuant to subsection (b) of this section is dismissed by the Commission, or if within one hundred and eighty days from the filing of such charge or the expiration of any period of reference under subsection (c) or (d) of this section, whichever is later, the Commission has not filed a civil action under this section or the Attorney General has not filed a civil action in a case involving a government, governmental agency, or political subdivision, or the Commission has not entered into a conciliation agreement to which the person aggrieved is a party, the Commission, or the Attorney General in a case involving a government, governmental agency, or political subdivision, shall so notify the person aggrieved and within ninety days after the giving of such notice a civil action may be brought against the respondent named in the charge (A) by the person claiming to be aggrieved or (B) if such charge was filed by a member of the Commission, by any person whom the charge alleges was aggrieved by the alleged unlawful employment practice. Upon application by the complainant and in such circumstances as the court may deem just, the court may appoint an attorney for such complainant and may authorize the commencement of the action without the payment of fees, costs, or security. Upon timely application, the court may, in its discretion, permit the Commission, or the Attorney General in a case involving a government, governmental agency, or political subdivision, to intervene in such civil action upon certification that the case is of general public importance. Upon request, the court may, in its discretion, stay further proceedings for not more than sixty days pending the termination of State or local proceedings described in subsections [ ] (c) or (d) of this section or further efforts of the Commission to obtain voluntary compliance.

(2) Whenever a charge is filed with the Commission and the Commission concludes on the basis of a preliminary investigation that prompt judicial action is necessary to carry out the purposes of this Act, the Commission, or the Attorney General in a case involving a government, governmental agency, or political subdivision, may bring an action for appropriate temporary or preliminary relief pending final disposition of such charge. Any temporary restraining order or other order granting preliminary or temporary relief shall be issued in accordance with rule 65 of the Federal Rules of Civil Procedure. It shall be the duty of a court having jurisdiction over proceedings under this section to assign cases for hearing at the earliest practicable date and to cause such cases to be in every way expedited.

(3) Each United States district court and each United States court of a place subject to the jurisdiction of the United States shall have jurisdiction of actions brought under this subchapter. Such an action may be brought in any judicial district in the State in which the unlawful employment practice is alleged to have been committed, in the judicial district in which the employment records relevant to such practice are maintained and administered, or in the judicial district in which the aggrieved person would have worked but for the alleged unlawful employment practice, but if the respondent is not found within any such district, such an action may be brought within the judicial district in which the respondent has his principal office. For purposes of sections 1404 and 1406 of Title 28, the judicial district in which the respondent has his principal office shall in all cases be considered a district in which the action might have been brought.

(4) It shall be the duty of the chief judge of the district (or in his absence, the acting chief judge) in which the case is pending immediately to designate a judge in such district to hear and determine the case. In the event that no judge in the district is available to hear and determine the case, the chief judge of the district, or the acting chief judge, as the case may be, shall certify this fact to the chief judge of the circuit (or in his absence, the acting chief judge) who shall then designate a district or circuit judge of the circuit to hear and determine the case.

(5) It shall be the duty of the judge designated pursuant to this subsection to assign the case for hearing at the earliest practicable date and to cause the case to be in every way expedited. If such judge has not scheduled the case for trial within one hundred and twenty days

after issue has been joined, that judge may appoint a master pursuant to rule 53 of the Federal Rules of Civil Procedure.

(g)(1) If the court finds that the respondent has intentionally engaged in or is intentionally engaging in an unlawful employment practice charged in the complaint, the court may enjoin the respondent from engaging in such unlawful employment practice, and order such affirmative action as may be appropriate, which may include, but is not limited to, reinstatement or hiring of employees, with or without back pay (payable by the employer, employment agency, or labor organization, as the case may be, responsible for the unlawful employment practice), or any other equitable relief as the court deems appropriate. Back pay liability shall not accrue from a date more than two years prior to the filing of a charge with the Commission. Interim earnings or amounts earnable with reasonable diligence by the person or persons discriminated against shall operate to reduce the back pay otherwise allowable.

(2)(A) No order of the court shall require the admission or reinstatement of an individual as a member of a union, or the hiring, reinstatement, or promotion of an individual as an employee, or the payment to him of any back pay, if such individual was refused admission, suspended, or expelled, or was refused employment or advancement or was suspended or discharged for any reason other than discrimination on account of race, color, religion, sex, or national origin or in violation of section 2000e–3(a) of this title.

*(B) On a claim in which an individual proves a violation under section 2000e-2(m) of this title and a respondent demonstrates that the respondent would have taken the same action in the absence of the impermissible motivating factor, the court—*

> *(i) may grant declaratory relief, injunctive relief (except as provided in clause (ii)), and attorney's fees and costs demonstrated to be directly attributable only to the pursuit of a claim under section 2000e–2(m) of this title; and*

> *(ii) shall not award damages or issue an order requiring any admission, reinstatement, hiring, promotion, or payment, described in subparagraph (A).*

(h) The provisions of chapter 6 of Title 29 shall not apply with respect to civil actions brought under this section.

(i) In any case in which an employer, employment agency, or labor organization fails to comply with an order of a court issued in a civil action brought under this section, the Commission may commence proceedings to compel compliance with such order.

(j) Any civil action brought under this section and any proceedings brought under subsection (i) of this section shall be subject to appeal as provided in sections 1291 and 1292, Title 28.

(k) In any action or proceeding under this subchapter the court, in its discretion, may allow the prevailing party, other than the Commission or the United States, a reasonable attorney's fee (including expert fees) as part of the costs, and the Commission and the United States shall be liable for costs the same as a private person.

### Sec. 707 [§ 2000e–6]. Civil actions by the Attorney General

(a) Whenever the Attorney General has reasonable cause to believe that any person or group of persons is engaged in a pattern or practice of resistance to the full enjoyment of any of the rights secured by this subchapter, and that the pattern or practice is of such a nature and is intended to deny the full exercise of the rights herein described, the Attorney General may bring a civil action in the appropriate district court of the United States by filing with it a complaint (1) signed by him (or in his absence the Acting Attorney General), (2) setting forth facts pertaining to such pattern or practice, and (3) requesting such relief, including an application for a permanent or temporary injunction, restraining order or other order against the person or persons responsible for such pattern or practice, as he deems necessary to insure the full enjoyment of the rights herein described.

(b) The district courts of the United States shall have and shall exercise jurisdiction of proceedings instituted pursuant to this section, and in any such proceeding the Attorney General may file with the clerk of such court a request that a court of three judges be convened to hear and determine the case.  Such request by the Attorney General shall be accompanied by a certificate that, in his opinion, the case is of general public importance.  A copy of the certificate and request for a three-judge court shall be immediately furnished by such clerk to the chief judge of the circuit (or in his absence, the presiding circuit judge of the circuit) in which the case is pending.  Upon receipt of such request it shall be the duty of the chief judge of the circuit or the presiding circuit judge, as the case may be, to designate immediately three judges in such circuit, of whom at least one shall be a circuit judge and another of whom shall be a district judge of the court in which the proceeding was instituted, to hear and determine such case, and it shall be the duty of the judges so designated to assign the case for hearing at the earliest practicable date, to participate in the hearing and determination thereof, and to cause the case to be in every way expedited.  An appeal from the final judgment of such court will lie to the Supreme Court.

In the event the Attorney General fails to file such a request in any such proceeding, it shall be the duty of the chief judge of the district (or in his absence, the acting chief judge) in which the case is pending immediately to designate a judge in such district to hear and determine the case.  In the event that no judge in the district is available to hear and determine the case, the chief judge of the district, or the acting chief judge, as the case may be, shall certify this fact to the chief judge of the circuit (or in his absence, the acting chief judge) who shall then designate a district or circuit judge of the circuit to hear and determine the case.

It shall be the duty of the judge designated pursuant to this section to assign the case for hearing at the earliest practicable date and to cause the case to be in every way expedited.

(c) Effective two years after March 24, 1972, the functions of the Attorney General under this section shall be transferred to the Commission, together with such personnel, property, records, and unexpended balances of appropriations, allocations, and other funds employed, used, held, available, or to be made available in connection with such functions unless the President submits, and neither House of Congress vetoes, a reorganization plan pursuant to chapter 9 of Title 5, inconsistent with the provisions of this subsection. The Commission shall carry out such functions in accordance with subsections (d) and (e) of this section.

(d) Upon the transfer of functions provided for in subsection (c) of this section, in all suits commenced pursuant to this section prior to the date of such transfer, proceedings shall continue without abatement, all court orders and decrees shall remain in effect, and the Commission shall be substituted as a party for the United States of America, the Attorney General, or the Acting Attorney General, as appropriate.

(e) Subsequent to March 24, 1972, the Commission shall have authority to investigate and act on a charge of a pattern or practice of discrimination, whether filed by or on behalf of a person claiming to be aggrieved or by a member of the Commission. All such actions shall be conducted in accordance with the procedures set forth in section 706 [2000e–5] of this title.

### Sec. 708 [§ 2000e–7]. Effect on State laws

Nothing in this subchapter shall be deemed to exempt or relieve any person from any liability, duty, penalty, or punishment provided by any present or future law of any State or political subdivision of a State, other than any such law which purports to require or permit the doing of any act which would be an unlawful employment practice under this subchapter.

### Sec. 709 [§ 2000e–8]. Investigations

(a) In connection with any investigation of a charge filed under section 2000e–5 of this title, the Commission or its designated representative shall at all reasonable times have access to, for the purposes of examination, and the right to copy any evidence of any person being investigated or proceeded against that relates to unlawful employment practices covered by this subchapter and is relevant to the charge under investigation.

(b) The Commission may cooperate with State and local agencies charged with the administration of State fair employment practices laws and, with the consent of such agencies, may, for the purpose of carrying out its functions and duties under this subchapter and within the limitation of funds appropriated specifically for such purpose, engage in and contribute to the cost of research and other projects of mutual interest undertaken by such agencies, and utilize the services of such agencies and their employees, and, notwithstanding any other provision of law, pay by advance or reimbursement such agencies and their employees for services rendered to assist the Commission in carrying out this subchapter. In furtherance of such cooperative efforts, the Commission may enter into written agreements with such State or local agencies and such agreements may include provisions under which the Commission shall refrain from processing a charge in any cases or class of cases specified in such agreements or under which the Commission shall relieve any person or class of persons in such State or locality from requirements imposed under this section. The Commission shall rescind any such agreement whenever it determines that the agreement no longer serves the interest of effective enforcement of this subchapter.

(c) Every employer, employment agency, and labor organization subject to this subchapter shall (1) make and keep such records relevant to the determinations of whether unlawful employment practices have been or are being committed, (2) preserve such records for such periods, and (3) make such reports therefrom as the Commission shall prescribe by regulation or order, after public hearing, as reasonable, necessary, or appropriate for the enforcement of this subchapter or the regulations or orders thereunder. The Commission shall, by regulation, require each employer, labor organization, and joint labor-management committee subject to this subchapter which controls an apprenticeship or other training program to maintain such records as are reasonably necessary to carry out the purposes of this subchapter, including, but not limited to, a list of applicants who wish to participate in such program, including the chronological order in which applications were received, and to furnish to the Commission upon request, a detailed description of the manner in which persons are selected to participate in the apprenticeship or other training program. Any employer, employment agency, labor organization, or joint labor-management committee which believes that the application to it of any regulation or order issued under this section would result in undue hardship may apply to the Commission for an exemption from the application of such regulation or order, and, if such application for an exemption is denied, bring a civil action in the United States district court for the district where such records are kept. If the Commission or the court, as the case may be, finds that the application of the regulation or order to the employer, employment agency, or labor organization in question would impose an undue hardship, the Commission or the court, as the case may be, may grant appropriate relief. If any person required to comply with the provisions of this subsection fails or refuses to do so, the United States district court for the district in which such person is found, resides, or transacts business, shall, upon application of the Commission, or the Attorney General in a case involving a government, governmental agency or political subdivision, have jurisdiction to issue to such person an order requiring him to comply.

(d) In prescribing requirements pursuant to subsection (c) of this section, the Commission shall consult with other interested State and

Federal agencies and shall endeavor to coordinate its requirements with those adopted by such agencies. The Commission shall furnish upon request and without cost to any State or local agency charged with the administration of a fair employment practice law information obtained pursuant to subsection (c) of this section from any employer, employment agency, labor organization, or joint labor-management committee subject to the jurisdiction of such agency. Such information shall be furnished on condition that it not be made public by the recipient agency prior to the institution of a proceeding under State or local law involving such information. If this condition is violated by a recipient agency, the Commission may decline to honor subsequent requests pursuant to this subsection.

(e) It shall be unlawful for any officer or employee of the Commission to make public in any manner whatever any information obtained by the Commission pursuant to its authority under this section prior to the institution of any proceeding under this subchapter involving such information. Any officer or employee of the Commission who shall make public in any manner whatever any information in violation of this subsection shall be guilty of a misdemeanor and upon conviction thereof, shall be fined not more than $1,000, or imprisoned not more than one year.

### Sec. 710 [§ 2000e–9]. Conduct of hearings and investigations pursuant to section 161 of Title 29

For the purpose of all hearings and investigations conducted by the Commission or its duly authorized agents or agencies, [Section 11 of the National Labor Relations Act] shall apply.

### Sec. 711 [§ 2000e–10]. Posting of notices; penalties

(a) Every employer, employment agency, and labor organization, as the case may be, shall post and keep posted in conspicuous places upon its premises where notices to employees, applicants for employment, and members are customarily posted a notice to be prepared or approved by the Commission setting forth excerpts from or, summaries of, the pertinent provisions of this subchapter and information pertinent to the filing of a complaint.

(b) A willful violation of this section shall be punishable by a fine of not more than $100 for each separate offense.

### Sec. 712 [§ 2000e–11]. Veterans' special rights or preference

Nothing contained in this subchapter shall be construed to repeal or modify any Federal, State, territorial, or local law creating special rights or preference for veterans.

### Sec. 713 [§ 2000e–12]. Regulations; conformity of regulations with administrative procedure provisions; reliance on interpretations and instructions of Commission

(a) The Commission shall have authority from time to time to issue, amend, or rescind suitable procedural regulations to carry out the provisions of this subchapter. Regulations issued under this section shall be in conformity with the standards and limitations of subchapter II of chapter 5 of Title 5.

(b) In any action or proceeding based on any alleged unlawful employment practice, no person shall be subject to any liability or punishment for or on account of (1) the commission by such person of an unlawful employment practice if he pleads and proves that the act or omission complained of was in good faith, in conformity with, and in reliance on any written interpretation or opinion of the Commission, or (2) the failure of such person to publish and file any information required by any provision of this subchapter if he pleads and proves that he failed to publish and file such information in good faith, in conformity with the instructions of the Commission issued under this subchapter regarding the filing of such information. Such a defense, if established, shall be a bar to the action or proceeding, notwithstanding that (A) after such act or omission, such interpretation or opinion is modified or rescinded or is determined by judicial authority to be invalid or of no legal effect, or (B) after publishing or filing the description and annual reports, such publication or filing is determined by judicial authority not to be in conformity with the requirements of this subchapter.

---

# AGE DISCRIMINATION IN EMPLOYMENT ACT OF 1967, AS AMENDED*

29 U.S.C. §§ 621–634

**Sec. 2.** **(§ 621)** Congressional statement of findings and purpose

**(a)** The Congress hereby finds and declares that—

**(1)** in the face of rising productivity and affluence, older workers find themselves disadvantaged in their efforts to retain employment, and especially to regain employment when displaced from jobs;

**(2)** the setting of arbitrary age limits regardless of potential for job performance has become a common practice, and certain otherwise desirable practices may work to the disadvantage of older persons;

**(3)** the incidence of unemployment, especially long-term unemployment with resultant deterioration of skill, morale, and employer acceptability is, relative to the younger ages, high among older workers; their numbers are great and growing; and their employment problems grave;

* The provisions of the 1967 Act are in roman type; provisions added in 1974 are underlined; provisions added in 1978 are in bold face; provisions added in 1984 are in bold face; provisions added in 1986 are in bold-face italics. Material enclosed by brackets was deleted by the legislation adding these provisions.

**(4)** the existence in industries affecting commerce, of arbitrary discrimination in employment because of age, burdens commerce and the free flow of goods in commerce.

**(b)** It is therefore the purpose of this chapter to promote employment of older persons based on their ability rather than age; to prohibit arbitrary age discrimination in employment; to help employers and workers find ways of meeting problems arising from the impact of age on employment.

**Sec. 3.** **(§ 622)** Education and research program; recommendation to Congress

**(a)** The Secretary of Labor* shall undertake studies and provide information to labor unions, management, and the general public concerning the needs and abilities of older workers, and their potentials for continued employment and contribution to the economy. * * *

**Study and Proposed Guidelines Relating to Police Officers and Firefighters.** Pub.L. 99–592, § 5, Oct. 31, 1986, 100 Stat. 3343, provided that:

*"(a) Study.—Not later than 4 years after the date of enactment of this Act [Oct. 31, 1986], the Secretary of Labor and the Equal Employment Opportunity Commission, jointly, shall—*

*"(1) conduct a study—*

*"(A) to determine whether physical and mental fitness tests are valid measurements of the ability and competency of police officers and firefighters to perform the requirements of their jobs,*

*"(B) if such tests are found to be valid measurements of such ability and competency, to determine which particular types of tests most effectively measure such ability and competency, and*

*"(C) to develop recommendations with respect to specific standards that such tests, and the administration of such tests should satisfy, and*

*"(2) submit a report to the Speaker of the House of Representatives and the President pro tempore of the Senate that includes—*

*"(A) a description of the results of such study, and*

*"(B) a statement of the recommendations developed under paragraph (1)(C).*

---

**\* Transfer of Functions.** "Equal Employment Opportunity Commission" and "Commission" were substituted for "Secretary", meaning the Secretary of Labor, pursuant to Reorg.Plan No. 1 of 1978, § 2, 43 F.R. 19807, 92 Stat. 3781, set out in Appendix 1 to Title 5, Government Organization and Employees, which transferred all functions vested by this section in the Secretary of Labor to the Equal Employment Opportunity Commission, effective Jan. 1, 1979, as provided by section 1–101 of Ex.Ord. No. 12106, Dec. 28, 1978, 44 F.R. 1053.

*"(b) Consultation requirement.—The Secretary of Labor and the Equal Employment Opportunity Commission shall, during the conduct of the study required under subsection (a) and prior to the development of recommendations under paragraph (1)(C), consult with the United States Fire Administration, the Federal Emergency Management Agency, organizations representing law enforcement officers, firefighters, and their employers, and organizations representing older Americans.*

*"(c) Proposed guidelines.—Not later than 5 years after the date of the enactment of this Act [Oct. 31, 1986] the Equal Employment Opportunity Commission shall propose, in accordance with subchapter II of chapter 5 of title 5 of the United States Code [5 U.S.C.A. § 551 et seq.] guidelines for the administration and use of physical and mental fitness tests to measure the ability and competency of police officers and firefighters to perform the requirements of their jobs."*

**Sec. 4 (§ 623).** Prohibition of age discrimination

### (a) Employer practices

It shall be unlawful for an employer—

**(1)** to fail or refuse to hire or to discharge any individual or otherwise discriminate against any individual with respect to his compensation, terms, conditions, or privileges of employment, because of such individual's age;

**(2)** to limit, segregate, or classify his employees in any way which would deprive or tend to deprive any individual of employment opportunities or otherwise adversely affect his status as an employee, because of such individual's age; or

**(3)** to reduce the wage rate of any employee in order to comply with this chapter.

### (b) Employment agency practices

It shall be unlawful for an employment agency to fail or refuse to refer for employment, or otherwise to discriminate against, any individual because of such individual's age, or to classify or refer for employment any individual on the basis of such individual's age.

### (c) Labor organization practices

It shall be unlawful for a labor organization—

**(1)** to exclude or to expel from its membership, or otherwise to discriminate against, any individual because of his age;

**(2)** to limit, segregate, or classify its membership, or to classify or fail or refuse to refer for employment any individual, in any way which would deprive or tend to deprive any individual of employment opportunities, or would limit such employment opportunities or otherwise adversely affect his status as an employee or as an applicant for employment, because of such individual's age;

**(3)** to cause or attempt to cause an employer to discriminate against an individual in violation of this section.

(d) Opposition to unlawful practices; participation in investigations, proceedings, or litigation

It shall be unlawful for an employer to discriminate against any of his employees or applicants for employment, for an employment agency to discriminate against any individual, or for a labor organization to discriminate against any member thereof or applicant for membership, because such individual, member or applicant for membership has opposed any practice made unlawful by this section, or because such individual, member or applicant for membership has made a charge, testified, assisted, or participated in any manner in an investigation, proceeding, or litigation under this chapter.

\* \* \*

(f) Lawful practices; age an occupational qualification; other reasonable factors; laws of foreign workplace; seniority system; employee benefit plans; discharge or discipline for good cause

It shall not be unlawful for an employer, employment agency, or labor organization—

**(1)** to take any action otherwise prohibited under subsections (a), (b), (c), or (e) of this section where age is a bona fide occupational qualification reasonably necessary to the normal operation of the particular business, or where the differentiation is based on reasonable factors other than age, *or where such practices involve an employee in a workplace in a foreign country, and compliance with such subsections would cause such employer, or a corporation controlled by such employer, to violate the laws of the country in which such workplace is located;*

**(2)** to observe the terms of a bona fide seniority system or any bona fide employee benefit plan such as a retirement, pension, or insurance plan, which is not a subterfuge to evade the purposes of this chapter, except that no such employee benefit plan shall excuse the failure to hire any individual, **and no such seniority system or employee benefit plan shall require or permit the involuntary retirement of any individual specified by section 631(a) of this title because of the age of such individual,** or

**(3)** to discharge or otherwise discipline an individual for good cause.

(g) Entitlement to coverage under group health plan

**(1)** For purposes of this section, any employer must provide that any employee aged 65 *or older,* and any employee's spouse aged 65 *or older,* shall be entitled to coverage under any group health plan offered to such employees under the same conditions as any employee, *and the spouse of such employee,* under age 65.

**(2)** For purposes of paragraph (1), the term "group health plan" has the meaning given to such term in section 162(i)(2) of Title 26. {subsec. (g) added in 1982}

(h) *Practices of foreign corporations controlled by American employers; foreign persons not controlled by American employers; factors determining control*

*(1) If an employer controls a corporation whose place of incorporation is in a foreign country, any practice by such corporation prohibited under this section shall be presumed to be such practice by such employer.*

*(2) The prohibitions of this section shall not apply where the employer is a foreign person not controlled by an American employer.*

*(3) For the purpose of this subsection the determination of whether an employer controls a corporation shall be based upon the—*

*(A) interrelation of operations,*

*(B) common management,*

*(C) centralized control of labor relations, and*

*(D) common ownership or financial control,*

of the employer and the corporation.

(i) *Firefighters and law enforcement officers attaining hiring or retiring age under State or local law on March 3, 1983*

**It shall not be unlawful for an employer which is a State, a political subdivision of a State, an agency or instrumentality of a State or a political subdivision of a State, or an interstate agency to fail or refuse to hire or to discharge any individual because of such individual's age if such action is taken—**

**(1) with respect to the employment of an individual as a firefighter or as a law enforcement officer and the individual has attained the age of hiring or retirement in effect under applicable State or local law on March 3, 1983, and**

**(2) pursuant to a bona fide hiring or retirement plan that is not a subterfuge to evade the purposes of this chapter.** {subsec. (i) repealed Dec. 31, 1993}

(i) [1] Employee pension benefit plans; cessation or reduction of benefit accrual or of allocation to employee account; distribution of benefits after attainment of normal retirement age; compliance; highly compensated employees

**(1) Except as otherwise provided in this subsection, it shall be unlawful for an employer, an employment agency, a labor organization, or any combination thereof to establish or maintain an employee pension benefit plan which requires or permits—**

---

**1.** So in original

*(A) in the case of a defined benefit plan, the cessation of an employee's benefit accrual, or the reduction of the rate of an employee's benefit accrual, because of age, or*

*(B) in the case of a defined contribution plan, the cessation of allocations to an employee's account, or the reduction of the rate at which amounts are allocated to an employee's account, because of age.*

*(2) Nothing in this section shall be construed to prohibit an employer, employment agency, or labor organization from observing any provision of an employee pension benefit plan to the extent that such provision imposes (without regard to age) a limitation on the amount of benefits that the plan provides or a limitation on the number of years of service or years of participation which are taken into account for purposes of determining benefit accrual under the plan.*

*(3) In the case of any employee who, as of the end of any plan year under a defined benefit plan, has attained normal retirement age under such plan—*

*(A) if distribution of benefits under such plan with respect to such employee has commenced as of the end of such plan year, then any requirement of this subsection for continued accrual of benefits under such plan with respect to such employee during such plan year shall be treated as satisfied to the extent of the actuarial equivalent of in-service distribution of benefits, and*

*(B) if distribution of benefits under such plan with respect to such employee has not commenced as of the end of such year in accordance with section 1056(a)(3) of this title and section 401(a)(14)(C) of title 26, and the payment of benefits under such plan with respect to such employee is not suspended during such plan year pursuant to section 1053(a)(3)(B) of this title or section 411(a)(3)(B) of title 26, then any requirement of this subsection for continued accrual of benefits under such plan with respect to such employee during such plan year shall be treated as satisfied to the extent of any adjustment in the benefit payable under the plan during such plan year attributable to the delay in the distribution of benefits after the attainment of normal retirement age.*

*The provisions of this paragraph shall apply in accordance with regulations of the Secretary of the Treasury. Such regulations shall provide for the application of the preceding provisions of this paragraph to all employee pension benefit plans subject to this subsection and may provide for the application of such provisions, in the case of any such employee, with respect to any period of time within a plan year.*

*(4) Compliance with the requirements of this subsection with respect to an employee pension benefit plan shall constitute compliance with the requirements of this section relating to benefit accrual under such plan.*

*(5) Paragraph (1) shall not apply with respect to any employee who is a highly compensated employee (within the meaning of section 414(q) of title 26) to the extent provided in regulations prescribed by the Secretary of the Treasury for purposes of precluding discrimination in favor of highly compensated employees within the meaning of subchapter D of chapter 1 of title 26.*

*(6) A plan shall not be treated as failing to meet the requirements of paragraph (1) solely because the subsidized portion of any early retirement benefit is disregarded in determining benefit accruals.*

*(7) Any regulations prescribed by the Secretary of the Treasury pursuant to clause (v) of section 411(b)(1)(H) of title 26 and subparagraphs (C) and (D) of section 411(b)(2) of title 26 shall apply with respect to the requirements of this subsection in the same manner and to the same extent as such regulations apply with respect to the requirements of such sections 411(b)(1)(H) and 411(b)(2) of title 26.*

*(8) A plan shall not be treated as failing to meet the requirements of this section solely because such plan provides a normal retirement age described in section 1002(24)(B) of this title and section 411(a)(8)(B) of title 26.*

*(9) For purposes of this subsection—*

*(A) The terms "employee pension benefit plan", "defined benefit plan", "defined contribution plan", and "normal retirement age" have the meanings provided such terms in section 1002 of this title.*

*(B) The term "compensation" has the meaning provided by section 414(s) of title 26.*

**Sec. 7 (§ 626).** Recordkeeping investigation, and enforcement

\* \* \*

(b) Enforcement; prohibition of age discrimination under fair labor standards: unpaid minimum wages and unpaid overtime compensation; liquidated damages; judicial relief; conciliation, conference, and persuasion

The provisions of this chapter shall be enforced in accordance with the powers, remedies, and procedures provided in sections 211(b), 216 (except for subsection (a) thereof), and 217 of this title, and subsection (c) of this section. Any act prohibited under section 623 of this title shall be deemed to be a prohibited act under section 215 of this title. Amounts owing to a person as a result of a violation of this chapter shall be deemed to be unpaid minimum wages or unpaid overtime compensation for purposes of sections 216 and 217 of this title: *Provided*, That liquidated damages shall be payable only in cases of willful violations of this chapter. In any action brought to enforce this chapter the court shall have jurisdiction to grant such legal or equitable relief as may be appropriate to effectuate the purposes of this chapter, including without limitation judgments compelling employment, reinstatement or promotion, or enforcing the liability for amounts deemed to be unpaid minimum wages or unpaid overtime compensation under this section. Before instituting any action under this section, the Equal Employment Opportunity Commission shall attempt to eliminate the discriminatory practice or practices alleged, and to effect voluntary compliance with the requirements of this chapter through informal methods of conciliation, conference, and persuasion.

 (c) Civil actions; persons aggrieved; jurisdiction; judicial relief;
termination of individual action upon commencement of
action by Commission; jury trial

 **(1)** Any person aggrieved may bring a civil action in any court of competent jurisdiction for such legal or equitable relief as will effectuate the purposes of this chapter: *Provided*, That the right of any person to bring such action shall terminate upon the commencement of an action by the Equal Employment Opportunity Commission to enforce the right of such employee under this chapter.

 **(2) In an action brought under paragraph (1), a person shall be entitled to a trial by jury of any issue of fact in any such action for recovery of amounts owing as a result of a violation of this chapter, regardless of whether equitable relief is sought by any party in such action.**

 (d) Filing of charge with Commission; timeliness;
conciliation, conference, and persuasion

 No civil action may be commenced by an individual under this section until **60 days after a charge alleging unlawful discrimination has been filed with the Equal Employment Opportunity Commission. Such a charge shall be filed—**

  **(1)** within 180 days after the alleged unlawful practice occurred; or

  **(2)** in a case to which section 633(b) of this title applies, within 300 days after the alleged unlawful practice occurred, or within 30 days after receipt by the individual of notice of termination of proceedings under State law, whichever is earlier.

 Upon receiving **such a charge, the Commission** shall promptly notify all persons named **in such charge** as prospective defendants in the action and shall promptly seek to eliminate any alleged unlawful practice by informal methods of conciliation, conference, and persuasion.

(e) Statute of limitations;  reliance in future
on administrative ruling, etc.;  tolling

**(1)** Sections 255 and 259 of this title shall apply to actions under this chapter.

**(2) For the period during which the Equal Employment Opportunity Commission is attempting to effect voluntary compliance with requirements of this chapter through informal methods of conciliation, conference, and persuasion pursuant to subsection (b) of this section, the statute of limitations as provided in section 255 of this title shall be tolled, but in no event for a period in excess of one year.**

\* \* \*

### Sec. 11   (§ 630).   Definitions

For the purposes of this chapter—

**(a)** The term "person" means one or more individuals, partnerships, associations, labor organizations, corporations, business trusts, legal representatives, or any organized groups of persons.

**(b)** The term "employer" means a person engaged in an industry affecting commerce who has twenty or more employees for each working day in each of twenty or more calendar weeks in the current or preceding calendar year: *Provided*, That prior to June 30, 1968, employers having fewer than fifty employees shall not be considered employers. The term also means (1) any agent of such a person, and (2) a State or political subdivision of a State and any agency or instrumentality of a State or a political subdivision of a State, and any interstate agency, but such term does not include the United States, or a corporation wholly owned by the Government of the United States.

**(c)** The term "employment agency" means any person regularly undertaking with or without compensation to procure employees for an employer and includes an agent of such a person;  but shall not include an agency of the United States.

**(d)** The term "labor organization" means a labor organization engaged in an industry affecting commerce, and any agent of such an organization, and includes any organization of any kind, any agency, or employee representation committee, group, association, or plan so engaged in which employees participate and which exists for the purpose, in whole or in part, of dealing with employers concerning grievances, labor disputes, wages, rates of pay, hours, or other terms or conditions of employment, and any conference, general committee, joint or system board, or joint council so engaged which is subordinate to a national or international labor organization.

**(e)** A labor organization shall be deemed to be engaged in an industry affecting commerce if (1) it maintains or operates a hiring hall or hiring office which procures employees for an employer or procures for employees opportunities to work for an employer, or (2) the number of its members (or, where it is a labor organization composed of other labor organizations or their representatives, if the aggregate number of the members of such other labor organization) is fifty or more prior to July 1, 1968, or twenty-five or more on or after July 1, 1968, and such labor organization—

**(1)** is the certified representative of employees under the provisions of the National Labor Relations Act, as amended [29 U.S.C.A. § 151 et seq.], or the Railway Labor Act, as amended [45 U.S.C.A. § 151 et seq.]; or

**(2)** although not certified, is a national or international labor organization or a local labor organization recognized or acting as the representative of employees of an employer or employers engaged in an industry affecting commerce; or

**(3)** has chartered a local labor organization or subsidiary body which is representing or actively seeking to represent employees of employers within the meaning of paragraph (1) or (2); or

**(4)** has been chartered by a labor organization representing or actively seeking to represent employees within the meaning of paragraph (1) or (2) as the local or subordinate body through which such employees may enjoy membership or become affiliated with such labor organization; or

**(5)** is a conference, general committee, joint or system board, or joint council subordinate to a national or international labor organization, which includes a labor organization engaged in an industry affecting commerce within the meaning of any of the preceding paragraphs of this subsection.

**(f)** The term "employee" means an individual employed by any employer except that the term "employee" shall not include any person elected to public office in any State or political subdivision of any State by the qualified voters thereof, or any person chosen by such officer to be on such officer's personal staff, or an appointee on the policymaking level or an immediate adviser with respect to the exercise of the constitutional or legal powers of the office. The exemption set forth in the preceding sentence shall not include employees subject to the civil service laws of a State government, governmental agency, or political subdivision. *The term "employee" includes any individual who is a citizen of the United States employed by an employer in a workplace in a foreign country.*

**(g)** The term "commerce" means trade, traffic, commerce, transportation, transmission, or communication among the several States; or between a State and any place outside thereof; or within the District of Columbia, or a possession of the United States; or between points in the same State but through a point outside thereof.

**(h)** The term "industry affecting commerce" means any activity, business, or industry in commerce or in which a labor dispute would hinder or obstruct commerce or the free flow of commerce and includes any activity or industry "affecting commerce" within the meaning of the Labor–Management Reporting and Disclosure Act of 1959 [29 U.S.C.A. § 401 et seq.].

(i) The term "State" includes a State of the United States, the District of Columbia, Puerto Rico, the Virgin Islands, American Samoa, Guam, Wake Island, the Canal Zone, and Outer Continental Shelf lands defined in the Outer Continental Shelf Lands Act [43 U.S.C.A. § 1331 et seq.].

(j) The term "firefighter" means an employee, the duties of whose position are primarily to perform work directly connected with the control and extinguishment of fires or the maintenance and use of firefighting apparatus and equipment, including an employee engaged in this activity who is transferred to a supervisory or administrative position.

(k) The term "law enforcement officer" means an employee, the duties of whose position are primarily the investigation, apprehension, or detention of individuals suspected or convicted of offenses against the criminal laws of a State, including an employee engaged in this activity who is transferred to a supervisory or administrative position. For the purpose of this subsection, "detention" includes the duties of employees assigned to guard individuals incarcerated in any penal institution.

**Sec. 12   (§ 631).**   Age limits

(a) Individuals at least 40 [but less than 70] years of age

The prohibitions in this chapter shall be limited to individuals who are at least 40 years of age [but less than 70 years of age].

(b) Employees or applicants for employment in Federal Government

**In the case of any personnel action affecting employees or applicants for employment which is subject to the provisions of section 633a of this title, the prohibitions established in section 633a of this title shall be limited to individuals who are at least 40 years of age.**

(c) Bona fide executives or high policymakers

**(1) Nothing in this chapter shall be construed to prohibit compulsory retirement of any employee who has attained 65 years of age [but not 70 years of age,] and who, for the 2–year period immediately before retirement, is employed in a bona fide executive or a high policymaking position, if such employee is entitled to an immediate nonforfeitable annual retirement benefit from a pension, profit-sharing, savings, or deferred compensation plan, or any combination of such plans, of the employer of such employee, which equals, in the aggregate, at least *$44,000*.**

**(2) In applying the retirement benefit test of paragraph (1) of this subsection, if any such retirement benefit is in a form other than a straight life annuity (with no ancillary benefits), or**

if employees contribute to any such plan or make rollover contributions, such benefit shall be adjusted in accordance with regulations prescribed by the Equal Employment Opportunity Commission, after consultation with the Secretary of the Treasury, so that the benefit is the equivalent of a straight life annuity (with no ancillary benefits) under a plan to which employees do not contribute and under which no rollover contributions are made.

(d) Tenured employee at institution of higher education

*Nothing in this chapter shall be construed to prohibit compulsory retirement of any employee who has attained 70 years of age, and who is serving under a contract of unlimited tenure (or similar arrangement providing for unlimited tenure) at an institution of higher education (as defined by section 1141(a) of Title 20).*

{Subsec. (d) repealed Dec. 31, 1993}

* * *

**Sec. 13 (§ 632).** Annual report to Congress * * *

**Sec. 14 (§ 633).** Federal–State relationship

(a) Federal action superseding State action

Nothing in this chapter shall affect the jurisdiction of any agency of any State performing like functions with regard to discriminatory employment practices on account of age except that upon commencement of action under this chapter such action shall supersede any State action.

(b) Limitation of Federal action upon commencement
of State proceedings

In the case of an alleged unlawful practice occurring in a State which has a law prohibiting discrimination in employment because of age and establishing or authorizing a State authority to grant or seek relief from such discriminatory practice, no suit may be brought under section 626 of this title before the expiration of sixty days after proceedings have been commenced under the State law, unless such proceedings have been earlier terminated: *Provided,* That such sixty-day period shall be extended to one hundred and twenty days during the first year after the effective date of such State law. If any requirement for the commencement of such proceedings is imposed by a State authority other than a requirement of the filing of a written and signed statement of the facts upon which the proceeding is based, the proceeding shall be deemed to have been commenced for the purposes of this subsection at the time such statement is sent by registered mail to the appropriate State authority.

# VOCATIONAL REHABILITATION ACT OF 1973
## (29 U.S.C. SECTIONS 701 ET SEQ.)

**§ 790.  * * ***

Approved State plans for vocational rehabilitation, approved projects, and contractual arrangements authorized under the Vocational Rehabilitation Act will be recognized under comparable provisions of this chapter so that there is no disruption of ongoing activities for which there is continuing authority.  * * *

## § 791.  Employment of handicapped individuals

* * *

(b) Federal agencies;  affirmative action program plans

Each department, agency, and instrumentality (including the United States Postal Service and the Postal Rate Commission) in the executive branch shall, within one hundred and eighty days after September 26, 1973, submit to the Office of Personnel Management and to the Committee an affirmative action program plan for the hiring, placement, and advancement of handicapped individuals in such department, agency, or instrumentality.  Such plan shall include a description of the extent to which and methods whereby the special needs of handicapped employees are being met.  Such plan shall be updated annually, and shall be reviewed annually and approved by the Office, if the Office determines, after consultation with the Committee, that such plan provides sufficient assurances, procedures and commitments to provide adequate hiring, placement, and advancement opportunities for handicapped individuals.

* * *

## § 793.  Employment under Federal contracts

(a) Amount of contracts or subcontracts;  provision
for employment and advancement of qualified
handicapped individuals;  regulations

Any contract in excess of $2,500 entered into by any Federal department or agency for the procurement of personal property and nonpersonal services (including construction) for the United States shall contain a provision requiring that, in employing persons to carry out such contract the party contracting with the United States shall take affirmative action to employ and advance in employment qualified handicapped individuals as defined in section 706(7) of this title.  The provisions of this section shall apply to any subcontract in excess of $2,500 entered into by a prime contractor in carrying out any contract for the procurement of personal property and nonpersonal services (including construction) for the United States.  * * *

(b) Administrative enforcement;  complaints;
investigations;  departmental action

If any handicapped individual believes any contractor has failed or refuses to comply with the provisions of his contract with the United

States, relating to employment of handicapped individuals, such individual may file a complaint with the Department of Labor. The Department shall promptly investigate such complaint and shall take such action thereon as the facts and circumstances warrant, consistent with the terms of such contract and the laws and regulations applicable thereto.

\* \* \*

### § 794. Nondiscrimination under federal grants and programs; promulgation of rules and regulations

No otherwise qualified handicapped individual in the United States, as defined in section 706(7) of this title, shall, solely by reason of his handicap, be excluded from the participation in, be denied the benefits of, or be subjected to discrimination under any program or activity receiving Federal financial assistance or under any program or activity conducted by any Executive agency or by the United States Postal Service. The head of each such agency shall promulgate such regulations as may be necessary to carry out the amendments to this section made by the Rehabilitation, Comprehensive Services, and Developmental Disabilities Act of 1978.[1] Copies of any proposed regulation shall be submitted to appropriate authorizing committees of the Congress, and such regulation may take effect no earlier than the thirtieth day after the date on which such regulation is so submitted to such committees.

### § 794a. Remedies and attorney fees

(a)(1) The remedies, procedures, and rights set forth in section 717 of the Civil Rights Act of 1964 (42 U.S.C. 2000e–16), including the application of sections 706(f) through 706(k) (42 U.S.C. 2000e–5(f) through (k)), shall be available, with respect to any complaint under section 791 of this title, to any employee or applicant for employment aggrieved by the final disposition of such complaint, or by the failure to take final action on such complaint. In fashioning an equitable or affirmative action remedy under such section, a court may take into account the reasonableness of the cost of any necessary work place accommodation, and the availability of alternatives therefor or other appropriate relief in order to achieve an equitable and appropriate remedy.

(2) The remedies, procedures, and rights set forth in title VI of the Civil Rights Act of 1964 [42 U.S.C.A. § 2000d et seq.] shall be available to any person aggrieved by any act or failure to act by any recipient of Federal assistance or Federal provider of such assistance under section 794 of this title.

(b) In any action or proceeding to enforce or charge a violation of a provision of this subchapter, the court, in its discretion, may allow the

---

**1.** Pub.L. 95–602, Nov. 6, 1978, 92 Stat. 2955.

prevailing party, other than the United States, a reasonable attorney's fee as part of the costs.

---

# AMERICANS WITH DISABILITIES ACT

42 U.S.C. Sec. 12101–12213

### Sec. 2   [§ 1210].   Congressional statement of findings and purposes

(a) The Congress finds that—

(1) some 43,000,000 Americans have one or more physical or mental disabilities, and this number is increasing as the population as a whole is growing older;

(2) historically, society has tended to isolate and segregate individuals with disabilities, and, despite some improvements, such forms of discrimination against individuals with disabilities continue to be a serious and pervasive social problem;

(3) discrimination against individuals with disabilities persists in such critical areas as employment, housing, public accommodations, education, transportation, communication, recreation, institutionalization, health services, voting, and access to public services;

(4) unlike individuals who have experienced discrimination on the basis of race, color, sex, national origin, religion, or age, individuals who have experienced discrimination on the basis of disability have often had no legal recourse to redress such discrimination;

(5) individuals with disabilities continually encounter various forms of discrimination, including outright intentional exclusion, the discriminatory effects of architectural, transportation, and communication barriers, overprotective rules and policies, failure to make modifications to existing facilities and practices, exclusionary qualification standards and criteria, segregation, and relegation to lesser services, programs, activities, benefits, jobs, or other opportunities;

(6) census data, national polls, and other studies have documented that people with disabilities, as a group, occupy an inferior status in our society, and are severely disadvantaged socially, vocationally, economically, and educationally;

(7) individuals with disabilities are a discrete and insular minority who have been faced with restrictions and limitations, subjected to a history of purposeful unequal treatment, and relegated to a position of political powerlessness in our society, based on characteristics that are beyond the control of such individuals and resulting from stereotypic assumptions not truly indicative of the individual ability of such individuals to participate in, and contribute to, society;

(8) the Nation's proper goals regarding individuals with disabilities are to assure equality of opportunity, full participation, independent living, and economic self-sufficiency for such individuals; and

(9) the continuing existence of unfair and unnecessary discrimination and prejudice denies people with disabilities the opportunity to compete on an equal basis and to pursue those opportunities for which our free society is justifiably famous, and costs the United States billions of dollars in unnecessary expenses resulting from dependency and nonproductivity.

(b) It is the purpose of this chapter—

(1) to provide a clear and comprehensive national mandate for the elimination of discrimination against individuals with disabilities;

(2) to provide clear, strong, consistent, enforceable standards addressing discrimination against individuals with disabilities;

(3) to ensure that the Federal Government plays a central role in enforcing the standards established in this chapter on behalf of individuals with disabilities; and

(4) to invoke the sweep of congressional authority, including the power to enforce the fourteenth amendment and to regulate commerce, in order to address the major areas of discrimination faced day-to-day by people with disabilities.

## Sec. 3 [§ 12102]. Definitions

As used in this chapter:

(1) The term "auxiliary aids and services" includes—

(A) qualified interpreters or other effective methods of making aurally delivered materials available to individuals with hearing impairments;

(B) qualified readers, taped texts, or other effective methods of making visually delivered materials available to individuals with visual impairments;

(C) acquisition or modification of equipment or devices; and

(D) other similar services and actions.

(2) The term "disability" means, with respect to an individual—

(A) a physical or mental impairment that substantially limits one or more of the major life activities of such individual;

(B) a record of such an impairment; or

(C) being regarded as having such an impairment.

(3) The term "State" means each of the several States, the District of Columbia, the Commonwealth of Puerto Rico, Guam, American Samoa, the Virgin Islands, the Trust Territory of the Pacific Islands, and the Commonwealth of the Northern Mariana Islands.

### Sec. 101  [§ 12111].  Definitions

As used in this subchapter:

(1) The term "Commission" means the Equal Employment Opportunity Commission established by section 2000e–4 of this title.

(2) The term "covered entity" means an employer, employment agency, labor organization, or joint labor-management committee.

(3) The term "direct threat" means a significant risk to the health or safety of others that cannot be eliminated by reasonable accommodation.

(4) The term "employee" means an individual employed by an employer. *With respect to employment in a foreign country, such term includes an individual who is a citizen of the United States.*

(5)(A) The term "employer" means a person engaged in an industry affecting commerce who has 15 or more employees for each working day in each of 20 or more calendar weeks in the current or preceding calendar year, and any agent of such person, except that, for two years following the effective date of this subchapter, an employer means a person engaged in an industry affecting commerce who has 25 or more employees for each working day in each of 20 or more calendar weeks in the current or preceding year, and any agent of such person.

(B) The term "employer" does not include—

(i) the United States, a corporation wholly owned by the government of the United States, or an Indian tribe; or

(ii) a bona fide private membership club (other than a labor organization) that is exempt from taxation under section 501(c) of Title 26.

(6)(A) The term "illegal use of drugs" means the use of drugs, the possession or distribution of which is unlawful under the Controlled Substances Act (21 U.S.C. 812).  Such term does not include the use of a drug taken under supervision by a licensed health care professional, or other uses authorized by the Controlled Substances Act [21 U.S.C.A. § 801 et seq.] or other provisions of Federal law.

(B) The term "drug" means a controlled substance, as defined in schedules I through V of section 202 of the Controlled Substances Act [21 U.S.C.A. § 812].

(7) The terms "person", "labor organization", "employment agency", "commerce", and "industry affecting commerce", shall have the same meaning given such terms in section 2000e of this title.

(8) The term "qualified individual with a disability" means an individual with a disability who, with or without reasonable accommodation, can perform the essential functions of the employment position that such individual holds or desires.  For the purposes of this subchapter, consideration shall be given to the employer's judgment as to what functions of a job are essential, and if an employer has prepared a written description before advertising or interviewing applicants for the

job, this description shall be considered evidence of the essential functions of the job.

(9) The term "reasonable accommodation" may include—

(A) making existing facilities used by employees readily accessible to and usable by individuals with disabilities; and

(B) job restructuring, part-time or modified work schedules, reassignment to a vacant position, acquisition or modification of equipment or devices, appropriate adjustment or modifications of examinations, training materials or policies, the provision of qualified readers or interpreters, and other similar accommodations for individuals with disabilities.

(10) Undue hardship

(A) The term "undue hardship" means an action requiring significant difficulty or expense, when considered in light of the factors set forth in subparagraph (B).

(B) In determining whether an accommodation would impose an undue hardship on a covered entity, factors to be considered include—

(i) the nature and cost of the accommodation needed under this chapter;

(ii) the overall financial resources of the facility or facilities involved in the provision of the reasonable accommodation; the number of persons employed at such facility; the effect on expenses and resources, or the impact otherwise of such accommodation upon the operation of the facility;

(iii) the overall financial resources of the covered entity; the overall size of the business of a covered entity with respect to the number of its employees; the number, type, and location of its facilities; and

(iv) the type of operation or operations of the covered entity, including the composition, structure, and functions of the workforce of such entity; the geographic separateness, administrative, or fiscal relationship of the facility or facilities in question to the covered entity.

## Sec. 102 [§ 12112]. Discrimination

(a) No covered entity shall discriminate against a qualified individual with a disability because of the disability of such individual in regard to job application procedures, the hiring, advancement, or discharge of employees, employee compensation, job training, and other terms, conditions, and privileges of employment.

(b) As used in subsection (a) of this section, the term "discriminate" includes—

(1) limiting, segregating, or classifying a job applicant or employee in a way that adversely affects the opportunities or status of such applicant or employee because of the disability of such applicant or employee;

(2) participating in a contractual or other arrangement or relationship that has the effect of subjecting a covered entity's qualified applicant or employee with a disability to the discrimination prohibited by this subchapter (such relationship includes a relationship with an employment or referral agency, labor union, an organization providing fringe benefits to an employee of the covered entity, or an organization providing training and apprenticeship programs);

(3) utilizing standards, criteria, or methods of administration—

(A) that have the effect of discrimination on the basis of disability; or

(B) that perpetuate the discrimination of others who are subject to common administrative control;

(4) excluding or otherwise denying equal jobs or benefits to a qualified individual because of the known disability of an individual with whom the qualified individual is known to have a relationship or association;

(5)(A) not making reasonable accommodations to the known physical or mental limitations of an otherwise qualified individual with a disability who is an applicant or employee, unless such covered entity can demonstrate that the accommodation would impose an undue hardship on the operation of the business of such covered entity;  or

(B) denying employment opportunities to a job applicant or employee who is an otherwise qualified individual with a disability, if such denial is based on the need of such covered entity to make reasonable accommodation to the physical or mental impairments of the employee or applicant;

(6) using qualification standards, employment tests or other selection criteria that screen out or tend to screen out an individual with a disability or a class of individuals with disabilities unless the standard, test or other selection criteria, as used by the covered entity, is shown to be job-related for the position in question and is consistent with business necessity;  and

(7) failing to select and administer tests concerning employment in the most effective manner to ensure that, when such test is administered to a job applicant or employee who has a disability that impairs sensory, manual, or speaking skills, such test results accurately reflect the skills, aptitude, or whatever other factor of such applicant or employee that such test purports to measure, rather than reflecting the impaired sensory, manual, or speaking skills of such employee or applicant (except where such skills are the factors that the test purports to measure).

(c)(1) *It shall not be unlawful under this section for a covered entity to take any action that constitutes discrimination under this section with respect to an employee in a workplace in a foreign country if compliance with this section would cause such covered entity to violate the law of the foreign country in which such workplace is located.*

*(2)(A) If an employer controls a corporation whose place of incorporation is a foreign country, any practice that constitutes discrimination under this section and is engaged in by such corporation shall be presumed to be engaged in by such employer.*

*(B) This section shall not apply with respect to the foreign operations of an employer that is a foreign person not controlled by an American employer.*

*(C) For purposes of this paragraph, the determination of whether an employer controls a corporation shall be based on—*

*(i) the interrelation of operations;*

*(ii) the common management;*

*(iii) the centralized control of labor relations; and*

*(iv) the common ownership or financial control,*

*of the employer and the corporation.*

(d)(1) The prohibition against discrimination as referred to in subsection (a) of this section shall include medical examinations and inquiries.

(2)(A) Except as provided in paragraph (3), a covered entity shall not conduct a medical examination or make inquiries of a job applicant as to whether such applicant is an individual with a disability or as to the nature or severity of such disability.

(B) Acceptable inquiry

A covered entity may make preemployment inquiries into the ability of an applicant to perform job-related functions.

(3) A covered entity may require a medical examination after an offer of employment has been made to a job applicant and prior to the commencement of the employment duties of such applicant, and may condition an offer of employment on the results of such examination, if—

(A) all entering employees are subjected to such an examination regardless of disability;

(B) information obtained regarding the medical condition or history of the applicant is collected and maintained on separate forms and in separate medical files and is treated as a confidential medical record, except that—

(i) supervisors and managers may be informed regarding necessary restrictions on the work or duties of the employee and necessary accommodations;

(ii) first aid and safety personnel may be informed, when appropriate, if the disability might require emergency treatment; and

(iii) government officials investigating compliance with this chapter shall be provided relevant information on request; and

(C) the results of such examination are used only in accordance with this subchapter.

(4)(A) A covered entity shall not require a medical examination and shall not make inquiries of an employee as to whether such employee is an individual with a disability or as to the nature or severity of the disability, unless such examination or inquiry is shown to be job-related and consistent with business necessity.

(B) A covered entity may conduct voluntary medical examinations, including voluntary medical histories, which are part of an employee health program available to employees at that work site. A covered entity may make inquiries into the ability of an employee to perform job-related functions.

(C) Information obtained under subparagraph (B) regarding the medical condition or history of any employee are subject to the requirements of subparagraphs (B) and (C) of paragraph (3).

## Sec. 103   [§ 12113].   Defenses

(a) It may be a defense to a charge of discrimination under this chapter that an alleged application of qualification standards, tests, or selection criteria that screen out or tend to screen out or otherwise deny a job or benefit to an individual with a disability has been shown to be job-related and consistent with business necessity, and such performance cannot be accomplished by reasonable accommodation, as required under this subchapter.

(b) The term "qualification standards" may include a requirement that an individual shall not pose a direct threat to the health or safety of other individuals in the workplace.

(c)(1) This subchapter shall not prohibit a religious corporation, association, educational institution, or society from giving preference in employment to individuals of a particular religion to perform work connected with the carrying on by such corporation, association, educational institution, or society of its activities.

(2) Under this subchapter, a religious organization may require that all applicants and employees conform to the religious tenets of such organization.

(d)(1) The Secretary of Health and Human Services, not later than 6 months after July 26, 1990, shall—

(A) review all infectious and communicable diseases which may be transmitted through handling the food supply;

(B) publish a list of infectious and communicable diseases which are transmitted through handling the food supply;

(C) publish the methods by which such diseases are transmitted; and

(D) widely disseminate such information regarding the list of diseases and their modes of transmissability to the general public.

Such list shall be updated annually.

(2) In any case in which an individual has an infectious or communicable disease that is transmitted to others through the handling of food, that is included on the list developed by the Secretary of Health and Human Services under paragraph (1), and which cannot be eliminated by reasonable accommodation, a covered entity may refuse to assign or continue to assign such individual to a job involving food handling.

(3) Nothing in this chapter shall be construed to preempt, modify, or amend any State, county, or local law, ordinance, or regulation applicable to food handling which is designed to protect the public health from individuals who pose a significant risk to the health or safety of others, which cannot be eliminated by reasonable accommodation, pursuant to the list of infectious or communicable diseases and the modes of transmissability published by the Secretary of Health and Human Services.

### Sec. 104 [§ 12114]. Illegal use of drugs and alcohol

(a) For purposes of this subchapter, the term "qualified individual with a disability" shall not include any employee or applicant who is currently engaging in the illegal use of drugs, when the covered entity acts on the basis of such use.

(b) Nothing in subsection (a) of this section shall be construed to exclude as a qualified individual with a disability an individual who—

(1) has successfully completed a supervised drug rehabilitation program and is no longer engaging in the illegal use of drugs, or has otherwise been rehabilitated successfully and is no longer engaging in such use;

(2) is participating in a supervised rehabilitation program and is no longer engaging in such use; or

(3) is erroneously regarded as engaging in such use, but is not engaging in such use;

except that it shall not be a violation of this chapter for a covered entity to adopt or administer reasonable policies or procedures, including but not limited to drug testing, designed to ensure that an individual described in paragraph (1) or (2) is no longer engaging in the illegal use of drugs.

(c) A covered entity—

(1) may prohibit the illegal use of drugs and the use of alcohol at the workplace by all employees;

(2) may require that employees shall not be under the influence of alcohol or be engaging in the illegal use of drugs at the workplace;

(3) may require that employees behave in conformance with the requirements established under the Drug–Free Workplace Act of 1988 (41 U.S.C. 701 et seq.);

(4) may hold an employee who engages in the illegal use of drugs or who is an alcoholic to the same qualification standards for employment

or job performance and behavior that such entity holds other employees, even if any unsatisfactory performance or behavior is related to the drug use or alcoholism of such employee; and

(5) may, with respect to Federal regulations regarding alcohol and the illegal use of drugs, require that—

(A) employees comply with the standards established in such regulations of the Department of Defense, if the employees of the covered entity are employed in an industry subject to such regulations, including complying with regulations (if any) that apply to employment in sensitive positions in such an industry, in the case of employees of the covered entity who are employed in such positions (as defined in the regulations of the Department of Defense);

(B) employees comply with the standards established in such regulations of the Nuclear Regulatory Commission, if the employees of the covered entity are employed in an industry subject to such regulations, including complying with regulations (if any) that apply to employment in sensitive positions in such an industry, in the case of employees of the covered entity who are employed in such positions (as defined in the regulations of the Nuclear Regulatory Commission); and

(C) employees comply with the standards established in such regulations of the Department of Transportation, if the employees of the covered entity are employed in a transportation industry subject to such regulations, including complying with such regulations (if any) that apply to employment in sensitive positions in such an industry, in the case of employees of the covered entity who are employed in such positions (as defined in the regulations of the Department of Transportation).

(d)(1) For purposes of this subchapter, a test to determine the illegal use of drugs shall not be considered a medical examination.

(2) Nothing in this subchapter shall be construed to encourage, prohibit, or authorize the conducting of drug testing for the illegal use of drugs by job applicants or employees or making employment decisions based on such test results.

(e) Nothing in this subchapter shall be construed to encourage, prohibit, restrict, or authorize the otherwise lawful exercise by entities subject to the jurisdiction of the Department of Transportation of authority to—

(1) test employees of such entities in, and applicants for, positions involving safety-sensitive duties for the illegal use of drugs and for on-duty impairment by alcohol; and

(2) remove such persons who test positive for illegal use of drugs and on-duty impairment by alcohol pursuant to paragraph (1) from safety-sensitive duties in implementing subsection (c) of this section.

## Sec. 105 [§ 12115]. Posting notices

Every employer, employment agency, labor organization, or joint labor-management committee covered under this subchapter shall post notices in an accessible format to applicants, employees, and members describing the applicable provisions of this chapter, in the manner prescribed by section 2000e–10 of this title.

### Sec. 106 [§ 12116]. Regulations

Not later than 1 year after July 26, 1990, the Commission shall issue regulations in an accessible format to carry out this title in accordance with subchapter II of chapter 5 of Title 5.

### Sec. 107 [§ 12117]. Enforcement

(a) The powers, remedies, and procedures set forth in sections 2000e–4, 2000e–5, 2000e–6, 2000e–8, and 2000e–9 of this title shall be the powers, remedies, and procedures this subchapter provides to the Commission, to the Attorney General, or to any person alleging discrimination on the basis of disability in violation of any provision of this chapter, or regulations promulgated under section 12116 of this title, concerning employment.

(b) The agencies with enforcement authority for actions which allege employment discrimination under this subchapter and under the Rehabilitation Act of 1973 [29 U.S.C.A. § 701 et seq.] shall develop procedures to ensure that administrative complaints filed under this subchapter and under the Rehabilitation Act of 1973 [29 U.S.C.A. § 701 et seq.] are dealt with in a manner that avoids duplication of effort and prevents imposition of inconsistent or conflicting standards for the same requirements under this subchapter and the Rehabilitation Act of 1973 [29 U.S.C.A. § 701 et seq.]. The Commission, the Attorney General, and the Office of Federal Contract Compliance Programs shall establish such coordinating mechanisms (similar to provisions contained in the joint regulations promulgated by the Commission and the Attorney General at part 42 of title 28 and part 1691 of title 29, Code of Federal Regulations, and the Memorandum of Understanding between the Commission and the Office of Federal Contract Compliance Programs dated January 16, 1981 (46 Fed.Reg. 7435, January 23, 1981)) in regulations implementing this subchapter and Rehabilitation Act of 1973 [29 U.S.C.A. § 701 et seq.] not later than 18 months after July 26, 1990.

SUBCHAPTER V—MISCELLANEOUS PROVISIONS

### Sec. 501 [§ 12201]. Construction

(a) Except as otherwise provided in this chapter, nothing in this chapter shall be construed to apply a lesser standard than the standards applied under title V of the Rehabilitation Act of 1973 (29 U.S.C. 790 et seq.) or the regulations issued by Federal agencies pursuant to such title.

(b) Nothing in this chapter shall be construed to invalidate or limit the remedies, rights, and procedures of any Federal law or law of any State or political subdivision of any State or jurisdiction that provides greater or equal protection for the rights of individuals with disabilities than are afforded by this chapter. Nothing in this chapter shall be construed to preclude the prohibition of, or the imposition of restrictions on, smoking in places of employment covered by subchapter I of this chapter, in transportation covered by subchapter II or III of this chapter, or in places of public accommodation covered by subchapter III of this chapter.

(c) [The employment sections] of this Act shall not be construed to prohibit or restrict—

(1) an insurer, hospital or medical service company, health maintenance organization, or any agent, or entity that administers benefit plans, or similar organizations from underwriting risks, classifying risks, or administering such risks that are based on or not inconsistent with State law; or

(2) a person or organization covered by this chapter from establishing, sponsoring, observing or administering the terms of a bona fide benefit plan that are based on underwriting risks, classifying risks, or administering such risks that are based on or not inconsistent with State law; or

(3) a person or organization covered by this chapter from establishing, sponsoring, observing or administering the terms of a bona fide benefit plan that is not subject to State laws that regulate insurance.

Paragraphs (1), (2), and (3) shall not be used as a subterfuge to evade the purposes of [the e,employment sections of this Act]

## Sec. 502 [§ 12202]. State immunity

A State shall not be immune under the eleventh amendment to the Constitution of the United States from an action in Federal or State court of competent jurisdiction for a violation of this chapter. In any action against a State for a violation of the requirements of this chapter, remedies (including remedies both at law and in equity) are available for such a violation to the same extent as such remedies are available for such a violation in an action against any public or private entity other than a State.

## Sec. 505 [§ 12203]. Prohibition against retaliation and coercion

(a) No person shall discriminate against any individual because such individual has opposed any act or practice made unlawful by this chapter or because such individual made a charge, testified, assisted, or participated in any manner in an investigation, proceeding, or hearing under this chapter.

(b) It shall be unlawful to coerce, intimidate, threaten, or interfere with any individual in the exercise or enjoyment of, or on account of his or her having exercised or enjoyed, or on account of his or her having aided or encouraged any other individual in the exercise or enjoyment of, any right granted or protected by this chapter.

(c) The remedies and procedures available under section [107] shall be available to aggrieved persons for violations of subsections (a) and (b) of this section. . . .

### Sec. 507 [§ 12205]. Attorney's fees

In any action or administrative proceeding commenced pursuant to this chapter, the court or agency, in its discretion, may allow the prevailing party, other than the United States, a reasonable attorney's fee, including litigation expenses, and costs, and the United States shall be liable for the foregoing the same as a private individual. . . .

### Sec. 508 [§ 12208]. Transvestites

For the purposes of this chapter, the term "disabled" or "disability" shall not apply to an individual solely because that individual is a transvestite.

### Sec. 510 [§ 12210]. Illegal use of drugs

(a) For purposes of this chapter, the term "individual with a disability" does not include an individual who is currently engaging in the illegal use of drugs, when the covered entity acts on the basis of such use.

(b) Nothing in subsection (a) of this section shall be construed to exclude as an individual with a disability an individual who—

(1) has successfully completed a supervised drug rehabilitation program and is no longer engaging in the illegal use of drugs, or has otherwise been rehabilitated successfully and is no longer engaging in such use;

(2) is participating in a supervised rehabilitation program and is no longer engaging in such use; or

(3) is erroneously regarded as engaging in such use, but is not engaging in such use;

except that it shall not be a violation of this chapter for a covered entity to adopt or administer reasonable policies or procedures, including but not limited to drug testing, designed to ensure that an individual described in paragraph (1) or (2) is no longer engaging in the illegal use of drugs; however, nothing in this section shall be construed to encourage, prohibit, restrict, or authorize the conducting of testing for the illegal use of drugs.

(c) Notwithstanding subsection (a) of this section and section 12211(b)(3) of this title, an individual shall not be denied health services, or services provided in connection with drug rehabilitation, on the basis of the current illegal use of drugs if the individual is otherwise entitled to such services.

(d)(1) The term "illegal use of drugs" means the use of drugs, the possession or distribution of which is unlawful under the Controlled Substances Act (21 U.S.C. 812). Such term does not include the use of a drug taken under supervision by a licensed health care professional, or other uses authorized by the Controlled Substances Act [21 U.S.C.A. § 801 et seq.] or other provisions of Federal law.

(2) The term "drug" means a controlled substance, as defined in schedules I through V of section 202 of the Controlled Substances Act [21 U.S.C.A. § 812].

### Sec. 511  [§ 12211].  Definitions

(a) For purposes of the definition of "disability" in section 12102(2) of this title, homosexuality and bisexuality are not impairments and as such are not disabilities under this chapter.

(b) Under this chapter, the term "disability" shall not include—

(1) transvestism, transsexualism, pedophilia, exhibitionism, voyeurism, gender identity disorders not resulting from physical impairments, or other sexual behavior disorders;

(2) compulsive gambling, kleptomania, or pyromania; or

(3) psychoactive substance use disorders resulting from current illegal use of drugs.

### Sec. 513  [§ 12212].  Alternative means of dispute resolution

Where appropriate and to the extent authorized by law, the use of alternative means of dispute resolution, including settlement negotiations, conciliation, facilitation, mediation, factfinding, minitrials, and arbitration, is encouraged to resolve disputes arising under this chapter.

---

# EXECUTIVE ORDER 11246—EQUAL EMPLOYMENT OPPORTUNITY

**Source:** The provisions of Executive Order 11246 of Sept. 24, 1965, appear at 30 FR 12319, 12935, 3 CFR, 1964–1965 Comp., p. 339, as amended.

Under and by virtue of the authority vested in me as President of the United States by the Constitution and statutes of the United States, it is ordered as follows:

\* \* \*

Part II.  Nondiscrimination in Employment by Government Contractors and Subcontractors

\* \* \*

SUBPART B.  CONTRACTORS' AGREEMENTS

**Sec. 202.**  Except in contracts exempted in accordance with Section 204 of this Order, all Government contracting agencies shall include in every Government contract hereafter entered into the following provisions:

During the performance of this contract, the contractor agrees as follows:

(1) The contractor will not discriminate against any employee or applicant for employment because of race, color, religion, sex, or national origin. The contractor will take affirmative action to ensure that applicants are employed, and that employees are treated during employment, without regard to their race, color, religion, sex or national origin. Such action shall include, but not be limited to the following: employment, upgrading, demotion, or transfer; recruitment or recruitment advertising; layoff or termination; rates of pay or other forms of compensation; and selection for training, including apprenticeship. The contractor agrees to post in conspicuous places, available to employees and applicants for employment, notices to be provided by the contracting officer setting forth the provisions of this nondiscrimination clause.

(2) The contractor will, in all solicitations or advertisements for employees placed by or on behalf of the contractor, state that all qualified applicants will receive consideration for employment without regard to race, color, religion, sex or national origin.

(3) The contractor will send to each labor union or representative of workers with which he has a collective bargaining agreement or other contract or understanding, a notice, to be provided by the agency contracting officer, advising the labor union or workers' representative of the contractor's commitments under Section 202 of Executive Order No. 11246 of September 24, 1965, and shall post copies of the notice in conspicuous places available to employees and applicants for employment.

\* \* \*

(6) In the event of the contractor's noncompliance with the nondiscrimination clauses of this contract or with any of such rules, regulations, or orders, this contract may be cancelled, terminated or suspended in whole or in part and the contractor may be declared ineligible for further Government contracts in accordance with procedures authorized in Executive Order No. 11246 of Sept. 24, 1965, and such other sanctions may be imposed and remedies invoked as provided in Executive Order No. 11246 of September 24, 1965, or by rule, regulation, or order of the Secretary of Labor, or as otherwise provided by law.

\* \* \*

[Sec. 202 amended by EO 11375 of Oct. 13, 1967, 32 FR 14303, 3 CFR, 1966–1970 Comp., p. 684; EO 12086 of Oct. 5, 1978, 43 FR 46501, 3 CFR, 1978 Comp., p. 230]

\* \* \*

SUBPART D.   SANCTIONS AND PENALTIES

**Sec. 209.**  (a) In accordance with such rules, regulations, or orders as the Secretary of Labor may issue or adopt, the Secretary may:

(1) Publish, or cause to be published, the names of contractors or unions which it has concluded have complied or have failed to comply with the provisions of this Order or of the rules, regulations, and orders of the Secretary of Labor.

(2) Recommend to the Department of Justice that, in cases in which there is substantial or material violation or the threat of substantial or material violation of the contractual provisions set forth in Section 202 of this Order, appropriate proceedings be brought to enforce those provisions, including the enjoining, within the limitations of applicable law, of organizations, individuals, or groups who prevent directly or indirectly, or seek to prevent directly or indirectly, compliance with the provisions of this Order.

(3) Recommend to the Equal Employment Opportunity Commission or the Department of Justice that appropriate proceedings be instituted under Title VII of the Civil Rights Act of 1964.

(4) Recommend to the Department of Justice that criminal proceedings be brought for the furnishing of false information to any contracting agency or to the Secretary of Labor as the case may be.

(5) After consulting with the contracting agency, direct the contracting agency to cancel, terminate, suspend, or cause to be cancelled, terminated, or suspended, any contract, or any portion or portions thereof, for failure of the contractor or subcontractor to comply with equal employment opportunity provisions of the contract.  Contracts may be cancelled, terminated, or suspended absolutely or continuance of contracts may be conditioned upon a program for future compliance approved by the Secretary of Labor.

(6) Provide that any contracting agency shall refrain from entering into further contracts, or extensions or other modifications of existing contracts, with any noncomplying contractor, until such contractor has satisfied the Secretary of Labor that such contractor has established and will carry out personnel and employment policies in compliance with the provisions of this Order.

(b) Pursuant to rules and regulations prescribed by the Secretary of Labor, the Secretary shall make reasonable efforts, within a reasonable time limitation, to secure compliance with the contract provisions of this Order by methods of conference, conciliation, mediation, and persuasion before proceedings shall be instituted under subsection (a)(2) of this Section, or before a contract shall be cancelled or terminated in whole or in part under subsection (a)(5) of this Section.

[Sec. 209 amended by EO 12086 of Oct. 5, 1978, 43 FR 46501, 3 CFR, 1978 Comp., p. 230]

\* \* \*

# FEDERAL LAWS RELATING TO LABOR RELATIONS

## NORRIS–LAGUARDIA ACT

47 Stat. 70 (1932), 29 U.S.C. §§ 101–15 (1982).

**Sec. 1.** (§ 101) No court of the United States, as herein defined, shall have jurisdiction to issue any restraining order or temporary or permanent injunction in a case involving or growing out of a labor dispute, except in a strict conformity with the provisions of this Act; nor shall any such restraining order or temporary or permanent injunction be issued contrary to the public policy declared in this Act.

**Sec. 2.** (§ 102) In the interpretation of this Act and in determining the jurisdiction and authority of the courts of the United States, as such jurisdiction and authority are herein defined and limited, the public policy of the United States is hereby declared as follows:

Whereas under prevailing economic conditions, developed with the aid of governmental authority for owners of property to organize in the corporate and other forms of ownership association, the individual unorganized worker is commonly helpless to exercise actual liberty of contract and to protect his freedom of labor, and thereby to obtain acceptable terms and conditions of employment, wherefore, though he should be free to decline to associate with his fellows, it is necessary that he have full freedom of association, self-organization, and designation of representatives of his own choosing, to negotiate the terms and conditions of his employment, and that he shall be free from the interference, restraint, or coercion of employers of labor, or their agents, in the designation of such representatives or in self-organization or in other concerted activities for the purpose of collective bargaining or other mutual aid or protection; therefore, the following definitions of, and limitations upon, the jurisdiction and authority of the courts of the United States are hereby enacted.

**Sec. 3.** (§ 103) Any undertaking or promise, such as is described in this section, or any other undertaking or promise in conflict with the public policy declared in section 2 of this Act, is hereby declared to be contrary to the public policy of the United States, shall not be enforceable in any court of the United States and shall not afford any basis for the granting of legal or equitable relief by any such court, including specifically the following:

Every undertaking or promise hereafter made, whether written or oral, express or implied, constituting or contained in any contract or agreement of hiring or employment between any individual, firm, company, association, or corporation, and any employee or prospective employee of the same whereby

(a) Either party to such contract or agreement undertakes or promises not to join, become, or remain a member of any labor organization or of any employer organization; or

(b) Either party to such contract or agreement undertakes or promises that he will withdraw from an employment relation in the event that he joins, becomes, or remains a member of any labor organization or of any employer organization.

**Sec. 4.**   (§ 104) No court of the United States shall have jurisdiction to issue any restraining order or temporary or permanent injunction in any case involving or growing out of any labor dispute to prohibit any person or persons participating or interested in such dispute (as these terms are herein defined) from doing, whether singly or in concert, any of the following acts:

(a) Ceasing or refusing to perform any work or to remain in any relation of employment;

(b) Becoming or remaining a member of any labor organization or of any employer organization, regardless of any such undertaking or promise as is described in section 3 of this Act;

(c) Paying or giving to, or withholding from, any person participating or interested in such labor dispute, any strike or unemployment benefits or insurance, or other moneys or things of value;

(d) By all lawful means aiding any person participating or interested in any labor dispute who is being proceeded against in, or is prosecuting, any action or suit in any court of the United States or of any State;

(e) Giving publicity to the existence of, or the facts involved in, any labor dispute, whether by advertising, speaking, patrolling, or by any other method not involving fraud or violence;

(f) Assembling peaceably to act or to organize to act in promotion of their interests in a labor dispute;

(g) Advising or notifying any person of an intention to do any of the Acts heretofore specified;

(h) Agreeing with other persons to do or not to do any of the acts heretofore specified; and

(i) Advising, urging, or otherwise causing or inducing without fraud or violence the acts heretofore specified, regardless of any such undertaking or promise as is described in section 3 of this Act.

**Sec. 5.**   (§ 105) No court of the United States shall have jurisdiction to issue a restraining order or temporary or permanent injunction upon the ground that any of the persons participating or interested in a labor dispute constitute or are engaged in an unlawful combination or conspiracy because of the doing in concert of the acts enumerated in section 4 of this Act.

**Sec. 6.** (§ 106) No officer or member of any association or organization, and no association or organization participating or interested in a labor dispute, shall be held responsible or liable in any court of the United States for the unlawful acts of individual officers, members, or agents, except upon clear proof of actual participation in, or actual authorization of, such acts, or of ratification of such acts after actual knowledge thereof.

**Sec. 7.** (§ 107) No court of the United States shall have jurisdiction to issue a temporary or permanent injunction in any case involving or growing out of a labor dispute, as herein defined, except after hearing the testimony of witnesses in open court (with opportunity for cross-examination) in support of the allegations of a complaint made under oath, and testimony in opposition thereto, if offered, and except after findings of fact by the court, to the effect—

(a) That unlawful acts have been threatened and will be committed unless restrained or have been committed and will be continued unless restrained, but no injunction or temporary restraining order shall be issued on account of any threat or unlawful act excepting against the person or persons, association, or organization making the threat or committing the unlawful act or actually authorizing or ratifying the same after actual knowledge thereof;

(b) That substantial and irreparable injury to complainant's property will follow:

(c) That as to each item of relief granted greater injury will be inflicted upon complainant by the denial of relief than will be inflicted upon defendants by the granting of relief;

(d) That complainant has no adequate remedy at law; and

(e) That the public officers charged with the duty to protect complainant's property are unable or unwilling to furnish adequate protection.

Such hearing shall be held after due and personal notice thereof has been given, in such manner as the court shall direct, to all known persons against whom relief is sought, and also to the chief of those public officials of the county and city within which the unlawful acts have been threatened or committed charged with the duty to protect complainant's property: *Provided, however,* That if a complainant shall also allege that, unless a temporary restraining order shall be issued without notice, a substantial and irreparable injury to complainant's property will be unavoidable, such a temporary restraining order may be issued upon testimony under oath, sufficient, if sustained, to justify the court in issuing a temporary injunction upon a hearing after notice. Such a temporary restraining order shall be effective for no longer than five days and shall become void at the expiration of said five days. No temporary restraining order or temporary injunction shall be issued except on condition that complainant shall first file an undertaking with adequate security in an amount to be fixed by the court sufficient to recompense those enjoined for any loss, expense, or damage caused by the improvident or erroneous issuance of such order or injunction, including all reasonable costs (together with a reasonable attorney's fee) and expense of defense against the order or against the granting of any injunctive relief sought in the same proceeding and subsequently denied by the court.

The undertaking herein mentioned shall be understood to signify an agreement entered into by the complainant and the surety upon which a decree may be rendered in the same suit or proceeding against said complainant and surety, upon a hearing to assess damages of which hearing complainant and surety shall have reasonable notice, the said complainant and surety submitting themselves to the jurisdiction of the court for that purpose. But nothing herein contained shall deprive any party having a claim or cause of action under or upon such undertaking from electing to pursue his ordinary remedy by suit at law or in equity.

**Sec. 8.** (§ 108) No restraining order or injunctive relief shall be granted to any complainant who has failed to comply with any obligation imposed by law which is involved in the labor dispute in question, or who has failed to make every reasonable effort to settle such dispute either by negotiation or with the aid of any available governmental machinery of mediation or voluntary arbitration.

**Sec. 9.** (§ 109) No restraining order or temporary or permanent injunction shall be granted in a case involving or growing out of a labor dispute, except on the basis of findings of fact made and filed by the court in the record of the case prior to the issuance of such restraining order or injunction; and every restraining order or injunction granted in a case involving or growing out of a labor dispute shall include only a prohibition of such specific act or acts as may be expressly complained of in the bill of complaint or petition filed in such case and as shall be expressly included in said findings of fact made and filed by the court as provided herein.

**Sec. 10.** (§ 110) Whenever any court of the United States shall issue or deny any temporary injunction in a case involving or growing out of a labor dispute, the court shall, upon the request of any party to the proceedings and on his filing the usual bond for costs, forthwith certify as in ordinary cases the record of the case to the circuit court of appeals for its review. Upon the filing of such record in the circuit court of appeals, the appeal shall be heard and the temporary injunctive order affirmed, modified, or set aside with the greatest possible expedition, giving the proceedings precedence over all other matters except older matters of the same character.

**Sec. 11.**\* In all cases arising under this Act in which a person shall be charged with contempt in a court of the United States (as herein

---

\* Sections 11 and 12 were repealed in 1948, 62 Stat. 862. The text of Section 11 is now in 18 U.S.C. § 3692 (1982); Rule 42 of the Federal Rules of Criminal Procedure

defined), the accused shall enjoy the right to a speedy and public trial by an impartial jury of the State and district wherein the contempt shall have been committed: *Provided,* That this right shall not apply to contempts committed in the presence of the court or so near thereto as to interfere directly with the administration of justice or to apply to the misbehavior, misconduct, or disobedience of any officer of the court in respect to the writs, orders, or process of the court.

**Sec. 12.**\* The defendant in any proceeding for contempt of court may file with the court a demand for the retirement of the judge sitting in the proceeding, if the contempt arises from an attack upon the character or conduct of such judge and if the attack occurred elsewhere than in the presence of the court or so near thereto as to interfere directly with the administration of justice. Upon the filing of any such demand the judge shall thereupon proceed no further, but another judge shall be designated in the same manner as is provided by law. The demand shall be filed prior to the hearing in the contempt proceeding.

**Sec. 13.** (§ 113) When used in this Act, and for the purposes of this Act—

(a) A case shall be held to involve or to grow out of a labor dispute when the case involves persons who are engaged in the same industry, trade, craft, or occupation; or have direct or indirect interests therein; or who are employees of the same employer; or who are members of the same or an affiliated organization of employers or employees; whether such dispute is (1) between one or more employers or associations of employers and one or more employees or associations of employees; (2) between one or more employers or associations of employers and one or more employers or associations of employers; or (3) between one or more employees or associations of employees and one or more employees or associations of employees; or when the case involves any conflicting or competing interests in a "labor dispute" (as hereinafter defined) of "persons participating or interested" therein (as hereinafter defined).

(b) A person or association shall be held to be a person participating or interested in a labor dispute if relief is sought against him or it, and if he or it is engaged in the same industry, trade, craft, or occupation in which such dispute occurs, or has a direct or indirect interest therein, or is a member, officer, or agent of any association composed in whole or in part of employers or employees engaged in such industry, trade, craft, or occupation.

(c) The term "labor dispute" includes any controversy concerning terms or conditions of employment, or concerning the association or representation of persons in negotiating, fixing, maintaining, changing, or seeking to arrange terms or conditions of employment, regardless of whether or not the disputants stand in the proximate relation of employer and employee.

now governs the matters formerly treated
in Section 12.

(d) The term "court of the United States" means any court of the United States whose jurisdiction has been or may be conferred or defined or limited by Act of Congress, including the courts of the District of Columbia.

**Sec. 14.** (§ 114) If any provision of this Act or the application thereof to any person or circumstance is held unconstitutional or otherwise invalid, the remaining provisions of the Act and the application of such provisions to other persons or circumstances shall not be affected thereby.

**Sec. 15.** (§ 115) All Acts and parts of Acts in conflict with the provisions of this Act are hereby repealed.

---

# LABOR MANAGEMENT RELATIONS ACT

*Act of June 23, 1947, 61 Stat. 136, as amended,*
*29 U.S.C. §§ 141 et seq.*

SHORT TITLE AND DECLARATION OF POLICY

§ 1. (§ 141) (A) THIS ACT MAY BE CITED AS THE "LABOR MANAGEMENT RELATIONS ACT, 1947".

(b) Industrial strife which interferes with the normal flow of commerce and with the full production of articles and commodities for commerce, can be avoided or substantially minimized if employers, employees, and labor organizations each recognize under law one another's legitimate rights in their relations with each other, and above all recognize under law that neither party has any right in its relations with any other to engage in acts or practices which jeopardize the public health, safety, or interest.

It is the purpose and policy of this Act, in order to promote the full flow of commerce, to prescribe the legitimate rights of both employees and employers in their relations affecting commerce, to provide orderly and peaceful procedures for preventing the interference by either with the legitimate rights of the other, to protect the rights of individual employees in their relations with labor organizations whose activities affect commerce, to define and proscribe practices on the part of labor and management which affect commerce and are inimical to the general welfare, and to protect the rights of the public in connection with labor disputes affecting commerce.

TITLE I—AMENDMENT OF NATIONAL LABOR RELATIONS ACT

[49 Stat. 449 (1935)]

§ 101. The National Labor Relations Act is hereby amended to read as follows:*

---

\* The provisions of the original NLRA are in roman type; provisions added by the Labor Management Relations Act (1947) are in bold face; provisions added by the

FINDINGS AND POLICIES

§ 1.   (§ 151) The denial by **some** employers of the right of employees to organize and the refusal by **some** employers to accept the procedure of collective bargaining lead to strikes and other forms of industrial strife or unrest, which have the intent or the necessary effect of burdening or obstructing commerce by (a) impairing the efficiency, safety, or operation of the instrumentalities of commerce; (b) occurring in the current of commerce; (c) materially affecting, restraining, or controlling the flow of raw materials or manufactured or processed goods from or into the channels of commerce, or the prices of such materials or goods in commerce; or (d) causing diminution of employment and wages in such volume as substantially to impair or disrupt the market for goods flowing from or into the channels of commerce.

The inequality of bargaining power between employees who do not possess full freedom of association or actual liberty of contract, and employers who are organized in the corporate or other forms of ownership association substantially burdens and affects the flow of commerce, and tends to aggravate recurrent business depressions, by depressing wage rates and the purchasing power of wage earners in industry and by preventing the stabilization of competitive wage rates and working conditions within and between industries.

Experience has proved that protection by law of the right of employees to organize and bargain collectively safeguards commerce from injury, impairment, or interruption, and promotes the flow of commerce by removing certain recognized sources of industrial strife and unrest, by encouraging practices fundamental to the friendly adjustment of industrial disputes arising out of differences as to wages, hours, or other working conditions, and by restoring equality of bargaining power between employers and employees.

**Experience has further demonstrated that certain practices by some labor organizations, their officers, and members have the intent or the necessary effect of burdening or obstructing commerce by preventing the free flow of goods in such commerce through strikes and other forms of industrial unrest or through concerted activities which impair the interest of the public in the free flow of such commerce. The elimination of such practices is a necessary condition to the assurance of the rights herein guaranteed.**

It is hereby declared to be the policy of the United States to eliminate the causes of certain substantial obstructions to the free flow of commerce and to mitigate and eliminate these obstructions when they have occurred by encouraging the practice and procedure of collective bargaining and by protecting the exercise by workers of full freedom of

Labor–Management Reporting and Disclosure Act (1959) are in italics; provisions added by Public Law 93–360 (enacted July 26, 1974) are in bold-face italics.  Material deleted by any of those statutes is enclosed by brackets.

association, self-organization, and designation of representatives of their own choosing, for the purpose of negotiating the terms and conditions of their employment or other mutual aid or protection.

### DEFINITIONS

§ 2. (§ 152) When used in this Act—

(1) The term "person" includes one or more individuals, labor organizations, partnerships, associations, corporations, legal representatives, trustees, trustees in bankruptcy, or receivers.*

(2) The term "employer" includes any person acting [in the interest] **as an agent** of an employer, directly or indirectly, but shall not include the United States **or any wholly owned Government corporation, or any Federal Reserve Bank**, or any State or political subdivision thereof, [**or any corporation or association operating a hospital, if no part of the net earnings inures to the benefit of any private shareholder or individual,**] or any person subject to the Railway Labor Act, as amended from time to time, or any labor organization (other than when acting as an employer), or anyone acting in the capacity of officer or agent of such labor organization.

(3) The term "employee" shall include any employee, and shall not be limited to the employees of a particular employer, unless the Act explicitly states otherwise, and shall include any individual whose work has ceased as a consequence of, or in connection with, any current labor dispute or because of any unfair labor practice, and who has not obtained any other regular and substantially equivalent employment, but shall not include any individual employed as an agricultural laborer, or in the domestic service of any family or person at his home, or any individual employed by his parent or spouse, **or any individual having the status of an independent contractor, or any individual employed as a supervisor, or any individual employed by an employer subject to the Railway Labor Act, as amended from time to time, or by any other person who is not an employer as herein defined.**

(4) The term "representatives" includes any individual or labor organization.

(5) The term "labor organization" means any organization of any kind, or any agency or employee representation committee or plan, in which employees participate and which exists for the purpose, in whole or in part, of dealing with employers concerning grievances, labor disputes, wages, rates of pay, hours of employment, or conditions of work.

(6) The term "commerce" means trade, traffic commerce, transportation, or communication among the several States, or between the

---

* Section 2(1) was amended by P.L. 95–598, effective October 1, 1979, to add the words "cases under Title II of the United States Code" and to delete the material enclosed in brackets.

District of Columbia or any Territory of the United States and any State or other Territory, or between any foreign country and any State, Territory, or the District of Columbia, or within the District of Columbia or any Territory, or between points in the same State but through any other State or any Territory or the District of Columbia or any foreign country.

(7) The term "affecting commerce" means in commerce, or burdening or obstructing commerce or the free flow of commerce, or having led or tending to lead to a labor dispute burdening or obstructing commerce or the free flow of commerce.

(8) The term "unfair labor practice" means any unfair labor practice listed in section 8.

(9) The term "labor dispute" includes any controversy concerning terms, tenure or conditions of employment, or concerning the association or representation of persons in negotiating, fixing, maintaining, changing, or seeking to arrange terms or conditions of employment, regardless of whether the disputants stand in the proximate relation of employer and employee.

(10) The term "National Labor Relations Board" means the National Labor Relations Board provided for in section 3 of this Act.

**(11) The term "supervisor" means any individual having authority, in the interest of the employer, to hire, transfer, suspend, lay off, recall, promote, discharge, assign, reward, or discipline other employees, or responsibly to direct them, or to adjust their grievances, or effectively to recommend such action, if in connection with the foregoing the exercise of such authority is not of a merely routine or clerical nature, but requires the use of independent judgment.**

**(12) The term "professional employee" means—**

**(a) any employee engaged in work (i) predominantly intellectual and varied in character as opposed to routine mental, manual, mechanical, or physical work; (ii) involving the consistent exercise of discretion and judgment in its performance; (iii) of such a character that the output produced or the result accomplished cannot be standardized in relation to a given period of time; (iv) requiring knowledge of an advanced type in a field of science or learning customarily acquired by a prolonged course of specialized intellectual instruction and study in an institution of higher learning or a hospital, as distinguished from a general academic education or from an apprenticeship or from training in the performance of routine mental, manual, or physical processes; or**

**(b) any employee, who (i) has completed the courses of specialized intellectual instruction and study described in clause (iv) of paragraph (a), and (ii) is performing related**

work under the supervision of a professional person to qualify himself to become a professional employee as defined in paragraph (a).

(13) In determining whether any person is acting as an "agent" of another person so as to make such other person responsible for his acts, the question of whether the specific acts performed were actually authorized or subsequently ratified shall not be controlling.

*(14) The term "health care institution" shall include any hospital, convalescent hospital, health maintenance organization, health clinic, nursing home, extended care facility, or other institution devoted to the care of sick, infirm, or aged person.*

§ 3.    (§ 153) **(a) The National Labor Relations Board (hereinafter called the "Board") created by this Act prior to its amendment by the Labor Management Relations Act, 1947, is hereby continued as an agency of the United States, except that the Board shall consist of five instead of three members, appointed by the President by and with the advice and consent of the Senate. Of the two additional members so provided for, one shall be appointed for a term of five years and the other for a term of two years. Their successors, and the successors of the other members, shall be appointed for terms of five years each, excepting that any individual chosen to fill a vacancy shall be appointed only for the unexpired term of the member whom he shall succeed. The President shall designate one member to serve as Chairman of the Board. Any member of the Board may be removed by the President, upon notice and hearing, for neglect of duty or malfeasance in office, but for no other cause.**

**(b) The Board is authorized to delegate to any group of three or more members any or all of the powers which it may itself exercise.** *The Board is also authorized to delegate to its regional directors its powers under section 9 to determine the unit appropriate for the purpose of collective bargaining, to investigate and provide for hearings, and determine whether a question of representation exists, and to direct an election or take a secret ballot under subsection (c) or (e) of section 9 and certify the results thereof, except that upon the filing of a request therefor with the Board by any interested person, the Board may review any action of a regional director delegated to him under this paragraph, but such a review shall not, unless specifically ordered by the Board, operate as a stay of any action taken by the regional director.* **A vacancy in the Board shall not impair the right of the remaining members to exercise all of the powers of the Board, and three members of the Board shall, at all times, constitute a quorum of the Board, except that two members shall constitute a quorum of any group designated pursuant to the first sentence thereof. The Board shall have an official seal which shall be judicially noticed.**

(c) The Board shall at the close of each fiscal year make a report in writing to Congress and to the President stating in detail the cases it has heard, the decisions it has rendered, [the names, salaries, and duties of all employees and officers in the employ or under the supervision of the Board,]* and an account of all moneys it has disbursed.

(d) There shall be a General Counsel of the Board who shall be appointed by the President, by and with the advice and consent of the Senate, for a term of four years. The General Counsel of the Board shall exercise general supervision over all attorneys employed by the Board (other than trial examiners and legal assistants to Board members) and over the officers and employees in the regional offices. He shall have final authority, on behalf of the Board, in respect of the investigation of charges and issuance of complaints under section 10, and in respect of the prosecution of such complaints before the Board, and shall have such other duties as the Board may prescribe or as may be provided by law. *In case of a vacancy in the office of the General Counsel the President is authorized to designate the officer or employee who shall act as General Counsel during such vacancy, but no person or persons so designated shall so act (1) for more than forty days when the Congress is in session unless a nomination to fill such vacancy shall have been submitted to the Senate, or (2) after the adjournment sine die of the session of the Senate in which such nomination was submitted.*

§ 4. (§ 154) **(a)** Each member of the Board and the General Counsel of the Board shall receive a salary of $12,000** a year, shall be eligible for reappointment, and shall not engage in any other business, vocation, or employment. The Board shall appoint an executive secretary, and such attorneys, examiners, and regional directors, and such other employees as it may from time to time find necessary for the proper performance of its duties. The Board may not employ any attorneys for the purpose of reviewing transcripts of hearings or preparing drafts of opinions except that any attorney employed for assignment as a legal assistant to any Board member may for such Board member review such transcripts and prepare such drafts. No trial examiner's report shall be reviewed, either before or after its publication, by any person other than a member of the Board or his legal assistant, and no trial examiner shall advise or consult with the Board with respect to exceptions taken to his findings, rulings, or recommendations. The Board may establish or utilize such regional, local, or other agencies, and utilize such voluntary and uncompensated services, as may from time to

* Section 3(c) was amended by P.L. 93–608, approved January 2, 1975, to delete the material enclosed by brackets.

** Pursuant to P.L. 96–369, approved October 1, 1980, the salary of the Chairman of the Board shall be $55,387 per year and the salaries of the General Counsel and each Board member shall be $52,750 per year.

time be needed. Attorneys appointed under this section may, at the direction of the Board, appear for and represent the Board in any case in court. Nothing in this Act shall be construed to authorize the Board to appoint individuals for the purpose of conciliation or mediation, or for economic analysis.

(b) All the expenses of the Board, including all necessary traveling and subsistence expenses outside the District of Columbia incurred by the members or employees of the Board under its orders, shall be allowed and paid on the presentation of itemized vouchers therefor approved by the Board or by any individual it designates for that purpose.

§ 5. (§ 155) The principal office of the Board shall be in the District of Columbia, but it may meet and exercise any or all of its powers at any other place. The Board may, by one or more of its members or by such agents or agencies as it may designate, prosecute any inquiry necessary to its functions in any part of the United States. A member who participates in such an inquiry shall not be disqualified from subsequently participating in a decision of the Board in the same case.

§ 6. (§ 156) The Board shall have authority from time to time to make, amend, and rescind, **in the manner prescribed by the Administrative Procedure Act,** such rules and regulations as may be necessary to carry out the provisions of this Act.

## Rights of Employees

§ 7. (§ 157) Employees shall have the right to self-organization, to form, join, or assist labor organizations, to bargain collectively through representatives of their own choosing, and to engage in **other** concerted activities for the purpose of collective bargaining or other mutual aid or protection, **and shall also have the right to refrain from any or all of such activities except to the extent that such right may be affected by an agreement requiring membership in a labor organization as a condition of employment as authorized in section 8(a)(3).**

## Unfair Labor Practices

§ 8. (§ 158) **(a)** It shall be an unfair labor practice for an employer—

(1) to interfere with, restrain, or coerce employees in the exercise of the rights guaranteed in section 7;

(2) to dominate or interfere with the formation or administration of any labor organization or contribute financial or other support to it: *Provided,* That subject to rules and regulations made and published by the Board pursuant to section 6, an employer shall not be prohibited from permitting employees to confer with him during working hours without loss of time or pay;

(3) by discrimination in regard to hire or tenure of employment or any term or condition of employment to encourage or discourage membership in any labor organization: *Provided,* That nothing in this Act, or in any other statute of the United States, shall preclude an employer from making an agreement with a labor organization (not established, maintained, or assisted by any action defined in section 8(**a**) of this Act as an unfair labor practice) to require as a condition of employment membership therein **on or after the thirtieth day following the beginning of such employment or the effective date of such agreement, whichever is the later,** (i) if such labor organization is the representative of the employees as provided in section 9(a), in the appropriate collective-bargaining unit covered by such agreement when made [**and has at the time the agreement was made or within the preceding twelve months received from the Board a notice of compliance with section 9(f), (g), (h)** ], **and (ii) unless following an election held as provided in section 9(e) within one year preceding the effective date of such agreement, the Board shall have certified that at least a majority of the employees eligible to vote in such election have voted to rescind the authority of such labor organization to make such an agreement:** *Provided further,* **That no employer shall justify any discrimination against an employee for nonmembership in a labor organization (A) if he has reasonable grounds for believing that such membership was not available to the employee on the same terms and conditions generally applicable to other members, or (B) if he has reasonable grounds for believing that membership was denied or terminated for reasons other than the failure of the employee to tender the periodic dues and the initiation fees uniformly required as a condition of acquiring or retaining membership;**

(4) to discharge or otherwise discriminate against an employee because he has filed charges or given testimony under this Act;

(5) to refuse to bargain collectively with the representatives of his employees, subject to the provisions of section 9(a).

**(b) It shall be an unfair labor practice for a labor organization or its agents—**

**(1) to restrain or coerce (A) employees in the exercise of the rights guaranteed in section 7:** *Provided,* **That this paragraph shall not impair the right of a labor organization to prescribe its own rules with respect to the acquisition or retention of membership therein; or (B) an employer in the selection of his representatives for the purposes of collective bargaining or the adjustment of grievances;**

**(2) to cause or attempt to cause an employer to discriminate against an employee in violation of subsection (a)(3) or to discriminate against an employee with respect to whom**

membership in such organization has been denied or terminated on some ground other than his failure to tender the periodic dues and the initiation fees uniformly required as a condition of acquiring or retaining membership;

(3) to refuse to bargain collectively with an employer, provided it is the representative of his employees subject to the provisions of section 9(a);

(4)(i) to engage in, or to induce or encourage [the employees of any employer] *any individual employed by any person engaged in commerce or in an industry affecting commerce* to engage in, a strike or a [concerted] refusal in the course of [their] *his* employment to use, manufacture, process, transport, or otherwise handle or work on any goods, articles, materials, or commodities or to perform any services[,]; *or (ii) to threaten, coerce, or restrain any person engaged in commerce or in an industry affecting commerce,* where *in either case* an object thereof is:

(A) forcing or requiring any employer or self-employed person to join any labor or employer organization or [any employer or other person to cease using, selling, handling, transporting, or otherwise dealing in the products of any other producer, processor, or manufacturer, or to cease doing business with any other person] *to enter into any agreement which is prohibited by section 8(e);*

(B) *forcing or requiring any person to cease using, selling, handling, transporting, or otherwise dealing in the products of any other producer, processor, or manufacturer, or to cease doing business with any other person, or* forcing or requiring any other employer to recognize or bargain with a labor organization as the representative of his employees unless such labor organization has been certified as the representative of such employees under the provisions of section 9[;]: *Provided, That nothing contained in this clause (B) shall be construed to make unlawful, where not otherwise unlawful, any primary strike or primary picketing;*

(C) forcing or requiring any employer to recognize or bargain with a particular labor organization as the representative of his employees if another labor organization has been certified as the representative of such employees under the provisions of section 9;

(D) forcing or requiring any employer to assign particular work to employees in a particular labor organization or in a particular trade, craft, or class rather than to employees in another labor organization or in another trade, craft, or class, unless such employer is failing to conform to an order or certification of the Board deter-

**mining the bargaining representative for employees performing such work;**

*Provided,* **That nothing contained in this subsection (b) shall be construed to make unlawful a refusal by any person to enter upon the premises of any employer (other than his own employer), if the employees of such employer are engaged in a strike ratified or approved by a representative of such employees whom such employer is required to recognize under this Act[;]:** *Provided further, That for the purposes of this paragraph (4) only, nothing contained in such paragraph shall be construed to prohibit publicity, other than picketing, for the purpose of truthfully advising the public, including consumers and members of a labor organization, that a product or products are produced by an employer with whom the labor organization has a primary dispute and are distributed by another employer, as long as such publicity does not have an effect of inducing any individual employed by any person other than the primary employer in the course of his employment to refuse to pick up, deliver, or transport any goods, or not to perform any services, at the establishment of the employer engaged in such distribution;*

**(5) to require of employees covered by an agreement authorized under subsection (a)(3) the payment, as a condition precedent to becoming a member of such organization, of a fee in an amount which the Board finds excessive or discriminatory under all the circumstances. In making such a finding, the Board shall consider, among other relevant factors, the practices and customs of labor organizations in the particular industry, and the wages currently paid to the employees affected; [and]**

**(6) to cause or attempt to cause an employer to pay or deliver or agree to pay or deliver any money or other thing of value, in the nature of an exaction, for services which are not performed or not to be performed[.];** *and*

*(7) to picket or cause to be picketed, or threaten to picket or cause to be picketed, any employer where an object thereof is forcing or requiring an employer to recognize or bargain with a labor organization as the representative of his employees, or forcing or requiring the employees of an employer to accept or select such labor organization as their collective bargaining representative, unless such labor organization is currently certified as the representative of such employees:*

*(A) where the employer has lawfully recognized in accordance with this Act any other labor organization and a question concerning representation may not appropriately be raised under section 9(c) of this Act,*

*(B) where within the preceding twelve months a valid election under section 9(c) of this Act has been conducted, or*

*(C) where such picketing has been conducted without a petition under section 9(c) being filed within a reasonable period of time not to exceed thirty days from the commencement of such picketing: Provided, That when such a petition has been filed the Board shall forthwith, without regard to the provisions of section 9(c)(1) or the absence of a showing of a substantial interest on the part of the labor organization, direct an election in such unit as the Board finds to be appropriate and shall certify the results thereof: Provided further, That nothing in this subparagraph (C) shall be construed to prohibit any picketing or other publicity for the purpose of truthfully advising the public (including consumers) that an employer does not employ members of, or have a contract with, a labor organization, unless an effect of such picketing is to induce any individual employed by any other person in the course of his employment, not to pick up, deliver or transport any goods or not to perform any services.*

*Nothing in this paragraph (7) shall be construed to permit any act which would otherwise be an unfair labor practice under this section 8(b).*

**(c) The expressing of any views, argument, or opinion, or the dissemination thereof, whether in written, printed, graphic, or visual form, shall not constitute or be evidence of an unfair labor practice under any of the provisions of this Act, if such expression contains no threat of reprisal or force or promise of benefit.**

**(d) For the purposes of this section, to bargain collectively is the performance of the mutual obligation of the employer and the representative of the employees to meet at reasonable times, and confer in good faith with respect to wages, hours, and other terms and conditions of employment, or the negotiation of an agreement, or any question arising thereunder, and the execution of a written contract incorporating any agreement reached if requested by either party, but such obligation does not compel either party to agree to a proposal or require the making of a concession:** *Provided,* **That where there is in effect a collective-bargaining contract covering employees in an industry affecting commerce, the duty to bargain collectively shall also mean that no party to such contract shall terminate or modify such contract, unless the party desiring such termination or modification—**

**(1) serves a written notice upon the other party to the contract of the proposed termination or modification sixty days prior to the expiration date thereof, or in the event such contract contains no expiration date, sixty days prior to the time it is proposed to make such termination or modification;**

(2) offers to meet and confer with the other party for the purpose of negotiating a new contract or a contract containing the proposed modifications;

(3) notifies the Federal Mediation and Conciliation Service within thirty days after such notice of the existence of a dispute, and simultaneously therewith notifies any State or Territorial agency established to mediate and conciliate disputes within the State or Territory where the dispute occurred, provided no agreement has been reached by that time; and

(4) continues in full force and effect, without resorting to strike or lockout, all the terms and conditions of the existing contract for a period of sixty days after such notice is given or until the expiration date of such contract, whichever occurs later:

The duties imposed upon employers, employees, and labor organizations by paragraphs (2), (3), and (4) shall become inapplicable upon an intervening certification of the Board, under which the labor organization or individual, which is a party to the contract, has been superseded as or ceased to be the representative of the employees subject to the provisions of section 9(a), and the duties so imposed shall not be construed as requiring either party to discuss or agree to any modification of the terms and conditions contained in a contract for a fixed period, if such modification is to become effective before such terms and conditions can be re-opened under the provisions of the contract. Any employee who engages in a strike within [the sixty-day] *any notice* period specified in this subsection, *or who engages in any strike within the appropriate period specified in subsection (g) of this section* shall lose his status as an employee of the employer engaged in the particular labor dispute, for the purposes of sections 8, 9, and 10 of this Act, as amended, but such loss of status for such employee shall terminate if and when he is reemployed by such employer. *Whenever the collective bargaining involves employees of a health care institution, the provisions of this section 8(d) shall be modified as follows:*

*(A) The notice of section 8(d)(1) shall be ninety days; the notice of section 8(d)(3) shall be sixty days; and the contract period of section 8(d)(4) shall be ninety days.*

*(B) Where the bargaining is for an initial agreement following certification or recognition, at least thirty days' notice of the existence of a dispute shall be given by the labor organization to the agencies set forth in section 8(d)(3).*

*(C) After notice is given to the Federal Mediation and Conciliation Service under either clause (A) or (B) of this sentence, the Service shall promptly communicate with the parties and use its best efforts, by mediation and concilia-*

*tion, to bring them to agreement. The parties shall partici-*
*pate fully and promptly in such meetings as may be under-*
*taken by the Service for the purpose of aiding in a settlement*
*of the dispute.*

(e) *It shall be an unfair labor practice for any labor organization and any employer to enter into any contract or agreement, express or implied, whereby such employer ceases or refrains or agrees to cease or refrain from handling, using, selling, transporting or otherwise dealing in any of the products of any other employer, or to cease doing business with any other person, and any contract or agreement entered into heretofore or hereafter containing such an agreement shall be to such extent unenforceable and void:* Provided, *That nothing in this subsection (e) shall apply to an agreement between a labor organization and an employer in the construction industry relating to the contracting or subcontracting of work to be done at the site of the construction, alteration, painting, or repair of a building, structure, or other work:* Provided further, *That for the purposes of this subsection (e) and section 8(b)(4)(B) the terms "any employer", "any person engaged in commerce or in industry affecting commerce", and "any person" when used in relation to the terms "any other producer, processor, or manufacturer", "any other employer", or "any other person" shall not include persons in the relation of a jobber, manufacturer, contractor, or subcontractor working on the goods or premises of the jobber or manufacturer or performing parts of an integrated process of production in the apparel and clothing industry:* Provided further, *That nothing in this Act shall prohibit the enforcement of any agreement which is within the foregoing exception.*

(f) *It shall not be an unfair labor practice under subsections (a) and (b) of this section for an employer engaged primarily in the building and construction industry to make an agreement covering employees engaged (or who, upon their employment, will be engaged) in the building and construction industry with a labor organization of which building and construction employees are members (not established, maintained, or assisted by any action defined in section 8(a) of this Act as an unfair labor practice) because (1) the majority status of such labor organization has not been established under the provisions of section 9 of this Act prior to the making of such agreement, or (2) such agreement requires as a condition of employment, membership in such labor organization after the seventh day following the beginning of such employment or the effective date of the agreement, whichever is later, or (3) such agreement requires the employer to notify such labor organization of opportunities for employment with such employer, or gives such labor organization an opportunity to refer qualified applicants for such employment, or (4) such agreement specifies minimum training or experience qualifications for employment or provides for priority in opportunities for employment based upon length of service with such employer, in the industry or in the particular geographical area:* Provided, *That nothing in this subsection shall set aside the final proviso to section 8(a)(3) of this Act:* Provided further, *That any agreement which would be invalid, but for clause (1) of this* *subsection, shall not be a bar to a petition filed pursuant to section 9(c) or 9(e).* *

**(g) A labor organization before engaging in any strike, picketing, or other concerted refusal to work at any health care institution shall, not less than ten days prior to such action, notify the institution in writing and the Federal Mediation and Conciliation Service of that intention, except that in the case of bargaining for an initial agreement following certification or recognition the notice required by this subsection shall not be given until the expiration of the period specified in clause (B) of the last sentence of section 8(d) of this Act. The notice shall state the date and time that such action will commence. The notice, once given, may be extended by the written agreement of both parties.**

### REPRESENTATIVES AND ELECTIONS

§ 9. (§ 159) (a) Representatives designated or selected for the purposes of collective bargaining by the majority of the employees in a unit appropriate for such purposes, shall be the exclusive representatives of all the employees in such unit for the purposes of collective bargaining in respect to rates of pay, wages, hours of employment, or other conditions of employment: *Provided,* That any individual employee or a group of employees shall have the right at any time to present grievances to their employer **and to have such grievances adjusted, without the intervention of the bargaining representative, as long as the adjustment is not inconsistent with the terms of a collective-bargaining contract or agreement then in effect:** *Provided further,* **That the bargaining representative has been given opportunity to be present at such adjustment.**

(b) The Board shall decide in each case whether, in order to assure to employees the fullest freedom in exercising the rights guaranteed by this Act, the unit appropriate for the purposes of collective bargaining shall be the employer unit, craft unit, plant unit, or subdivision thereof: *Provided,* **That the Board shall not (1) decide that any unit is appropriate for such purposes if such unit includes both professional employees and employees who are not professional employees unless a majority of such professional employees vote for inclusion in such unit; or (2) decide that any craft unit is inappropriate for such purposes on the ground that a different unit has been established by a prior Board determination, unless a majority of the employees in the proposed craft unit vote against separate representation or (3) decide that any unit is**

---

* Section 8(f) was inserted in the Act by subsection (a) of Section 705 of Public Law 86–257. Section 705(b) provides: "Nothing contained in the amendment made by subsection (a) shall be construed as authorizing the execution or application of agreements requiring membership in a labor organization as a condition of employment in any State or Territory in which such execution or application is prohibited by State or Territorial law."

appropriate for such purposes if it includes, together with other employees, any individual employed as a guard to enforce against employees and other persons rules to protect property of the employer or to protect the safety of persons on the employer's premises; but no labor organization shall be certified as the representative of employees in a bargaining unit of guards if such organization admits to membership, or is affiliated directly or indirectly with an organization which admits to membership, employees other than guards.

[ (c) Whenever a question affecting commerce arises concerning the representation of employees, the Board may investigate such controversy and certify to the parties, in writing, the name or names of the representatives that have been designated or selected. In any such investigation, the Board shall provide for an appropriate hearing upon due notice, either in conjunction with a proceeding under section 10 or otherwise, and may take a secret ballot of employees, or utilize any other suitable method to ascertain such representatives.]

(c)(1) Wherever a petition shall have been filed, in accordance with such regulations as may be prescribed by the Board—

(A) by an employee or group of employees or any individual or labor organization acting in their behalf alleging that a substantial number of employees (i) wish to be represented for collective bargaining and that their employer declines to recognize their representative as the representative defined in section 9(a), or (ii) assert that the individual or labor organization, which has been certified or is being currently recognized by their employer as the bargaining representative, is no longer a representative as defined in section 9(a); or

(B) by an employer, alleging that one or more individuals or labor organizations have presented to him a claim to be recognized as the representative defined in section 9(a);

the Board shall investigate such petition and if it has reasonable cause to believe that a question of representation affecting commerce exists shall provide for an appropriate hearing upon due notice. Such hearing may be conducted by an officer or employee of the regional office, who shall not make any recommendations with respect thereto. If the Board finds upon the record of such hearing that such a question of representation exists, it shall direct an election by secret ballot and shall certify the results thereof.

(2) In determining whether or not a question of representation affecting commerce exists, the same regulations and rules of decision shall apply irrespective of the identity of the persons filing the petition or the kind of relief sought and in no case shall the Board deny a labor organization a place on the ballot

by reason of an order with respect to such labor organization or its predecessor not issued in conformity with section 10(c).

(3) No election shall be directed in any bargaining unit or any subdivision within which, in the preceding twelve-month period, a valid election shall have been held. Employees [on] engaged in an economic strike who are not entitled to reinstatement shall [not] be eligible to vote[.] *under such regulations as the Board shall find are consistent with the purposes and provisions of this Act in any election conducted within twelve months after the commencement of the strike.* In any election where none of the choices on the ballot receives a majority, a run-off shall be conducted, the ballot providing for a selection between the two choices receiving the largest and second largest number of valid votes cast in the election.

(4) Nothing in this section shall be construed to prohibit the waiving of hearings by stipulation for the purpose of a consent election in conformity with regulations and rules of decision of the Board.

(5) In determining whether a unit is appropriate for the purposes specified in subsection (b) the extent to which the employees have organized shall not be controlling.

(d) Whenever an order of the Board made pursuant to section 10(c) is based in whole or in part upon facts certified following an investigation pursuant to subsection (c) of this section and there is a petition for the enforcement or review of such order, such certification and the record of such investigation shall be included in the transcript of the entire record required to be filed under section 10(e) or 10(f), and thereupon the decree of the court enforcing, modifying, or setting aside in whole or in part the order of the Board shall be made and entered upon the pleadings, testimony, and proceedings set forth in such transcript.

(e)(1) Upon the filing with the Board, by 30 per centum or more of the employees in a bargaining unit covered by an agreement between their employer and a labor organization made pursuant to section 8(a)(3), of a petition alleging they desire that such authority be rescinded, the Board shall take a secret ballot of the employees in such unit and certify the results thereof to such labor organization and to the employer.

(2) No election shall be conducted pursuant to this subsection in any bargaining unit or any subdivision within which, in the preceding twelve-month period, a valid election shall have been held.

PREVENTION OF UNFAIR LABOR PRACTICES

§ 10. (§ 160) (a) The Board is empowered, as hereinafter provided, to prevent any person from engaging in any unfair labor practice (listed in section 8) affecting commerce. This power shall not be affected by any other means of adjustment or prevention that has been or may be established by agreement, law, or otherwise: ***Provided,* That the Board is empowered by agreement with any agency of any State or Territory to cede to such agency jurisdiction over any cases in any industry (other than mining, manufacturing, communications, and transportation except where predominantly local in character) even though such cases may involve labor disputes affecting commerce, unless the provision of the State or Territorial statute applicable to the determination of such cases by such agency is inconsistent with the corresponding provision of this Act or has received a construction inconsistent therewith.**

(b) Whenever it is charged that any person has engaged in or is engaging in any such unfair labor practice, the Board, or any agent or agency designated by the Board for such purposes, shall have power to issue and cause to be served upon such person a complaint stating the charges in that respect, and containing a notice of hearing before the Board or a member thereof, or before a designated agent or agency, at a place therein fixed, not less than five days after the serving of said complaint: ***Provided,* That no complaint shall issue based upon any unfair labor practice occurring more than six months prior to the filing of the charge with the Board and the service of a copy thereof upon the person against whom such charge is made, unless the person aggrieved thereby was prevented from filing such charge by reason of service in the armed forces, in which event the six-month period shall be computed from the day of his discharge.** Any such complaint may be amended by the member, agent, or agency conducting the hearing or the Board in its discretion at any time prior to the issuance of an order based thereon. The person so complained of shall have the right to file an answer to the original or amended complaint and to appear in person or otherwise and give testimony at the place and time fixed in the complaint. In the discretion of the member, agent, or agency conducting the hearing or the Board, any other person may be allowed to intervene in the said proceeding and to present testimony. [In any such proceeding the rules of evidence prevailing in courts of law or equity shall not be controlling.] **Any such proceeding shall, so far as practicable, be conducted in accordance with the rules of evidence applicable in the district courts of the United States under the rules of civil procedure for the district courts of the United States, adopted by the Supreme Court of the United States pursuant to the Act of June 19, 1934 (U.S.C., title 28, secs. 723–B, 723–C).**

(c) The testimony taken by such member, agent, or agency or the Board shall be reduced to writing and filed with the Board. Thereafter, in its discretion, the Board upon notice may take further testimony or hear argument. If upon [all] **the preponderance of** the testimony taken the Board shall be of the opinion that any person named in the complaint has engaged in or is engaging in any such unfair labor practice, then the Board shall state its findings of fact and shall issue and cause to be served on such person an order requiring such person to cease and desist from such unfair labor practice, and to take such affirmative action including reinstatement of employees with or without back pay, as will effectuate the policies of this Act: *Provided,* **That where an order directs reinstatement of an employee, back pay may be required of the employer or labor organization, as the case may be, responsible for the discrimination suffered by him:** *And provided further,* **That in determining whether a complaint shall issue alleging a violation of section 8(a)(1) or section 8(a)(2), and in deciding such cases, the same regulations and rules of decision shall apply irrespective of whether or not the labor organization affected is affiliated with a labor organization national or international in scope. Such order may further require such person to make reports from time to time showing the extent to which it has complied with the order.** If upon [all] **the preponderance of** the testimony taken the Board shall not be of the opinion that the person named in the complaint has engaged in or is engaging in any such unfair labor practice, then the Board shall state its findings of fact and shall issue an order dismissing the said complaint. **No order of the Board shall require the reinstatement of any individual as an employee who has been suspended or discharged, or the payment to him of any back pay, if such individual was suspended or discharged for cause. In case the evidence is presented before a member of the Board, or before an examiner or examiners thereof, such member, or such examiner or examiners, as the case may be, shall issue and cause to be served on the parties to the proceeding a proposed report, together with a recommended order, which shall be filed with the Board, and if no exceptions are filed within twenty days after service thereof upon such parties, or within such further period as the Board may authorize, such recommended order shall become the order of the Board and become effective as therein prescribed.**

(d) Until the record in a case shall have been filed in a court, as hereinafter provided, the Board may at any time, upon reasonable notice and in such manner as it shall deem proper, modify or set aside, in whole or in part, any finding or order made or issued by it.

(e) The Board shall have power to petition any court of appeals of the United States, or if all the courts of appeals to which application may be made are in vacation, any district court of the United States, within any circuit or district, respectively, wherein the unfair labor practice in question occurred or wherein such person resides or transacts business, for the enforcement of such order and for appropriate temporary relief or restraining order, and shall file in the court the record in the proceedings, as provided in section 2112 of title 28, United States Code. Upon the filing of such petition, the court shall cause notice thereof to be served upon such person, and thereupon shall have jurisdiction of the proceeding and of the question determined therein, and shall have power to grant such temporary relief or restraining order as it deems just and proper, and to make and enter a decree enforcing, modifying, and enforcing as so modified, or setting aside in whole or in part the order of the Board. No objection that has not been urged before the Board, its member, agent, or agency, shall be considered by the court, unless the failure or neglect to urge such objection shall be excused because of extraordinary circumstances. The findings of the Board with respect to questions of fact if supported by **substantial** evidence **on the record considered as a whole** shall be conclusive. If either party shall apply to the court for leave to adduce additional evidence and shall show to the satisfaction of the court that such additional evidence is material and that there were reasonable grounds for the failure to adduce such evidence in the hearing before the Board, its member, agent, or agency, the court may order such additional evidence to be taken before the Board, its member, agent, or agency, and to be made a part of the record. The Board may modify its findings as to the facts, or make new findings, by reason of additional evidence so taken and filed, and it shall file such modified or new findings, which findings with respect to questions of fact if supported by substantial evidence on the record considered as a whole shall be conclusive, and shall file its recommendations, if any, for the modification or setting aside of its original order. Upon the filing of the record with it the jurisdiction of the court shall be exclusive and its judgment and decree shall be final, except that the same shall be subject to review by the appropriate United States court of appeals if application was made to the district court as hereinabove provided, and by the Supreme Court of the United States upon writ of certiorari or certification as provided in section 1254 of title 28.

(f) Any person aggrieved by a final order of the Board granting or denying in whole or in part the relief sought may obtain a review of such order in any circuit court of appeals of the United States in the circuit wherein the unfair labor practice in question was alleged to have been engaged in or wherein such person resides or transacts business, or in the United States Court of Appeals for the District of Columbia, by filing in such court a written petition praying that the order of the Board be modified or set aside. A copy of such petition shall be forthwith transmitted by the clerk of the court to the Board, and thereupon the aggrieved party shall file in the court the record in the proceeding, certified by the Board, as provided in section 2112 of title 28, United States Code. Upon the filing of such petition, the court shall proceed in the same manner as in the case of an application by the Board under subsection (e) of this section, and shall have the same jurisdiction to grant to the Board such temporary relief or restraining order as it deems just and proper, and in like manner to make and enter a decree enforcing, modifying, and enforcing as so modified, or setting aside in whole or in part the order of the Board; the findings of the Board with respect to questions of fact if supported by **substantial** evidence **on the record considered as a whole** shall in like manner be conclusive.

(g) The commencement of proceedings under subsection (e) or (f) of this section shall not, unless specifically ordered by the court, operate as a stay of the Board's order.

(h) When granting appropriate temporary relief or a restraining order, or making and entering a decree enforcing, modifying, and enforcing as so modified, or setting aside in whole or in part an order of the Board, as provided in this section, the jurisdiction of courts sitting in equity shall not be limited by the Act entitled "An Act to amend the Judicial Code and to define and limit the jurisdiction of courts sitting in equity, and for other purposes," approved March 23, 1932 (U.S.C., Supp. VII, title 29, secs. 101–115).

(i) Petitions filed under this Act shall be heard expeditiously, and if possible within ten days after they have been docketed.

**(j) The Board shall have power, upon issuance of a complaint as provided in subsection (b) charging that any person has engaged in or is engaging in an unfair labor practice, to petition any district court of the United States (including the District Court of the United States for the District of Columbia), within any district wherein the unfair labor practice in question is alleged to have occurred or wherein such person resides or transacts business, for appropriate temporary relief or restraining order. Upon the filing of any such petition the court shall cause notice thereof to be served upon such person, and thereupon shall have jurisdiction to grant to the Board such temporary relief or restraining order as it deems just and proper.**

**(k) Whenever it is charged that any person has engaged in an unfair labor practice within the meaning of paragraph (4)(D) of section 8(b), the Board is empowered and directed to hear and determine the dispute out of which such unfair labor practice shall have arisen, unless, within ten days after notice that such charge has been filed, the parties to such dispute submit to the Board satisfactory evidence that they have adjusted, or agreed upon methods for the voluntary adjustment of, the dispute. Upon compliance by the parties to the dispute with the decision of the Board or upon such voluntary adjustment of the dispute, such charge shall be dismissed.**

**(l) Whenever it is charged that any person has engaged in an unfair labor practice within the meaning of paragraphs (4)(A), (B), or (C) of section 8(b), *or section 8(e) or section 8(b)(7)*, the preliminary investigation of such charge shall be made forthwith and given priority over all other cases except cases of like character in the office where it is filed or to which it is referred. If, after such investigation, the officer or regional attorney to whom the matter may be referred has reasonable cause to believe such charge is true and that a complaint should issue, he shall, on behalf of the Board, petition any district court of the United States (including the District Court of the United States**

for the District of Columbia) within any district where the unfair labor practice in question has occurred, is alleged to have occurred, or wherein such person resides or transacts business, for appropriate injunctive relief pending the final adjudication of the Board with respect to such matter. Upon the filing of any such petition the district court shall have jurisdiction to grant such injunctive relief or temporary restraining order as it deems just and proper, notwithstanding any other provision of law: *Provided further,* That no temporary restraining order shall be issued without notice unless a petition alleges that substantial and irreparable injury to the charging party will be unavoidable and such temporary restraining order shall be effective for no longer than five days and will become void at the expiration of such period [.]: *Provided further, That such officer or regional attorney shall not apply for any restraining order under section 8(b)(7) if a charge against the employer under section 8(a)(2) has been filed and after the preliminary investigation, he has reasonable cause to believe that such charge is true and that a complaint should issue.* Upon filing of any such petition the courts shall cause notice thereof to be served upon any person involved in the charge and such person, including the charging party, shall be given an opportunity to appear by counsel and present any relevant testimony: *Provided further,* That for the purposes of this subsection district courts shall be deemed to have jurisdiction of a labor organization (1) in the district in which such organization maintains its principal office, or (2) in any district in which its duly authorized officers or agents are engaged in promoting or protecting the interests of employee members. The service of legal process upon such officer or agent shall constitute service upon the labor organization and make such organization a party to the suit. In situations where such relief is appropriate the procedure specified herein shall apply to charges with respect to section 8(b)(4)(D).

*(m) Whenever it is charged that any person has engaged in an unfair labor practice within the meaning of subsection (a)(3) or (b)(2) of section 8, such charge shall be given priority over all other cases except cases of like character in the office where it is filed or to which it is referred and cases given priority under subsection (l).*

### INVESTIGATORY POWERS

§ 11. (§ 161) For the purpose of all hearings and investigations, which, in the opinion of the Board, are necessary and proper for the exercise of the powers vested in it by section 9 and section 10—

(1) The Board, or its duly authorized agents or agencies, shall at all reasonable times have access to, for the purpose of examination, and the right to copy any evidence of any person being investigated or proceeded against that relates to any matter under investigation or in question. The Board, or any member thereof, shall upon application of any party

to such proceedings, forthwith issue to such party subpenas requiring the attendance and testimony of witnesses or the production of any evidence in such proceeding or investigation requested in such application. Within five days after the service of a subpena on any person requiring the production of any evidence in his possession or under his control, such person may petition the Board to revoke, and the Board shall revoke, such subpena if in its opinion the evidence whose production is required does not relate to any matter under investigation, or any matter in question in such proceedings, or if in its opinion such subpena does not describe with sufficient particularity the evidence whose production is required. Any member of the Board, or any agent or agency designated by the Board for such purposes, may administer oaths and affirmations, examine witnesses, and receive evidence. Such attendance of witnesses and the production of such evidence may be required from any place in the United States or any Territory or possession thereof, at any designated place of hearing.

(2) In case of contumacy or refusal to obey a subpena issued to any person, any district court of the United States or the United States courts of any Territory or possession, or the District Court of the United States for the District of Columbia, within the jurisdiction of which the inquiry is carried on or within the jurisdiction of which said person guilty of contumacy or refusal to obey is found or resides or transacts business, upon application by the Board shall have jurisdiction to issue to such person an order requiring such person to appeal before the Board, its member, agent, or agency, there to produce evidence if so ordered, or there to give testimony touching the matter under investigation or in question; and any failure to obey such order of the court may be punished by said court as a contempt thereof.

[ (3) No person shall be excused from attending and testifying or from producing books, records, correspondence, documents, or other evidence in obedience to the subpena of the Board, on the ground that the testimony or evidence required of him may tend to incriminate him or subject him to a penalty or forfeiture; but no individual shall be prosecuted or subjected to any penalty or forfeiture for or on account of any transaction, matter, or thing concerning which he is compelled, after having claimed his privilege against self-incrimination, to testify or produce evidence, except that such individual so testifying shall not be exempt from prosecution and punishment for perjury committed in so testifying.]*

(4) Complaints, orders and other process and papers of the Board, its member, agent, or agency, may be served either personally or by registered or certified mail or by telegraph or by leaving a copy thereof at the principal office or place of business of the person required to be served. The verified return by the individual so serving the same

* Repealed by § 259 of the Organized Crime Control Act of 1970, 18 U.S.C. § 6001 n. See 18 U.S.C. §§ 6003–04.

setting forth the manner of such service shall be proof of the same, and the return post office receipt or telegraph receipt thereof when registered or certified and mailed or when telegraphed as aforesaid shall be proof of service of the same. Witnesses summoned before the Board, its member, agent, or agency, shall be paid the same fees and mileage that are paid witnesses in the courts of the United States, and witnesses whose depositions are taken and the persons taking the same shall severally be entitled to the same fees as are paid for like services in the courts of the United States.*

(5) All process of any court to which application may be made under this Act may be served in the judicial district wherein the defendant or other person required to be served resides or may be found.

(6) The several departments and agencies of the Government, when directed by the President, shall furnish the Board, upon its request, all records, papers, and information in their possession relating to any matter before the Board.

§ 12. (§ 162) Any person who shall willfully resist, prevent, impede, or interfere with any member of the Board or any of its agents or agencies in the performance of duties pursuant to this Act shall be punished by a fine of not more than $5,000 or by imprisonment for not more than one year, or both.

### LIMITATIONS

§ 13. (§ 163) Nothing in this Act, **except as specifically provided for herein,** shall be construed so as either to interfere with or impede or diminish in any way the right to strike, **or to affect the limitations or qualifications on that right.**

§ 14. (§ 164) **(a) Nothing herein shall prohibit any individual employed as a supervisor from becoming or remaining a member of a labor organization, but no employer subject to this Act shall be compelled to deem individuals defined herein as supervisors as employees for the purpose of any law, either national or local, relating to collective bargaining.**

**(b) Nothing in this Act shall be construed as authorizing the execution or application of agreements requiring membership in a labor organization as a condition of employment in any State or Territory in which such execution or application is prohibited by State or Territorial law.**

### FEDERAL–STATE JURISDICTION

(c)(1) *The Board, in its discretion, may, by rule of decision or by published rules adopted pursuant to the Administrative Procedure Act, decline to assert jurisdiction over any labor dispute involving any class or category of employers, where, in the opinion of the Board, the effect of such labor dispute on commerce is not sufficiently substantial to warrant*

* Section 11(4) was amended by P.L. 96–245, effective May 21, 1980.

*the exercise of its jurisdiction:*  Provided, *That the Board shall not decline to assert jurisdiction over any labor dispute over which it would assert jurisdiction under the standards prevailing upon August 1, 1959.*

(2) *Nothing in this Act shall be deemed to prevent or bar any agency or the courts of any State or Territory (including the Commonwealth of Puerto Rico, Guam, and the Virgin Islands), from assuming and asserting jurisdiction over labor disputes over which the Board declines, pursuant to paragraph (1) of this subsection, to assert jurisdiction.*

**§ 15.    (§ 165) Wherever the application of the provisions of section 272 of chapter 10 of the Act entitled "An Act to establish a uniform system of bankruptcy throughout the United States," approved July 1, 1898, and Acts amendatory thereof and supplementary thereto (U.S.C., title 11, sec. 672), conflicts with the application of the provisions of this Act, this Act shall prevail:** ***Provided,*** **That in any situation where the provisions of this Act cannot be validly enforced, the provisions of such other Acts shall remain in full force and effect.**

§ 16.    (§ 166) If any provision of this Act, or the application of such provision to any person or circumstances, shall be held invalid, the remainder of this Act, or the application of such provision to persons or circumstances other than those as to which it is held invalid, shall not be affected thereby.

§ 17.    (§ 167) This Act may be cited as the "National Labor Relations Act."

§ 18.    (§ 168) No petition entertained, no investigation made, no election held, and no certification issued by the National Labor Relations Board, under any of the provisions of section 9 of the National Labor Relations Act, as amended, shall be invalid by reason of the failure of the Congress of Industrial Organizations to have complied with the requirements of section 9(f), (g), or (h) of the aforesaid Act prior to December 22, 1949, or by reason of the failure of the American Federation of Labor to have complied with the provisions of section 9(f), (g), or (h) of the aforesaid Act prior to November 7, 1947: *Provided,* That no liability shall be imposed under any provision of this Act upon any person for failure to honor any election or certificate referred to above, prior to the effective date of this amendment: *Provided, however,* That this proviso shall not have the effect of setting aside or in any way affecting judgments or decrees heretofore entered under section 10(e) or (f) and which have become final.*

INDIVIDUALS WITH RELIGIOUS CONVICTIONS

**§ 19.    (§ 169)** *Any employee [of a health care institution] who is a member of and adheres to established and traditional tenets or teachings of a bona fide religion, body, or sect which has historically held conscientious objections to joining or financial-*

---

* Section 18 was added by P.L. 82–189, enacted October 22, 1951.

*ly supporting labor organizations shall not be required to join or financially support any labor organization as a condition of employment; except that such employee may be required* in a contract between such employees' employer and a labor organization *in lieu of periodic dues and initiation fees, to pay sums equal to such dues and initiation fees to a nonreligious* nonlabor organization *charitable fund exempt from taxation under section 501(c)(3) of title 26 of the Internal Revenue Code, chosen by such employee from a list of at least three such funds, designated in such [a] contract [between such institution and a labor organization,] or if the contract fails to designate such funds, then to any such fund chosen by the employee.* If such employee who holds conscientious objections pursuant to this section requests the labor organization to use the grievance-arbitration procedure on the employee's behalf, the labor organization is authorized to charge the employee for the reasonable cost of using such procedure.*

EFFECTIVE DATE OF CERTAIN CHANGES**

**§ 102. No provision of this title shall be deemed to make an unfair labor practice any act which was performed prior to the date of the enactment of this Act which did not constitute an unfair labor practice prior thereto, and the provisions of section 8(a)(3) and section 8(b)(2) of the National Labor Relations Act as amended by this title shall not make an unfair labor practice the performance of any obligation under a collective bargaining agreement entered into prior to the date of the enactment of this Act, or (in the case of an agreement for a period of not more than one year) entered into on or after such date of enactment, but prior to the effective date of this title, if the performance of such obligation would not have constituted an unfair labor practice under section 8(3) of the National Labor Relations Act prior to the effective date of this title, unless such an agreement was renewed or extended subsequent thereto.**

**§ 103. No provisions of this title shall affect any certification of representatives or any determination as to the appropriate collective-bargaining unit, which was made under section 9 of the National Labor Relations Act prior to the effective date of this title until one year after the date of such certification or if, in respect of any such certification, a collective-bargaining contract was entered into prior to the effective date of this title, until the end of the contract period or until one year after such date, whichever first occurs.**

**§ 104. The amendments made by this title shall take effect sixty days after the date of the enactment of this Act, except**

* Section 19 was amended by P.L. 96–593, approved December 24, 1980, to add the material in roman type and to delete the material enclosed in brackets.

** The effective date referred to in Sections 102, 103, and 104 is August 22, 1947.

**that the authority of the President to appoint certain officers conferred upon him by section 3 of the National Labor Relations Act as amended by this title may be exercised forthwith.**

TITLE II—CONCILIATION OF LABOR DISPUTES; NATIONAL EMERGENCIES

§ 201.   (§ 171)   It is the policy of the United States that—

(a) sound and stable industrial peace and the advancement of the general welfare, health, and safety of the Nation and of the best interests of employers and employees can most satisfactorily be secured by the settlement of issues between employers and employees through the processes of conference and collective bargaining between employers and the representatives of their employees;

(b) the settlement of issues between employers and employees through collective bargaining may be advanced by making available full and adequate governmental facilities for conciliation, mediation, and voluntary arbitration to aid and encourage employers and the representatives of their employees to reach and maintain agreements concerning rates of pay, hours, and working conditions, and to make all reasonable efforts to settle their differences by mutual agreement reached through conferences and collective bargaining or by such methods as may be provided for in any applicable agreement for the settlement of disputes; and

(c) certain controversies which arise between parties to collective-bargaining agreements may be avoided or minimized by making available full and adequate governmental facilities for furnishing assistance to employers and the representatives of their employees in formulating for inclusion within such agreements provision for adequate notice of any proposed changes in the terms of such agreements, for the final adjustment of grievances or questions regarding the application or interpretation of such agreements, and other provisions designed to prevent the subsequent arising of such controversies.

§ 202.   (§ 172) (a) There is created an independent agency to be known as the Federal Mediation and Conciliation Service (herein referred to as the "Service", except that for sixty days after June 23, 1947, such term shall refer to the Conciliation Service of the Department of Labor).   The Service shall be under the direction of a Federal Mediation and Conciliation Director (hereinafter referred to as the "Director"), who shall be appointed by the President by and with the advice and consent of the Senate.   The Director shall not engage in any other business, vocation, or employment.

(b) The Director is authorized, subject to the civil service laws, to appoint such clerical and other personnel as may be necessary for the execution of the functions of the Service, and shall fix their compensation in accordance with the Classification Act of 1949, and may, without regard to the provisions of the civil service laws, appoint such conciliators and mediators as may be necessary to carry out the functions of the Service.   The Director is authorized to make such expenditures for supplies, facilities, and services as he deems necessary. Such expenditures shall be allowed and paid upon presentation of itemized vouchers therefor approved by the Director or by any employee designated by him for that purpose.

(c) The principal office of the Service shall be in the District of Columbia, but the Director may establish regional offices convenient to localities in which labor controversies are likely to arise. The Director may by order, subject to revocation at any time, delegate any authority and discretion conferred upon him by this chapter to any regional director, or other officer or employee of the Service. The Director may establish suitable procedures for cooperation with State and local mediation agencies. The Director shall make an annual report in writing to Congress at the end of the fiscal year.

(d) All mediation and conciliation functions of the Secretary of Labor or the United States Conciliation Service under section 8 of the Act entitled "An Act to create a Department of Labor", approved March 4, 1913 (U.S.C., title 29, sec. 51), and all functions of the United States Conciliation Service under any other law are transferred to the Federal Mediation and Conciliation Service, together with the personnel and records of the United States Conciliation Service. Such transfer shall take effect upon the sixtieth day after June 23, 1947. Such transfer shall not affect any proceedings pending before the United States Conciliation Service or any certification, order, rule, or regulation theretofore made by it or by the Secretary of Labor. The Director and the Service shall not be subject in any way to the jurisdiction or authority of the Secretary of Labor or any official or division of the Department of Labor.

### Functions of the Service

§ 203. (§ 173) (a) It shall be the duty of the Service, in order to prevent or minimize interruptions of the free flow of commerce growing out of labor disputes, to assist parties to labor disputes in industries affecting commerce to settle such disputes through conciliation and mediation.

(b) The Service may proffer its services in any labor dispute in any industry affecting commerce, either upon its own motion or upon the request of one or more of the parties to the dispute, whenever in its judgment such dispute threatens to cause a substantial interruption of commerce. The Director and the Service are directed to avoid attempting to mediate disputes which would have only a minor effect on interstate commerce if State or other conciliation services are available to the parties. Whenever the Service does proffer its services in any dispute, it shall be the duty of the Service promptly to put itself in communication with the parties and to use its best efforts, by mediation and conciliation, to bring them to agreement.

(c) If the Director is not able to bring the parties to agreement by conciliation within a reasonable time, he shall seek to induce the parties voluntarily to seek other means of settling the dispute without resort to strike, lock-out, or other coercion, including submission to the employees in the bargaining unit of the employer's last offer of settlement for approval or rejection in a secret ballot. The failure or refusal of either party to agree to any procedure suggested by the Director shall not be deemed a violation of any duty or obligation imposed by this Act.

(d) Final adjustment by a method agreed upon by the parties is declared to be the desirable method for settlement of grievance disputes arising over the application or interpretation of an existing collective-bargaining agreement. The Service is directed to make its conciliation and mediation services available in the settlement of such grievance disputes only as a last resort and in exceptional cases.

(e) The Service is authorized and directed to encourage and support the establishment and operation of joint labor management activities conducted by plant, area, and industrywide committees designed to improve labor management relationships, job security and organizational effectiveness, in accordance with the provisions of section 205A.*

§ 204. (§ 174) (a) In order to prevent or minimize interruptions of the free flow of commerce growing out of labor disputes, employers and employees and their representatives, in any industry affecting commerce, shall—

(1) exert every reasonable effort to make and maintain agreements concerning rates of pay, hours, and working conditions, including provision for adequate notice of any proposed change in the terms of such agreements;

(2) whenever a dispute arises over the terms or application of a collective-bargaining agreement and a conference is requested by a party or prospective party thereto, arrange promptly for such a conference to be held and endeavor in such conference to settle such dispute expeditiously; and

(3) in case such dispute is not settled by conference, participate fully and promptly in such meetings as may be undertaken by the Service under this Act for the purpose of aiding in a settlement of the dispute.

§ 205. (§ 175) (a) There is created a National Labor–Management Panel which shall be composed of twelve members appointed by the President, six of whom shall be selected from among persons outstanding in the field of management and six of whom shall be selected from among persons outstanding in the field of labor. Each member shall hold office for a term of three years, except that any member appointed to fill a vacancy occurring prior to the expiration of the term for which his predecessor was appointed shall be appointed for the remainder of such term, and the terms of office of the members first taking office shall expire, as designated by the President at the time of appointment, four at the end of the first year, four at the end of the second year, and four at the end of the third year after the date of appointment. Members of the panel, when serving on business of the panel, shall be paid compen-

* Section 203(e) was added by P.L. 95–
524, enacted October 27, 1978.

sation at the rate of $25 per day, and shall also be entitled to receive an allowance for actual and necessary travel and subsistence expenses while so serving away from their places of residence.

(b) It shall be the duty of the panel, at the request of the Director, to advise in the avoidance of industrial controversies and the manner in which mediation and voluntary adjustment shall be administered, particularly with reference to controversies affecting the general welfare of the country.

§ 205A. (§ 175a) (a)(1) The Service is authorized and directed to provide assistance in the establishment and operation of plant, area and industry-wide labor management committees which—

(A) have been organized jointly by employers and labor organizations representing employees in that plant, area, or industry; and

(B) are established for the purpose of improving labor management relationships, job security, organizational effectiveness, enhancing economic development or involving workers in decisions affecting their jobs including improving communication with respect to subjects of mutual interest and concern.

(2) The Service is authorized and directed to enter into contracts and to make grants, where necessary or appropriate, to fulfill its responsibilities under this section.

(b)(1) No grant may be made, no contract may be entered into and no other assistance may be provided under the provisions of this section to a plant labor management committee unless the employees in that plant are represented by a labor organization and there is in effect at that plant a collective bargaining agreement.

(2) No grant may be made, no contract may be entered into and no other assistance may be provided under the provisions of this section to an area or industrywide labor management committee unless its participants include any labor organizations certified or recognized as the representative of the employees of an employer participating in such committee. Nothing in this clause shall prohibit participation in an area or industrywide committee by an employer whose employees are not represented by a labor organization.

(3) No grant may be made under the provisions of this section to any labor management committee which the Service finds to have as one of its purposes the discouragement of the exercise of rights contained in section 7 of the National Labor Relations Act (29 U.S.C. 157), or the interference with collective bargaining in any plant, or industry.

(c) The Service shall carry out the provisions of this section through an office established for that purpose.

(d) There are authorized to be appropriated to carry out the provisions of this section $10,000,000 for the fiscal year 1979, and such sums as may be necessary thereafter.

(d) Section 302(c) of the Labor Management Relations Act, 1947, is amended by striking the word "or" after the semicolon at the end of subparagraph (7) thereof and by inserting the following before the period at the end thereof: ";" or (9) with respect to money or other things of value paid by an employer to a plant, area or industrywide labor management committee established for one or more of the purposes set forth in section 5(b) of the Labor Management Cooperation Act of 1978.

(e) Nothing in this section or the amendments made by this section shall affect the terms and conditions of any collective bargaining agreement whether in effect prior to or entered into after the date of enactment of this section.*

## NATIONAL EMERGENCIES

§ 206.   (§ 176) Whenever in the opinion of the President of the United States, a threatened or actual strike or lock-out affecting an entire industry or a substantial part thereof engaged in trade, commerce, transportation, transmission, or communication among the several States or with foreign nations, or engaged in the production of goods for commerce, will, if permitted to occur or to continue, imperil the national health or safety, he may appoint a board of inquiry to inquire into the issues involved in the dispute and to make a written report to him within such time as he shall prescribe.  Such report shall include a statement of the facts with respect to the dispute, including each party's statement of its position but shall not contain any recommendations. The President shall file a copy of such report with the Service and shall make its contents available to the public.

§ 207.   (§ 177) (a) A board of inquiry shall be composed of a chairman and such other members as the President shall determine, and shall have power to sit and act in any place within the United States and to conduct such hearings either in public or in private, as it may deem necessary or proper, to ascertain the facts with respect to the causes and circumstances of the dispute.

(b) Members of a board of inquiry shall receive compensation at the rate of $50 for each day actually spent by them in the work of the board, together with necessary travel and subsistence expenses.

(c) For the purpose of any hearing or inquiry conducted by any board appointed under this title, the provisions of sections 9 and 10 (relating to the attendance of witnesses and the production of books, papers, and documents) of the Federal Trade Commission Act of September 16, 1914, as amended (U.S.C. 19, title 15, secs. 49 and 50, as amended), are hereby made applicable to the powers and duties of such board.

§ 208.   (§ 178) (a) Upon receiving a report from a board of inquiry the President may direct the Attorney General to petition any district court of the United States having jurisdiction of the parties to enjoin

* Section 205A was added by P.L. 95–524, enacted October 27, 1978.

such strike or lock-out or the continuing thereof, and if the court finds
that such threatened or actual strike or lock-out—

(i) affects an entire industry or a substantial part thereof engaged in
trade, commerce, transportation, transmission, or communication among
the several States or with foreign nations, or engaged in the production
of goods for commerce; and

(ii) if permitted to occur or to continue, will imperil the national
health or safety, it shall have jurisdiction to enjoin any such strike or
lock-out, or the continuing thereof, and to make such other orders as
may be appropriate.

(b) In any case, the provisions of the Act of March 23, 1932, entitled
"An Act to amend the Judicial Code and to define and limit the
jurisdiction of courts sitting in equity, and for other purposes," shall not
be applicable.

(c) The order or orders of the court shall be subject to review by the
appropriate United States court of appeals and by the Supreme Court
upon writ of certiorari or certification as provided in sections 239 and
240 of the Judicial Code, as amended (U.S.C., title 29, secs. 346 and 347).

§ 209.  (§ 179) (a) Whenever a district court has issued an order
under section 208 enjoining acts or practices which imperil or threaten
to imperil the national health or safety, it shall be the duty of the parties
to the labor dispute giving rise to such order to make every effort to
adjust and settle their differences, with the assistance of the Service
created by this Act.  Neither party shall be under any duty to accept, in
whole or in part, any proposal of settlement made by the Service.

(b) Upon the issuance of such order, the President shall reconvene
the board of inquiry which has previously reported with respect to the
dispute.  At the end of a sixty-day period (unless the dispute has been
settled by that time), the board of inquiry shall report to the President
the current position of the parties and the efforts which have been made
for settlement, and shall include a statement by each party of its position
and a statement of the employer's last offer of settlement.  The President shall make such report available to the public.  The National Labor
Relations Board, within the succeeding fifteen days, shall take a secret
ballot of the employees of each employer involved in the dispute on the
question of whether they wish to accept the final offer of settlement
made by their employer as stated by him and shall certify the results
thereof to the Attorney General within five days thereafter.

§ 210.  (§ 180) Upon the certification of the results of such ballot
or upon a settlement being reached, whichever happens sooner, the
Attorney General shall move the court to discharge the injunction, which
motion shall then be granted and the injunction discharged.  When such
motion is granted, the President shall submit to the Congress a full and
comprehensive report of the proceedings, including the findings of the
board of inquiry and the ballot taken by the National Labor Relations

Board, together with such recommendations as he may see fit to make for consideration and appropriate action.

### COMPILATION OF COLLECTIVE-BARGAINING AGREEMENTS, ETC.

§ 211.    (§ 181) (a) For the guidance and information of interested representatives of employers, employees, and the general public, the Bureau of Labor Statistics of the Department of Labor shall maintain a file of copies of all available collective bargaining agreements and other available agreements and actions thereunder settling or adjusting labor disputes.    Such file shall be open to inspection under appropriate conditions prescribed by the Secretary of Labor, except that no specific information submitted in confidence shall be disclosed.

(b) The Bureau of Labor Statistics in the Department of Labor is authorized to furnish upon request of the Service, or employers, employees, or their representatives, all available data and factual information which may aid in the settlement of any labor dispute, except that no specific information submitted in confidence shall be disclosed.

### EXEMPTION OF RAILWAY LABOR ACT

§ 212.    (§ 182) The provisions of this title shall not be applicable with respect to any matter which is subject to the provisions of the Railway Labor Act, as amended from time to time.

### CONCILIATION OF LABOR DISPUTES IN THE HEALTH CARE INDUSTRY *

*§ 213.    (§ 183) (a) If, in the opinion of the Director of the Federal Mediation and Conciliation Service a threatened or actual strike or lockout affecting a health care institution will, if permitted to occur or to continue, substantially interrupt the delivery of health care in the locality concerned, the Director may further assist in the resolution of the impasse by establishing within 30 days after the notice to the Federal Mediation and Conciliation Service under clause (A) of the last sentence of section 8(d) (which is required by clause (3) of such section 8(d)), or within 10 days after the notice under clause (B), an impartial Board of Inquiry to investigate the issues involved in the dispute and to make a written report thereon to the parties within fifteen (15) days after the establishment of such a Board.    The written report shall contain the findings of fact together with the Board's recommendations for settling the dispute, with the objective of achieving a prompt, peaceful and just settlement of the dispute.    Each such Board shall be composed of such number of individuals as the Director may deem desirable.    No member appointed under this section shall have any interest or involvement in the health care institutions or the employee organizations involved in the dispute.*

*(b)(1) Members of any board established under this section who are otherwise employed by the Federal Government shall serve without compensation but shall be reimbursed for travel, subsistence, and other*

---

* Section 213 was added by P.L. 93-360, enacted July 26, 1974.

*necessary expenses incurred by them in carrying out its duties under this section.*

*(2) Members of any board established under this section who are not subject to paragraph (1) shall receive compensation at a rate prescribed by the Director but not to exceed the daily rate prescribed for GS–18 of the General Schedule under section 5332 of title 5, United States Code, including travel for each day they are engaged in the performance of their duties under this section and shall be entitled to reimbursement for travel, subsistence, and other necessary expenses incurred by them in carrying out their duties under this section.*

*(c) After the establishment of a board under subsection (a) of this section and for 15 days after any such board has issued its report, no change in the status quo in effect prior to the expiration of the contract in the case of negotiations for a contract renewal, or in effect prior to the time of the impasse in the case of an initial bargaining negotiation, except by agreement, shall be made by the parties to the controversy.*

*(d) There are authorized to be appropriated such sums as may be necessary to carry out the provisions of this section.*

TITLE III

SUITS BY AND AGAINST LABOR ORGANIZATIONS

§ 301. (§ 185) (a) Suits for violation of contracts between an employer and a labor organization representing employees in an industry affecting commerce as defined in this Act, or between any such labor organizations, may be brought in any district court of the United States having jurisdiction of the parties, without respect to the amount in controversy or without regard to the citizenship of the parties.

(b) Any labor organization which represents employees in an industry affecting commerce as defined in this Act and any employer whose activities affect commerce as defined in this Act shall be bound by the acts of its agents. Any such labor organization may sue or be sued as an entity and in behalf of the employees whom it represents in the courts of the United States. Any money judgment against a labor organization in a district court of the United States shall be enforceable only against the organization as an entity and against its assets, and shall not be enforceable against any individual member or his assets.

(c) For the purposes of actions and proceedings by or against labor organizations in the district courts of the United States, district courts shall be deemed to have jurisdiction of a labor organization (1) in the district in which such organization maintains its principal office, or (2) in any district in which its duly authorized officers or agents are engaged in representing or acting for employee members.

(d) The service of summons, subpena, or other legal process of any court of the United States upon an officer or agent of a labor organization, in his capacity as such, shall constitute service upon the labor organization.

(e) For the purposes of this section, in determining whether any person is acting as an "agent" of another person so as to make such other person responsible for his acts, the question of whether the specific acts performed were actually authorized or subsequently ratified shall not be controlling.

### RESTRICTIONS ON PAYMENTS TO EMPLOYEE REPRESENTATIVES *

§ 302.   (§ 186) (a) It shall be unlawful for any employer *or association of employers or any person who acts as a labor relations expert, adviser, or consultant to an employer or who acts in the interest of an employer* to pay, *lend,* or deliver, or [to] agree to pay, *lend,* or deliver, any money or other thing of value—

(1) to any representative of any of his employees who are employed in an industry affecting commerce[.]; *or*

(2) *to any labor organization, or any officer or employee thereof, which represents, seeks to represent, or would admit to membership, any of the employees of such employer who are employed in an industry affecting commerce; or*

(3) *to any employee or group or committee of employees of such employer employed in an industry affecting commerce in excess of their normal compensation for the purpose of causing such employee or group or committee directly or indirectly to influence any other employees in the exercise of the right to organize and bargain collectively through representatives of their own choosing; or*

(4) *to any officer or employee of a labor organization engaged in an industry affecting commerce with intent to influence him in respect to any of his actions, decisions, or duties as a representative of employees or as such officer or employee of such labor organization,*

(b)(1) It shall be unlawful for any [representative of any employees who are employed in an industry affecting commerce] *person* to request, demand, [to] receive or accept, or [to] agree to *receive or accept* [from the employer of such employees] *any payment, loan, or delivery of any money or other thing of value* [.] *prohibited by subsection (a) of this section.*

(2) *It shall be unlawful for any labor organization, or for any person acting as an officer, agent, representative, or employee of such labor organization, to demand or accept from the operator of any motor vehicle (as defined in part II of the Interstate Commerce Act) employed in the transportation of property in commerce, or the employer of any such operator, any money or other thing of value payable to such organization or to an officer, agent, representative or employee thereof as a fee or charge for the unloading, or in connection with the unloading, of the cargo of such vehicle:* Provided, *That*

---

* The provisions of §§ 302 and 303 contained in the LMRA are in roman type below; additions to those sections made by the LMRDA appear in italics; and deletions, in brackets.

*nothing in this paragraph shall be construed to make unlawful any payment by an employer to any of his employees as compensation for their services as employees.*

(c) The provisions of this section shall not be applicable (1) [with] *in respect to any money or other thing of value payable by an employer to any of his employees whose established duties include acting openly for such employer in matters of labor relations or personnel administration or to any representative of his employees, or to any officer or employee of a labor organization,* who is *also* an employee or former employee of such employer, as compensation for, or by reason of, his service[s] as an employee of such employer; (2) with respect to the payment or delivery of any money or other thing of value in satisfaction of a judgment of any court or a decision or award of an arbitrator or impartial chairman or in compromise, adjustment, settlement, or release of any claim, complaint, grievance, or dispute in the absence of fraud or duress; (3) with respect to the sale or purchase of an article or commodity at the prevailing market price in the regular course of business; (4) with respect to money deducted from the wages of employees in payment of membership dues in a labor organization: *Provided,* That the employer has received from each employee, on whose account such deductions are made, a written assignment which shall not be irrevocable for a period of more than one year, or beyond the termination date of the applicable collective agreement, whichever occurs sooner; [or] (5) with respect to money or other thing of value paid to a trust fund established by such representative, for the sole and exclusive benefit of the employees of such employer, and their families and dependents (or of such employees, families, and dependents jointly with the employees of other employers making similar payments, and their families and dependents): *Provided,* That (A) such payments are held in trust for the purpose of paying, either from principal or income or both, for the benefit of employees, their families and dependents, for medical or hospital care, pensions or retirement or death of employees, compensation for injuries or illness resulting from occupational activity or insurance to provide any of the foregoing, or unemployment benefits or life insurance, disability and sickness insurance, or accident insurance; (B) the detailed basis on which such payments are to be made is specified in a written agreement with the employer, and employees and employers are equally represented in the administration of such fund, together with such neutral persons as the representatives of the employers and the representatives of [the] employees may agree upon and in the event the employer and employee groups deadlock on the administration of such fund and there are no neutral persons empowered to break such deadlock, such agreement provides that the two groups shall agree on an impartial umpire to decide such dispute, or in the event of their failure to agree within a reasonable length of time, an impartial umpire to decide such dispute shall, on petition of either group, be appointed by the district court of the United States for the district where the trust fund has its principal office, and shall also contain provisions for an annual audit of the trust fund, a statement of the results of which shall be available for inspection by interested persons at the principal office of the trust fund and at such other places as may be designated in such written agreement; and (C) such payments as are intended to be used for the purpose of providing pensions or annuities for employees are made to a separate trust which provides that the funds held therein cannot be used for any purpose other than paying such pensions or annuities[.]; [or] (6) *with respect to money or other thing of value paid by any employer to a trust fund established by such representative for the purpose of pooled vacation, holiday, severance or similar benefits, or defraying costs of apprenticeship or other training programs:* Provided, *That the requirements of clause (B) of the proviso to clause (5) of this subsection shall apply to such trust funds;* [or] (7) with respect to money or other thing of value paid by any employer to a pooled or individual trust fund established by such representative for the purpose of (A) scholarships for the benefit of employees, their families, and dependents for study at educational institutions, or (B) child care centers for preschool and school age dependents of employees: *Provided,* that no labor organization or employer shall be required to bargain on the establishment of any such trust fund, and refusal to do so shall not constitute an unfair labor practice: *Provided further,* That the requirements of clause (B) of the proviso to clause (5) of this subsection shall apply to such trust funds; or (8) with respect to money or any other thing of value paid by any employer to a trust fund established by such representative for the purpose of defraying the costs of legal services for employees, their families, and dependents for counsel or plan of their choice: *Provided,* that the requirements of clause (B) of the proviso to clause (5) of this subsection shall apply to such trust funds: *Provided further,* that no such legal services shall be furnished: (A) to initiate any proceeding directed (i) against any such employer or its officers or agents except in workman's compensation cases, or (ii) against such labor organization, or its parent or subordinate bodies, or their officers or agents, or (iii) against any other employer or labor organization, or their officers or agents, in any matter arising under the National Labor Relations Act, as amended, or this Act; and (B) in any proceeding where a labor organization would be prohibited from defraying the costs of legal services by the provisions of the Labor–Management Reporting and Disclosure Act of 1959; or (9) with respect to money or other things of value paid by an employer to a plant, area or industrywide labor management committee established for one or more of the purposes set forth in section 5(b) of the Labor Management Cooperation Act of 1978.*

(d) Any person who willfully violates any of the provisions of this section shall, upon conviction thereof, be guilty of a misdemeanor and be subject to a fine of not more than $10,000 or to imprisonment for not more than one year, or both.

* Subsection (c)(7) was added by P.L. 91-86, enacted October 14, 1969. Subsection (c)(8) was added by P.L. 93-95, enacted August 15, 1973. Subsection (c)(9) was added by P.L. 95-524, enacted October 27, 1978.

(e) The district courts of the United States and the United States courts of the Territories and possessions shall have jurisdiction, for cause shown, and subject to the provisions of section 17 (relating to notice to opposite party) of the Act entitled "An Act to supplement existing laws against unlawful restraints and monopolies, and for other purposes", approved October 15, 1914, as amended (U.S.C., title 28, sec. 381), to restrain violations of this section, without regard to the provisions of sections 6 and 20 of such Act of October 15, 1914, as amended (U.S.C., title 15, sec. 17, and title 29, sec. 52), and the provisions of the Act entitled "An Act to amend the Judicial Code and to define and limit the jurisdiction of courts sitting in equity, and for other purposes", approved March 23, 1932 (U.S.C., title 29, secs. 101–115).

(f) This section shall not apply to any contract in force on June 23, 1947, until the expiration of such contract, or until July 1, 1948, whichever first occurs.

(g) Compliance with the restrictions contained in subsection (c)(5)(B) of this section upon contributions to trust funds, otherwise lawful, shall not be applicable to contributions to such trust funds established by collective agreement prior to January 1, 1946, nor shall subsection (c)(5)(A) of this section be construed as prohibiting contributions to such trust funds if prior to January 1, 1947, such funds contained provisions for pooled vacation benefits.

### Boycotts and Other Unlawful Combinations

§ 303. (§ 187) (a) It shall be unlawful, for the purpose[s] of this section only, in an industry or activity affecting commerce, for any labor organization to engage in *any activity or conduct defined as an unfair labor practice in section 8(b)(4) of the National Labor Relations Act, as amended.* [or to induce or encourage the employees of any employer to engage in, a strike or a concerted refusal in the course of their employment to use, manufacture, process, transport, or otherwise handle or work on any goods, articles, materials, or commodities or to perform any services, where an object thereof is—

(1) forcing or requiring any employer or self-employed person to join any labor or employer organization or any employer or other person to cease using, selling, handling, transporting, or otherwise dealing in the products of any other producer, processor, or manufacturer, or to cease doing business with any other person;

(2) forcing or requiring any other employer to recognize or bargain with a labor organization as the representative of his employees unless such labor organization has been certified as the representative of such employees under the provisions of section 9 of the National Labor Relations Act;

(3) forcing or requiring any employer to recognize or bargain with a particular labor organization as the representative of his employees if another labor organization has been certified as the

representative of such employees under the provisions of section 9 of the National Labor Relations Act;

(4) forcing or requiring any employer to assign particular work to employees in a particular labor organization or in a particular trade, craft, or class rather than to employees in another labor organization or in another trade, craft, or class unless such employer is failing to conform to an order or certification of the National Labor Relations Board determining the bargaining representative for employees performing such work. Nothing contained in this subsection shall be construed to make unlawful a refusal by any person to enter upon the premises of any employer (other than his own employer), if the employees of such employer are engaged in a strike ratified or approved by a representative of such employees whom such employer is required to recognize under the National Labor Relations Act.]

(b) Whoever shall be injured in his business or property by reason of any violation of subsection (a) may sue therefor in any district court of the United States subject to the limitations and provisions of section 301 hereof without respect to the amount in controversy, or in any other court having jurisdiction of the parties, and shall recover the damages by him sustained and the cost of the suit.

RESTRICTION ON POLITICAL CONTRIBUTIONS

[Note: Section 304 of the LMRA (ch. 120, 61 Stat. 159 (1947)) amended § 313 of the Federal Corrupt Practices Act (chs. 368, 369, 43 Stat. 1074 (1925)). Section 304 was repealed (ch. 645, 62 Stat. 868 (1948)). The same chapter that repealed § 304 enacted 18 U.S.C. § 610 (1970) in ch. 645, 62 Stat. 723 (1948), which was repealed, Pub.L. 94–283, Title II, § 201(a), May 11, 1976, 90 Stat. 496. Section 321 was enacted by the Federal Election Campaign Act, Pub.L. 94–283, Title I, § 112(a), May 11, 1976, 90 Stat. 490, and was renumbered (to § 316) and amended, Pub.L. 96–187, Title I, §§ 105(5), 112(d), Jan. 8, 1980, 93 Stat. 1354, 1366. Relevant parts of that Act are reprinted below.]

CONTRIBUTIONS OR EXPENDITURES BY NATIONAL BANKS, CORPORATIONS, OR LABOR ORGANIZATIONS

§ 316. (2 U.S.C. § 441b) (a) It is unlawful for any national bank, or any corporation organized by authority of any law of Congress, to make a contribution or expenditure in connection with any election to any political office, or in connection with any primary election or political convention or caucus held to select candidates for any political office, or for any corporation whatever, or any labor organization, to make a contribution or expenditure in connection with any election at which presidential and vice presidential electors or a Senator or Representative in, or a Delegate or Resident Commissioner to, Congress are to be voted for, or in connection with any primary election or political convention or caucus held to select candidates for any of the foregoing offices, or for any candidate, political committee, or other person knowingly to accept or receive any contribution prohibited by this section, or any officer or any director of any corporation or any national bank or any officer of any labor organization to consent to any contribution or expenditure by the corporation, national bank, or labor organization, as the case may be, prohibited by this section.

(b)(1) For the purposes of this section the term "labor organization" means any organization of any kind, or any agency or employee representation committee or plan, in which employees participate and which exists for the purpose, in whole or in part, of dealing with employers concerning grievances, labor disputes, wages, rates of pay, hours of employment, or conditions of work.

(2) For purposes of this section and section 12(h) of the Public Utility Holding Company Act (15 U.S.C. 791(h)), the term "contribution or expenditure" shall include any direct or indirect payment, distribution, loan, advance, deposit, or gift of money, or any services, or anything of value (except a loan of money by a national or State bank made in accordance with the applicable banking laws and regulations and in the ordinary course of business) to any candidate, campaign committee, or political party or organization, in connection with any election to any of the offices referred to in this section, but shall not include (A) communications by a corporation to its stockholders and executive or administrative personnel and their families or by a labor organization to its members and their families on any subject; (B) nonpartisan registration and get-out-the-vote campaigns by a corporation aimed at its stockholders and executive or administrative personnel and their families, or by a labor organization aimed at its members and their families; and (C) the establishment, administration, and solicitation of contributions to a separate segregated fund to be utilized for political purposes by a corporation, labor organization, membership organization, cooperative, or corporation without capital stock.

(3) It shall be unlawful—

    (A) For such a fund to make a contribution or expenditure by utilizing money or anything of value secured by physical force, job discrimination, financial reprisals, or the threat of force, job discrimination, or financial reprisal; or by dues, fees, or other moneys required as a condition of membership in a labor organization or as a condition of employment, or by moneys obtained in any commercial transaction;

    (B) for any person soliciting an employee for a contribution to such a fund to fail to inform such employee of the political purposes of such fund at the time of such solicitation; and

    (C) for any person soliciting an employee for a contribution to such a fund to fail to inform such employee, at the time of such solicitation, of his right to refuse to so contribute without any reprisal.

(4)(A) Except as provided in subparagraphs (B), (C), and (D), it shall be unlawful—

    (i) for a corporation, or a separate segregated fund established by a corporation, to solicit contributions to such a fund from any person other than its stockholders and their families and its executive or administrative personnel and their families, and

    (ii) for a labor organization, or a separate segregated fund established by a labor organization, to solicit contributions to such a fund from any person other than its members and their families.

(B) It shall not be unlawful under this section for a corporation, a labor organization, or a separate segregated fund established by such corporation or such labor organization, to make 2 written solicitations for contributions during the calendar year from any stockholder, executive or administrative personnel, or employee of a corporation or the families of such persons. A solicitation under this subparagraph may be made only by mail addressed to stockholders, executive or administrative personnel, or employees at their residence and shall be so designed that the corporation, labor organization, or separate segregated fund conducting such solicitation cannot determine who makes a contribution of $50 or less as a result of such solicitation and who does not make such a contribution.

(C) This paragraph shall not prevent a membership organization, cooperative, or corporation without capital stock, or a separate segregated fund established by a membership organization, cooperative, or corporation without capital stock, from soliciting contributions to such a fund from members of such organization, cooperative, or corporation without capital stock.

(D) This paragraph shall not prevent a trade association or a separate segregated fund established by a trade association from soliciting contributions from the stockholders and executive or administrative personnel of the member corporations of such trade association and the families of such stockholders or personnel to the extent that such solicitation of such stockholders and personnel, and their families, has been separately and specifically approved by the member corporation involved, and such member corporation does not approve any such solicitation by more than one such trade association in any calendar year.

    (5) Notwithstanding any other law, any method of soliciting voluntary contributions or of facilitating the making of voluntary contributions to a separate segregated fund established by a corporation, permitted by law to corporations with regard to stockholders and executive or administrative personnel, shall also be permitted to labor organizations with regard to their members.

    (6) Any corporation, including its subsidiaries, branches, divisions, and affiliates, that utilizes a method of soliciting voluntary contributions

or facilitating the making of voluntary contributions, shall make available such method, on written request and at a cost sufficient only to reimburse the corporation for the expenses incurred thereby, to a labor organization representing any members working for such corporation, its subsidiaries, branches, divisions, and affiliates.

(7) For purposes of this section, the term "executive or administrative personnel" means individuals employed by a corporation who are paid on a salary, rather than hourly, basis and who have policymaking, managerial, professional, or supervisory responsibilities.

### STRIKES BY GOVERNMENT EMPLOYEES

[§ 305. (§ 188) It shall be unlawful for any individual employed by the United States or any agency thereof including wholly owned Government corporations to participate in any strike. Any individual employed by the United States or by any such agency who strikes shall be discharged immediately from his employment, and shall forfeit his civil-service status, if any, and shall not be eligible for reemployment for three years by the United States or any such agency.]*

### TITLE IV

#### CREATION OF JOINT COMMITTEE TO STUDY AND REPORT ON BASIC PROBLEMS AFFECTING FRIENDLY LABOR RELATIONS AND PRODUCTIVITY

### TITLE V

#### DEFINITIONS

§ 501. (§ 142) When used in this Act—

(1) The term "industry affecting commerce" means any industry or activity in commerce or in which a labor dispute would burden or obstruct commerce or tend to burden or obstruct commerce or the free flow of commerce.

(2) The term "strike" includes any strike or other concerted stoppage of work by employees (including a stoppage by reason of the expiration of a collective-bargaining agreement) and any concerted slowdown or other concerted interruption of operations by employees.

(3) The terms "commerce," "labor disputes," "employer," "employee," "labor organization," "representative," "person," and "supervisor" shall have the same meaning as when used in the National Labor Relations Act as amended by this Act.

### SAVING PROVISION

§ 502. (§ 143) Nothing in this Act shall be construed to require an individual employee to render labor or service without his consent, nor shall anything in this Act be construed to make the quitting of his labor by an individual employee an illegal act; nor shall any court issue any

---

* Section 305 was repealed by Pub.L. No. 330, 84th Cong., 1st Sess., approved August 9, 1955, which added 5 U.S.C. §§ 118p– 118r, [now 5 U.S.C. §§ 3333, 7311, 18 U.S.C. § 1918]; those provisions retain the proscription of strikes by federal employees.

process to compel the performance by an individual employee of such labor or service, without his consent; nor shall the quitting of labor by an employee or employees in good faith because of abnormally dangerous conditions for work at the place of employment of such employee or employees be deemed a strike under this Act.

SEPARABILITY

§ 503. (§ 144) If any provision of this Act, or the application of such provision to any person or circumstance, shall be held invalid, the remainder of this Act, or the application of such provision to persons or circumstances other than those as to which it is held invalid, shall not be affected thereby.

———

# LABOR–MANAGEMENT REPORTING AND DISCLOSURE ACT*

*73 Stat. 519 (1959), as amended, 29 U.S.C. §§ 401–531*

AN ACT

To provide for the reporting and disclosure of certain financial transactions and administrative practices of labor organizations and employers, to prevent abuses in the administration of trusteeships by labor organizations, to provide standards with respect to the election of officers of labor organizations and for other purposes.

SHORT TITLE

§ 1. This Act may be cited as the "Labor–Management Reporting and Disclosure Act of 1959".

DECLARATION OF FINDINGS, PURPOSES, AND POLICY

§ 2. (§ 401) (a) The Congress finds that, in the public interest, it continues to be the responsibility of the Federal Government to protect employees' rights to organize, choose their own representatives, bargain collectively, and otherwise engage in concerted activities for their mutual aid or protection; that the relations between employers and labor organizations and the millions of workers they represent have a substantial impact on the commerce of the Nation; and that in order to accomplish the objective of a free flow of commerce it is essential that labor organizations, employers, and their officials adhere to the highest standards of responsibility and ethical conduct in administering the affairs of their organizations, particularly as they affect labor-management relations.

---

* Title VII, § 201(d) and (e) and § 505 of the LMRDA amends the National Labor Relations Act and the Labor Management Relations Act. These amendments, which have been incorporated in the appropriate sections of these statutes, are omitted here.

(b) The Congress further finds, from recent investigations in the labor and management fields, that there have been a number of instances of breach of trust, corruption, disregard of the rights of individual employees, and other failures to observe high standards of responsibility and ethical conduct which require further and supplementary legislation that will afford necessary protection of the rights and interests of employees and the public generally as they relate to the activities of labor organizations, employers, labor relations consultants, and their officers and representatives.

(c) The Congress, therefore, further finds and declares that the enactment of this Act is necessary to eliminate or prevent improper practices on the part of labor organizations, employers, labor relations consultants, and their officers and representatives which distort and defeat the policies of the Labor Management Relations Act, 1947, as amended, and the Railway Labor Act, as amended, and have the tendency or necessary effect of burdening or obstructing commerce by (1) impairing the efficiency, safety, or operation of the instrumentalities of commerce; (2) occurring in the current of commerce; (3) materially affecting, restraining, or controlling the flow of raw materials or manufactured or processed goods into or from the channels of commerce, or the prices of such materials or goods in commerce; or (4) causing diminution of employment and wages in such volume as substantially to impair or disrupt the market for goods flowing into or from the channels of commerce. * * *

### Title I—Bill of Rights of Members of Labor Organizations

#### Bill of Rights

§ 101. (§ 411) (a)(1) *Equal Rights.* Every member of a labor organization shall have equal rights and privileges within such organization to nominate candidates, to vote in elections or referendums of the labor organization, to attend membership meetings, and to participate in the deliberations and voting upon the business of such meetings, subject to reasonable rules and regulations in such organization's constitution and bylaws.

(2) *Freedom of Speech and Assembly.* Every member of any labor organization shall have the right to meet and assemble freely with other members; and to express any views, arguments, or opinions; and to express at meetings of the labor organization his views, upon candidates in an election of the labor organization or upon any business properly before the meeting, subject to the organization's established and reasonable rules pertaining to the conduct of meetings: *Provided,* That nothing herein shall be construed to impair the right of a labor organization to adopt and enforce reasonable rules as to the responsibility of every member toward the organization as an institution and to his refraining from conduct that would interfere with its performance of its legal or contractual obligations.

(3) *Dues, Initiation Fees, and Assessments.* Except in the case of a federation of national or international labor organizations, the rates of dues and initiation fees payable by members of any labor organization in effect on the date of enactment of this Act shall not be increased, and no general or special assessment shall be levied upon such members, except—

(A) in the case of a local labor organization, (i) by majority vote by secret ballot of the members in good standing voting at a general or special membership meeting, after reasonable notice of the intention to vote upon such question, or (ii) by majority vote of the members in good standing voting in a membership referendum conducted by secret ballot; or

(B) in the case of a labor organization, other than a local labor organization or a federation of national or international labor organizations, (i) by majority vote of the delegates voting at a regular convention, or at a special convention of such labor organization held upon not less than thirty days' written notice to the principal office of each local or constituent labor organization entitled to such notice, or (ii) by majority vote of the members in good standing of such labor organization voting in a membership referendum conducted by secret ballot, or (iii) by majority vote of the members of the executive board or similar governing body of such labor organization, pursuant to express authority contained in the constitution and bylaws of such labor organization: *Provided,* That such action on the part of the executive board or similar governing body shall be effective only until the next regular convention of such labor organization.

(4) *Protection of the Right To Sue.* No labor organization shall limit the right of any member thereof to institute an action in any court, or in a proceeding before any administrative agency, irrespective of whether or not the labor organization or its officers are named as defendants or respondents in such action or proceeding, or the right of any member of a labor organization to appear as a witness in any judicial, administrative, or legislative proceeding, or to petition any legislature or to communicate with any legislator: *Provided,* That any such member may be required to exhaust reasonable hearing procedures (but not to exceed a four-month lapse of time) within such organization, before instituting legal or administrative proceedings against such organizations or any officer thereof: *And provided further,* That no interested employer or employer association shall directly or indirectly finance, encourage, or participate in, except as a party, any such action, proceeding, appearance, or petition.

(5) *Safeguards Against Improper Disciplinary Action.* No member of any labor organization may be fined, suspended, expelled, or otherwise disciplined except for nonpayment of dues by such organization or by any officer thereof unless such member has been (A) served with written

specific charges; (B) given a reasonable time to prepare his defense; (C) afforded a full and fair hearing.

(b) Any provision of the constitution and bylaws of any labor organization which is inconsistent with the provisions of this section shall be of no force or effect.

## Civil Enforcement

§ 102. (§ 412) Any person whose rights secured by the provisions of this title have been infringed by any violation of this title may bring a civil action in a district court of the United States for such relief (including injunctions) as may be appropriate. Any such action against a labor organization shall be brought in the district court of the United States for the district where the alleged violation occurred, or where the principal office of such labor organization is located. * * *

## Title III—Trusteeships * * *
### Purposes for Which a Trusteeship May Be Established

§ 302. (§ 462) Trusteeships shall be established and administered by a labor organization over a subordinate body only in accordance with the constitution and bylaws of the organization which has assumed trusteeship over the subordinate body and for the purpose of correcting corruption or financial malpractice, assuring the performance of collective bargaining agreements or other duties of a bargaining representative, restoring democratic procedures, or otherwise carrying out the legitimate objects of such labor organization. * * *

## Title IV—Elections
### Terms of Office; Election Procedures

§ 401. (§ 481) (a) Every national or international labor organization, except a federation of national or international labor organizations, shall elect its officers not less often than once every five years either by secret ballot among the members in good standing or at a convention of delegates chosen by secret ballot.

(b) Every local labor organization shall elect its officers not less often than once every three years by secret ballot among the members in good standing.

(c) Every national or international labor organization, except a federation of national or international labor organizations, and every local labor organization, and its officers, shall be under a duty, enforceable at the suit of any bona fide candidate for office in such labor organization in the district court of the United States in which such labor organization maintains its principal office, to comply with all reasonable requests of any candidate to distribute by mail or otherwise at the candidate's expense campaign literature in aid of such person's candidacy to all members in good standing of such labor organization and to refrain from discrimination in favor of or against any candidate with respect to the use of lists of members, and whenever such labor organizations or its officers authorize the distribution by mail or otherwise to members of campaign literature on behalf of any candidate or of the labor organization itself with reference to such election, similar distribution at the request of any other bona fide candidate shall be made by such labor organization and its officers, with equal treatment as to the expense of such distribution. Every bona fide candidate shall have the right, once within 30 days prior to an election of a labor organization in which he is a candidate, to inspect a list containing the names and last known addresses of all members of the labor organization who are subject to a collective bargaining agreement requiring membership therein as a condition of employment, which list shall be maintained and kept at the principal office of such labor organization by a designated official thereof. Adequate safeguards to insure a fair election shall be provided including the right of any candidate to have an observer at the polls and at the counting of the ballots.

(d) Officers of intermediate bodies, such as general committees, system boards, joint boards, or joint councils, shall be elected not less often than once every four years by secret ballot among the members in good standing or by labor organization officers representative of such members who have been elected by secret ballot.

(e) In any election required by this section which is to be held by secret ballot a reasonable opportunity shall be given for the nomination of candidates and every member in good standing shall be eligible to be a candidate and to hold office (subject to section 504 and to reasonable qualifications uniformly imposed) and shall have the right to vote for or otherwise support the candidate or candidates of his choice, without being subject to penalty, discipline, or improper interference or reprisal of any kind by such organization or any member thereof. Not less than fifteen days prior to the election notice thereof shall be mailed to each member at his last known home address. Each member in good standing shall be entitled to one vote. No member whose dues have been withheld by his employer for payment to such organization pursuant to his voluntary authorization provided for in a collective bargaining agreement shall be declared ineligible to vote or be a candidate for office in such organization by reason of alleged delay or default in the payment of dues. The votes cast by members of each local labor organization shall be counted, and the results published, separately. The election officials designated in the constitution and bylaws or the secretary, if no other official is designated, shall preserve for one year the ballots and all other records pertaining to the election. The election shall be conducted in accordance with the constitution and bylaws of such organization insofar as they are not inconsistent with the provisions of this title.

(f) When officers are chosen by a convention of delegates elected by secret ballot, the convention shall be conducted in accordance with the constitution and bylaws of the labor organization insofar as they are not inconsistent with the provisions of this title. The officials designated in the constitution and bylaws or the secretary, if no other is designated, shall preserve for one year the credentials of the delegates and all minutes and other records of the convention pertaining to the election of officers.

(g) No moneys received by any labor organization by way of dues, assessment, or similar levy, and no moneys of an employer shall be contributed or applied to promote the candidacy of any person in an election subject to the provisions of this title. Such moneys of a labor organization may be utilized for notices, factual statements of issues not involving candidates, and other expenses necessary for the holding of an election.

(h) If the Secretary, upon application of any member of a local labor organization, finds after hearing in accordance with the Administrative Procedure Act that the constitution and bylaws of such labor organization do not provide an adequate procedure for the removal of an elected officer guilty of serious misconduct, such officer may be removed, for cause shown and after notice and hearing, by the members in good standing voting in a secret ballot conducted by the officers of such labor organization in accordance with its constitution and bylaws insofar as they are not inconsistent with the provisions of this title.

(i) The Secretary shall promulgate rules and regulations prescribing minimum standards and procedures for determining the adequacy of the removal procedures to which reference is made in subsection (h).

ENFORCEMENT

§ 402. (§ 482) (a) A member of a labor organization—

(1) who has exhausted the remedies available under the constitution and bylaws of such organization and of any parent body, or

(2) who has invoked such available remedies without obtaining a final decision within three calendar months after their invocation,

may file a complaint with the Secretary within one calendar month thereafter alleging the violation of any provision of section 401 (including violation of the constitution and bylaws of the labor organization pertaining to the election and removal of officers). The challenged election shall be presumed valid pending a final decision thereon (as hereinafter provided) and in the interim the affairs of the organization shall be conducted by the officers elected or in such other manner as its constitution and bylaws may provide.

(b) The Secretary shall investigate such complaint and, if he finds probable cause to believe that a violation of this title has occurred and has not been remedied, he shall, within sixty days after the filing of such complaint, bring a civil action against the labor organization as an entity in the district court of the United States in which such labor organization maintains its principal office to set aside the invalid election, if any, and to direct the conduct of an election or hearing and vote upon the removal of officers under the supervision of the Secretary and in accordance with the provisions of this title and such rules and regulations as the Secretary may prescribe. The court shall have power to take such action as it deems proper to preserve the assets of the labor organization.

(c) If, upon a preponderance of the evidence after a trial upon the merits, the court finds—

(1) that an election has not been held within the time prescribed by section 401, or

(2) that the violation of section 401 may have affected the outcome of an election,

that court shall declare the election, if any, to be void and direct the conduct of a new election under supervision of the Secretary and, so far as lawful and practicable, in conformity with the constitution and bylaws of the labor organization. The Secretary shall promptly certify to the court the names of the persons elected, and the court shall thereupon enter a decree declaring such persons to be the officers of the labor organization. If the proceeding is for the removal of officers pursuant to subsection (h) of section 401, the Secretary shall certify the results of the vote and the court shall enter a decree declaring whether such persons have been removed as officers of the labor organization.

(d) An order directing an election, dismissing a complaint, or designating elected officers of a labor organization shall be appealable in the same manner as the final judgment in a civil action, but an order directing an election shall not be stayed pending appeal.

### APPLICATION OF OTHER LAWS

§ 403. (§ 483) No labor organization shall be required by law to conduct elections of officers with greater frequency or in a different form or manner than is required by its own constitution or bylaws, except as otherwise provided by this title. Existing rights and remedies to enforce the constitution and bylaws of a labor organization with respect to elections prior to the conduct thereof shall not be affected by the provisions of this title. The remedy provided by this title for challenging an election already conducted shall be exclusive.

\* \* \*

### TITLE V—SAFEGUARDS FOR LABOR ORGANIZATIONS
### FIDUCIARY RESPONSIBILITY OF OFFICERS OF LABOR ORGANIZATIONS

§ 501. (§ 501) (a) The officers, agents, shop stewards, and other representatives of a labor organization occupy positions of trust in relation to such organization and its members as a group. It is, therefore, the duty of each such person, taking into account the special problems and functions of a labor organization, to hold its money and property solely for the benefit of the organization and its members and to manage, invest, and expend the same in accordance with its constitution and bylaws and any resolutions of the governing bodies adopted thereunder, to refrain from dealing with such organization as an adverse party or in behalf of an adverse party in any matter connected with his duties and from holding or acquiring any pecuniary or personal interest which conflicts with the interests of such organization, and to account to the organization for any profit received by him in whatever capacity in connection with transactions conducted by him or under his direction on behalf of the organization. A general exculpatory provision in the constitution and bylaws of such a labor organization or a general exculpatory resolution of a governing body purporting to relieve any such person of liability for breach of the duties declared by this section shall be void as against public policy. \* \* \*

---

# SHERMAN ACT

*Act of July 2, 1890, 26 Stat. 209, as amended, 15 U.S.C. §§ 1–7*

§ 1. (§ 1) Every contract, combination in the form of trust or otherwise, or conspiracy, in restraint of trade or commerce among the several States, or with foreign nations, is declared to be illegal. Every person who shall make any such contract or engage in any such combination or conspiracy hereby declared to be illegal shall be deemed guilty of a felony, and, on conviction thereof, shall be punished by fine not exceeding one million dollars if a corporation, or, in any other person, one hundred thousand dollars, or by imprisonment not exceeding three years, or by both said punishments, in the discretion of the court.

§ 2. (§ 2) Every person who shall monopolize, or attempt to monopolize, or combine or conspire with any other person or persons, to monopolize any part of the trade or commerce among the several States, or with foreign nations, shall be deemed guilty of a felony, and, on conviction thereof, shall be punished by fine not exceeding one million dollars if a corporation, or, if any other person, one hundred thousand dollars, or by imprisonment not exceeding three years, or by both said punishments, in the discretion of the court.

§ 3. (§ 3) Every contract, combination in form of trust or otherwise, or conspiracy, in restraint of trade or commerce in any Territory of the United States or of the District of Columbia, or in restraint of trade or commerce between any such Territory and another, or between any such Territory or Territories and any State or States or the District of Columbia, or with foreign nations, or between the District of Columbia and any State or States or foreign nations, is hereby declared illegal. Every person who shall make any such contract or engage in any such combination or conspiracy, shall be deemed guilty of a felony, and, on conviction thereof, shall be punished by fine not exceeding one million dollars if a corporation, or, if any other person, one hundred thousand dollars, or by imprisonment not exceeding three years, or by both said punishments, in the discretion of the court.

§ 4. (§ 4) The several district courts of the United States are invested with jurisdiction to prevent and restrain violations of this act;

and it shall be the duty of the several United States attorneys, in their respective districts, under the direction of the Attorney General, to institute proceedings in equity to prevent and restrain such violations. Such proceedings may be by way of petition setting forth the case and praying that such violation shall be enjoined or otherwise prohibited. When the parties complained of shall have been duly notified of such petition the court shall proceed, as soon as may be, to the hearing and determination of the case; and pending such petition and before final decree, the court may at any time make such temporary restraining order or prohibition as shall be deemed just in the premises.

§ 5. (§ 5) Whenever it shall appear to the court before which any proceeding under section 4 of this title may be pending, that the ends of justice require that other parties should be brought before the court, the court may cause them to be summoned, whether they reside in the district in which the court is held or not; and subpoenas to that end may be served in any district by the marshal thereof.

§ 6. (§ 6) Any property owned under any contract or by any combination, or pursuant to any conspiracy (and being the subject thereof) mentioned in section 1 of this act, and being in the course of transportation from one State to another, or to a foreign country, shall be forfeited to the United States, and may be seized and condemned by like proceedings as those provided by law for the forfeiture, seizure, and condemnation of property imported into the United States contrary to law.

§ 7. This Act shall not apply to conduct involving trade or commerce (other than important trade or import commerce) with foreign nations unless—

(1) such conduct has a direct, substantial, and reasonably foreseeable effect—

(A) on trade or commerce which is not trade or commerce with foreign nations, or on import trade or import commerce with foreign nations; or

(B) on export trade or export commerce with foreign nations, of a person engaged in such trade or commerce in the United States; and

(2) such effect gives rise to a claim under the provisions of this Act, other than this section.

If this Act applies to such conduct only because of the operation of paragraph (1)(B), then this Act shall apply to such conduct only for injury to export business in the United States.*

§ 8. (§ 7) The word "person," or "persons," wherever used in this act shall be deemed to include corporations and associations existing

* The old Section 7 concerning treble damages was repealed by 69 Stat. 283 (1955). Section 4 of the Clayton Act, 38 Stat. 731 (1914), 15 U.S.C. § 15 (1964), now authorizes private treble damage suits. A new Section 7 was added by P.L. 97–290, effective October 8, 1982.

under or authorized by the laws of either the United States, the laws of any of the Territories, the laws of any State, or the laws of any foreign country.

---

# CLAYTON ACT

*Act of October 15, 1914, 38 Stat. 730, as amended, 15 U.S.C. §§ 12–27*

*Be it enacted by the Senate and House of Representatives of the United States of America in Congress Assembled,* That "antitrust laws," as used herein, includes the Act entitled "An Act to protect trade and commerce against unlawful restraints and monopolies," approved July second, eighteen hundred and ninety [The Sherman Act].

\* \* \*

§ 6. (§ 17) That the labor of a human being is not a commodity or article of commerce. Nothing contained in the antitrust laws shall be construed to forbid the existence and operation of labor, agricultural, or horticultural organizations, instituted for the purposes of mutual help, and not having capital stock or conducted for profit, or to forbid or restrain individual members of such organizations from lawfully carrying out the legitimate objects thereof; nor shall such organizations, or the members thereof, be held or construed to be illegal combinations or conspiracies in restraint of trade, under the antitrust laws.

\* \* \*

§ 20. (29 U.S.C. § 52) That no restraining order or injunction shall be granted by any court of the United States, or a judge or the judges thereof, in any case between an employer and employees, or between employers and employees, or between employees, or between persons employed and persons seeking employment, involving, or growing out of, a dispute concerning terms or conditions of employment, unless necessary to prevent irreparable injury to property, or to a property right, of the party making the application, for which injury there is no adequate remedy at law, and such property or property right must be described with particularity in the application, which must be in writing and sworn to by the applicant or by his agent or attorney.

And no such restraining order or injunction shall prohibit any person or persons, whether singly or in concert, from terminating any relation of employment, or from ceasing to perform any work or labor, or from recommending, advising, or persuading others by peaceful means so to do; or from attending at any place where any such person or persons may lawfully be, for the purpose of peacefully obtaining or communicating information, or from peacefully persuading any person to work or to abstain from working; or from ceasing to patronize or to employ any party to such dispute, or from recommending, advising, or persuading others by peaceful and lawful means so to do; or from paying or giving to, or withholding from, any person engaged in such dispute, any strike benefits or other moneys or things of value; or from peaceably assembling in a lawful manner, and for lawful purposes; or from doing any act or thing which might lawfully be done in the absence of such dispute by any party thereto; nor shall any of the acts specified in this paragraph be considered or held to be violations of any law of the United States.

---

# OCCUPATIONAL SAFETY AND HEALTH ACT

29 U.S.C. §§ 651–678, as amended

DEFINITIONS

SEC. 3.　(§ 652) For the purposes of this Act—

(1) The term "Secretary" means the Secretary of Labor.

(2) The term "Commission" means the Occupational Safety and Health Review Commission established under this Act.

(3) The term "commerce" means trade, traffic, commerce, transportation, or communication among the several States, or between a State and any place outside thereof, or within the District of Columbia, or a possession of the United States (other than the Trust Territory of the Pacific Islands), or between points in the same State but through a point outside thereof.

(4) The term "person" means one or more individuals, partnerships, associations, corporations, business trusts, legal representatives, or any organized group of persons.

(5) The term "employer" means a person engaged in a business affecting commerce who has employees, but does not include the United States or any State or political subdivision of a State.

(6) The term "employee" means an employee of an employer who is employed in a business of his employer which affects commerce.

(7) The term "State" includes a State of the United States, the District of Columbia, Puerto Rico, the Virgin Islands, American Samoa, Guam, and the Trust Territory of the Pacific Islands.

(8) The term "occupational safety and health standard" means a standard which requires conditions, or the adoption or use of one or more practices, means, methods, operations, or processes, reasonably necessary or appropriate to provide safe or healthful employment and places of employment.

(9) The term "national consensus standard" means any occupational safety and health standard or modification thereof which (1) has been adopted and promulgated by a nationally recognized standards-producing organization under procedures whereby it can be determined by the Secretary that persons interested and affected by the scope or provisions of the standard have reached substantial agreement on its adoption, (2)

was formulated in a manner which afforded an opportunity for diverse views to be considered and (3) has been designated as such a standard by the Secretary, after consultation with other appropriate Federal agencies.

(10) The term "established Federal standard" means any operative occupational safety and health standard established by any agency of the United States and presently in effect, or contained in any Act of Congress in force on the date of enactment of this Act.

*  *  *

## APPLICABILITY OF THIS ACT

SEC. 4.  (§ 653) (a) This Act shall apply with respect to employment performed in a workplace in a State, the District of Columbia, the Commonwealth of Puerto Rico, the Virgin Islands, American Samoa, Guam, the Trust Territory of the Pacific Islands, Wake Island, Outer Continental Shelf lands defined in the Outer Continental Shelf Lands Act, Johnston Island, and the Canal Zone.  The Secretary of the Interior shall, by regulation, provide for judicial enforcement of this Act by the courts established for areas in which there are no United States district courts having jurisdiction.

(b)(1) Nothing in this Act shall apply to working conditions of employees with respect to which other Federal agencies, and State agencies acting under section 274 of the Atomic Energy Act of 1954, as amended (42 U.S.C. 2021), exercise statutory authority to prescribe or enforce standards or regulations affecting occupational safety or health.

(2) The safety and health standards promulgated under the Act of June 30, 1936, commonly known as the Walsh–Healey Act (41 U.S.C. 35 et seq.), the Service Contract Act of 1965 (41 U.S.C. 351 et seq.), Public Law 91–54, Act of August 9, 1969 (40 U.S.C. 333), Public Law 85–742, Act of August 23, 1958 (33 U.S.C. 941), and the National Foundation on Arts and Humanities Act (20 U.S.C. 951 et seq.) are superseded on the effective date of corresponding standards, promulgated under this Act, which are determined by the Secretary to be more effective.  Standards issued under the laws listed in this paragraph and in effect on or after the effective date of this Act shall be deemed to be occupational safety and health standards issued under this Act, as well as under such other Acts.

(3) The Secretary shall, within three years after the effective date of this Act, report to the Congress his recommendations for legislation to avoid unnecessary duplication and to achieve coordination between this Act and other Federal laws.

(4) Nothing in this Act shall be construed to supersede or in any manner affect any workmen's compensation law or to enlarge or diminish or affect in any other manner the common law or statutory rights, duties, or liabilities of employers and employees under any law with

respect to injuries, diseases, or death of employees arising out of, or in the course of, employment.

## DUTIES

**SEC. 5.** **(§ 654)** (a) Each employer—

(1) shall furnish to each of his employees employment and a place of employment which are free from recognized hazards that are causing or are likely to cause death or serious physical harm to his employees;

(2) shall comply with occupational safety and health standards promulgated under this Act.

(b) Each employee shall comply with occupational safety and health standards and all rules, regulations, and orders issued pursuant to this Act which are applicable to his own actions and conduct.

## OCCUPATIONAL SAFETY AND HEALTH STANDARDS

**SEC. 6.** **(§ 655)** (a) Without regard to chapter 5 of title 5, United States Code, or to the other subsections of this section, the Secretary shall, as soon as practicable during the period beginning with the effective date of this Act and ending two years after such date, by rule promulgate as an occupational safety or health standard any national consensus standard, and any established Federal standard, unless he determines that the promulgation of such a standard would not result in improved safety or health for specifically designated employees. In the event of conflict among any such standards, the Secretary shall promulgate the standard which assures the greatest protection of the safety or health of the affected employees.

(b) The Secretary may by rule promulgate, modify, or revoke any occupational safety or health standard in the following manner:

(1) Whenever the Secretary, upon the basis of information submitted to him in writing by an interested person, a representative of any organization of employers or employees, a nationally recognized standards-producing organization, the Secretary of Health and Human Services, the National Institute for Occupational Safety and Health, or a State or political subdivision, or on the basis of information developed by the Secretary or otherwise available to him, determines that a rule should be promulgated in order to serve the objectives of this Act, the Secretary may request the recommendations of an advisory committee appointed under section 7 of this Act. The Secretary shall provide such an advisory committee with any proposals of his own or of the Secretary of Health and Human Services, together with all pertinent factual information developed by the Secretary or the Secretary of Health and Human Services, or otherwise available, including the results of research, demonstrations, and experiments. An advisory committee shall submit to the Secretary its recommendations regarding the rule to be promulgated within ninety days from the date of its appointment or within such longer or shorter period as may be prescribed by the

Secretary, but in no event for a period which is longer than two hundred and seventy days.

(2) The Secretary shall publish a proposed rule promulgating, modifying, or revoking an occupational safety or health standard in the Federal Register and shall afford interested persons a period of thirty days after publication to submit written data or comments. Where an advisory committee is appointed and the Secretary determines that a rule should be issued, he shall publish the proposed rule within sixty days after the submission of the advisory committee's recommendations or the expiration of the period prescribed by the Secretary for such submission.

(3) On or before the last day of the period provided for the submission of written data or comments under paragraph (2), any interested person may file with the Secretary written objections to the proposed rule, stating the grounds therefor and requesting a public hearing on such objections. Within thirty days after the last day for filing such objections, the Secretary shall publish in the Federal Register a notice specifying the occupational safety or health standard to which objections have been filed and a hearing requested, and specifying a time and place for such hearing.

(4) Within sixty days after the expiration of the period provided for the submission of written data or comments under paragraph (2), or within sixty days after the completion of any hearing held under paragraph (3), the Secretary shall issue a rule promulgating, modifying, or revoking an occupational safety or health standard or make a determination that a rule should not be issued. Such a rule may contain a provision delaying its effective date for such period (not in excess of ninety days) as the Secretary determines may be necessary to insure that affected employers and employees will be informed of the existence of the standard and of its terms and that employers affected are given an opportunity to familiarize themselves and their employees with the existence of the requirements of the standard.

(5) The Secretary, in promulgating standards dealing with toxic materials or harmful physical agents under this subsection, shall set the standard which most adequately assures, to the extent feasible, on the basis of the best available evidence, that no employee will suffer material impairment of health or functional capacity even if such employee has regular exposure to the hazard dealt with by such standard for the period of his working life. Development of standards under this subsection shall be based upon research, demonstrations, experiments, and such other information as may be appropriate. In addition to the attainment of the highest degree of health and safety protection for the employee, other considerations shall be the latest available scientific data in the field, the feasibility of the standards, and experience gained under this and other health and safety laws. Whenever practicable, the standard promulgated shall be expressed in terms of objective criteria and of the performance desired.

(6)(A) Any employer may apply to the Secretary for a temporary order granting a variance from a standard or any provision thereof promulgated under this section. Such temporary order shall be granted only if the employer files an application which meets the requirements of clause (B) and establishes that (i) he is unable to comply with a standard by its effective date because of unavailability of professional or technical personnel or of materials and equipment needed to come into compliance with the standard or because necessary construction or alteration of facilities cannot be completed by the effective date, (ii) he is taking all available steps to safeguard his employees against the hazards covered by the standard, and (iii) he has an effective program for coming into compliance with the standard as quickly as practicable. Any temporary order issued under this paragraph shall prescribe the practices, means, methods, operations, and processes which the employer must adopt and use while the order is in effect and state in detail his program for coming into compliance with the standard. Such a temporary order may be granted only after notice to employees and an opportunity for a hearing: *Provided,* That the Secretary may issue one interim order to be effective until a decision is made on the basis of the hearing. No temporary order may be in effect for longer than the period needed by the employer to achieve compliance with the standard or one year, whichever is shorter, except that such an order may be renewed not more than twice (I) so long as the requirements of this paragraph are met and (II) if an application for renewal is filed at least 90 days prior to the expiration date of the order. No interim renewal of an order may remain in effect for longer than 180 days.

(B) An application for a temporary order under this paragraph (6) shall contain:

(i) a specification of the standard or portion thereof from which the employer seeks a variance,

(ii) a representation by the employer, supported by representations from qualified persons having firsthand knowledge of the facts represented, that he is unable to comply with the standard or portion thereof and a detailed statement of the reasons therefor,

(iii) a statement of the steps he has taken and will take (with specific dates) to protect employees against the hazard covered by the standard,

(iv) a statement of when he expects to be able to comply with the standard and what steps he has taken and what steps he will take (with dates specified) to come into compliance with the standard, and

(v) a certification that he has informed his employees of the application by giving a copy thereof to their authorized representative, posting a statement giving a summary of the application and specifying where a copy may be examined at the place or places where notices to employees are normally posted, and by other appropriate means.

A description of how employees have been informed shall be contained in the certification. The information to employees shall also inform them of their right to petition the Secretary for a hearing.

(C) The Secretary is authorized to grant a variance from any standard or portion thereof whenever he determines, or the Secretary of Health, Education, and Welfare certifies, that such variance is necessary to permit an employer to participate in an experiment approved by him or the Secretary of Health and Human Services designed to demonstrate or validate new and improved techniques to safeguard the health or safety of workers.

(7) Any standard promulgated under this subsection shall prescribe the use of labels or other appropriate forms of warning as are necessary to insure that employees are apprised of all hazards to which they are exposed, relevant symptoms and appropriate emergency treatment, and proper conditions and precautions of safe use or exposure. Where appropriate, such standard shall also prescribe suitable protective equipment and control or technological procedures to be used in connection with such hazards and shall provide for monitoring or measuring employee exposure at such locations and intervals, and in such manner as may be necessary for the protection of employees. In addition, where appropriate, any such standard shall prescribe the type and frequency of medical examinations or other tests which shall be made available, by the employer or at his cost, to employees exposed to such hazards in order to most effectively determine whether the health of such employees is adversely affected by such exposure. In the event such medical examinations are in the nature of research, as determined by the Secretary of Health and Human Services, such examinations may be furnished at the expense of the Secretary of Health and Human Services. The results of such examinations or tests shall be furnished only to the Secretary or the Secretary of Health and Human Services, and, at the request of the employee, to his physician. The Secretary, in consultation with the Secretary of Health and Human Services, may by rule promulgated pursuant to section 553 of title 5, United States Code, make appropriate modifications in the foregoing requirements relating to the use of labels or other forms of warning, monitoring or measuring, and medical examinations, as may be warranted by experience, information, or medical or technological developments acquired subsequent to the promulgation of the relevant standard.

(8) Whenever a rule promulgated by the Secretary differs substantially from an existing national consensus standard, the Secretary shall, at the same time, publish in the Federal Register a statement of the reasons why the rule as adopted will better effectuate the purposes of this Act than the national consensus standard.

(c)(1) The Secretary shall provide, without regard to the requirements of chapter 5, title 5, United States Code, for an emergency temporary standard to take immediate effect upon publication in the Federal Register if he determines (A) that employees are exposed to grave danger from exposure to substances or agents determined to be toxic or physically harmful or from new hazards, and (B) that such emergency standard is necessary to protect employees from such danger.

(2) Such standard shall be effective until superseded by a standard promulgated in accordance with the procedures prescribed in paragraph (3) of this subsection.

(3) Upon publication of such standard in the Federal Register the Secretary shall commence a proceeding in accordance with section 6(b) of this Act, and the standard as published shall also serve as a proposed rule for the proceeding.  The Secretary shall promulgate a standard under this paragraph no later than six months after publication of the emergency standard as provided in paragraph (2) of this subsection.

(d) Any affected employer may apply to the Secretary for a rule or order for a variance from a standard promulgated under this section. Affected employees shall be given notice of each such application and an opportunity to participate in a hearing.  The Secretary shall issue such rule or order if he determines on the record, after opportunity for an inspection where appropriate and a hearing, that the proponent of the variance has demonstrated by a preponderance of the evidence that the conditions, practices, means, methods, operations, or processes used or proposed to be used by an employer will provide employment and places of employment to his employees which are as safe and healthful as those which would prevail if he complied with the standard.  The rule or order so issued shall prescribe the conditions the employer must maintain, and the practices, means, methods, operations, and processes which he must adopt and utilize to the extent they differ from the standard in question. Such a rule or order may be modified or revoked upon application by an employer, employees, or by the Secretary on his own motion, in the manner prescribed for its issuance under this subsection at any time after six months from its issuance.

(e) Whenever the Secretary promulgates any standard, makes any rule, order, or decision, grants any exemption or extension of time, or compromises, mitigates, or settles any penalty assessed under this Act, he shall include a statement of the reasons for such action, which shall be published in the Federal Register.

(f) Any person who may be adversely affected by a standard issued under this section may at any time prior to the sixtieth day after such standard is promulgated file a petition challenging the validity of such standard with the United States court of appeals for the circuit wherein such person resides or has his principal place of business, for a judicial review of such standard.  A copy of the petition shall be forthwith transmitted by the clerk of the court to the Secretary.  The filing of such petition shall not, unless otherwise ordered by the court, operate as a stay of the standard.  The determinations of the Secretary shall be conclusive if supported by substantial evidence in the record considered as a whole.

(g) In determining the priority for establishing standards under this section, the Secretary shall give due regard to the urgency of the need for mandatory safety and health standards for particular industries, trades, crafts, occupations, businesses, workplaces or work environments. The Secretary shall also give due regard to the recommendations of the Secretary of Health and Human Services regarding the need for mandatory standards in determining the priority for establishing such standards.

\* \* \*

INSPECTIONS, INVESTIGATIONS, AND RECORDKEEPING

SEC. 8. (§ 657) (a) In order to carry out the purposes of this Act, the Secretary, upon presenting appropriate credentials to the owner, operator, or agent in charge, is authorized—

(1) to enter without delay and at reasonable times any factory, plant, establishment, construction site, or other area, workplace or environment where work is performed by an employee of an employer; and

(2) to inspect and investigate during regular working hours and at other reasonable times, and within reasonable limits and in a reasonable manner, any such place of employment and all pertinent conditions, structures, machines, apparatus, devices, equipment, and materials therein, and to question privately any such employer, owner, operator, agent or employee.

(b) In making his inspections and investigations under this Act the Secretary may require the attendance and testimony of witnesses and the production of evidence under oath. Witnesses shall be paid the same fees and mileage that are paid witnesses in the courts of the United States. In case of a contumacy, failure, or refusal of any person to obey such an order, any district court of the United States or the United States courts of any territory or possession, within the jurisdiction of which such person is found, or resides or transacts business, upon the application by the Secretary, shall have jurisdiction to issue to such person an order requiring such person to appear to produce evidence if, as, and when so ordered, and to give testimony relating to the matter under investigation or in question, and any failure to obey such order of the court may be punished by said court as a contempt thereof.

(c)(1) Each employer shall make, keep and preserve, and make available to the Secretary or the Secretary of Health and Human Services, such records regarding his activities relating to this Act as the Secretary, in cooperation with the Secretary of Health and Human Services, may prescribe by regulation as necessary or appropriate for the enforcement of this Act or for developing information regarding the causes and prevention of occupational accidents and illnesses. In order to carry out the provisions of this paragraph such regulations may include provisions requiring employers to conduct periodic inspections.

The Secretary shall also issue regulations requiring that employers, through posting of notices or other appropriate means, keep their employees informed of their protections and obligations under this Act, including the provisions of applicable standards.

(2) The Secretary, in cooperation with the Secretary of Health and Human Services, shall prescribe regulations requiring employers to maintain accurate records of, and to make periodic reports on, work-related deaths, injuries and illnesses other than minor injuries requiring only first aid treatment and which do not involve medical treatment, loss of consciousness, restriction of work or motion, or transfer to another job.

(3) The Secretary, in cooperation with the Secretary of Health and Human Services, shall issue regulations requiring employers to maintain accurate records of employee exposures to potentially toxic materials or harmful physical agents which are required to be monitored or measured under section 6. Such regulations shall provide employees or their representatives with an opportunity to observe such monitoring or measuring, and to have access to the records thereof. Such regulations shall also make appropriate provision for each employee or former employee to have access to such records as will indicate his own exposure to toxic materials or harmful physical agents. Each employer shall promptly notify any employee who has been or is being exposed to toxic materials or harmful physical agents in concentrations or at levels which exceed those prescribed by an applicable occupational safety and health standard promulgated under section 6, and shall inform any employee who is being thus exposed of the corrective action being taken.

(d) Any information obtained by the Secretary, the Secretary of Health and Human Services, or a State agency under this Act shall be obtained with a minimum burden upon employers, especially those operating small businesses. Unnecessary duplication of efforts in obtaining information shall be reduced to the maximum extent feasible.

(e) Subject to regulations issued by the Secretary a representative of the employer and a representative authorized by his employees shall be given an opportunity to accompany the Secretary or his authorized representative during the physical inspection of any workplace under subsection (a) for the purpose of aiding such inspection. Where there is no authorized employee representative, the Secretary or his authorized representative shall consult with a reasonable number of employees concerning matters of health and safety in the workplace.

(f)(1) Any employees or representative of employees who believe that a violation of a safety or health standard exists that threatens physical harm, or that an imminent danger exists, may request an inspection by giving notice to the Secretary or his authorized representative of such violation or danger. Any such notice shall be reduced to writing, shall set forth with reasonable particularity the grounds for the notice, and shall be signed by the employees or representative of employees, and a copy shall be provided the employer or his agent no later than at the time of inspection, except that, upon the request of the person giving such notice, his name and the names of individual employees referred to therein shall not appear in such copy or on any record published, released, or made available pursuant to subsection (g) of this section.  If upon receipt of such notification the Secretary determines there are reasonable grounds to believe that such violation or danger exists, he shall make a special inspection in accordance with the provisions of this section as soon as practicable, to determine if such violation or danger exists.  If the Secretary determines there are no reasonable grounds to believe that a violation or danger exists he shall notify the employees or representative of the employees in writing of such determination.

(2) Prior to or during any inspection of a workplace, any employees or representative of employees employed in such workplace may notify the Secretary or any representative of the Secretary responsible for conducting the inspection, in writing, of any violation of this Act which they have reason to believe exists in such workplace.  The Secretary shall, by regulation, establish procedures for informal review of any refusal by a representative of the Secretary to issue a citation with respect to any such alleged violation and shall furnish the employees or representative of employees requesting such review a written statement of the reasons for the Secretary's final disposition of the case.

(g)(1) The Secretary and Secretary of Health and Human Services are authorized to compile, analyze, and publish, either in summary or detailed form, all reports or information obtained under this section.

(2) The Secretary and the Secretary of Health and Human Services shall each prescribe such rules and regulations as he may deem necessary to carry out their responsibilities under this Act, including rules and regulations dealing with the inspection of an employer's establishment.

## CITATIONS

**SEC. 9.  (§ 658)** (a) If, upon inspection or investigation, the Secretary or his authorized representative believes that an employer has violated a requirement of section 5 of this Act, of any standard, rule or order promulgated pursuant to section 6 of this Act, or of any regulations prescribed pursuant to this Act, he shall with reasonable promptness issue a citation to the employer.  Each citation shall be in writing and shall describe with particularity the nature of the violation, including a reference to the provision of the Act, standard, rule, regulation, or order alleged to have been violated.  In addition, the citation shall fix a reasonable time for the abatement of the violation.  The Secretary may prescribe procedures for the issuance of a notice in lieu of a citation with respect to de minimis violations which have no direct or immediate relationship to safety or health.

(b) Each citation issued under this section, or a copy or copies thereof, shall be prominently posted, as prescribed in regulations issued by the Secretary, at or near each place a violation referred to in the citation occurred.

(c) No citation may be issued under this section after the expiration of six months following the occurrence of any violation.

## PROCEDURE FOR ENFORCEMENT

**SEC. 10.** (**§ 659**) (a) If, after an inspection or investigation, the Secretary issues a citation under section 9(a), he shall, within a reasonable time after the termination of such inspection or investigation, notify the employer by certified mail of the penalty, if any, proposed to be assessed under section 17 and that the employer has fifteen working days within which to notify the Secretary that he wishes to contest the citation or proposed assessment of penalty. If, within fifteen working days from the receipt of the notice issued by the Secretary the employer fails to notify the Secretary that he intends to contest the citation or proposed assessment of penalty, and no notice is filed by any employee or representative of employees under subsection (c) within such time, the citation and the assessment, as proposed, shall be deemed a final order of the Commission and not subject to review by any court or agency.

(b) If the Secretary has reason to believe that an employer has failed to correct a violation for which a citation has been issued within the period permitted for its correction (which period shall not begin to run until the entry of a final order by the Commission in the case of any review proceedings under this section initiated by the employer in good faith and not solely for delay or avoidance of penalties), the Secretary shall notify the employer by certified mail of such failure and of the penalty proposed to be assessed under section 17 by reason of such failure, and that the employer has fifteen working days within which to notify the Secretary that he wishes to contest the Secretary's notification or the proposed assessment of penalty. If, within fifteen working days from the receipt of notification issued by the Secretary, the employer fails to notify the Secretary that he intends to contest the notification or proposed assessment of penalty, the notification and assessment, as proposed, shall be deemed a final order of the Commission and not subject to review by any court or agency.

(c) If an employer notifies the Secretary that he intends to contest a citation issued under section 9(a) or notification issued under subsection (a) or (b) of this section, or if, within fifteen working days of the issuance of a citation under section 9(a), any employee or representative of employees files a notice with the Secretary alleging that the period of time fixed in the citation for the abatement of the violation is unreasonable, the Secretary shall immediately advise the Commission of such notification, and the Commission shall afford an opportunity for a hearing (in accordance with section 554 of title 5, United States Code, but without regard to subsection (a)(3) of such section). The Commission shall thereafter issue an order, based on findings of fact, affirming, modifying, or vacating the Secretary's citation or proposed penalty, or directing other appropriate relief, and such order shall become final thirty days after its issuance. Upon a showing by an employer of a good faith effort to comply with the abatement requirements of a citation, and that abatement has not been completed because of factors beyond his reasonable control, the Secretary, after an opportunity for a hearing as provided in this subsection, shall issue an order affirming or modifying the abatement requirements in such citation. The rules of procedure prescribed by the Commission shall provide affected employees or representatives of affected employees an opportunity to participate as parties to hearings under this subsection.

JUDICIAL REVIEW

**SEC. 11.** (§ **660**) (a) Any person adversely affected or aggrieved by an order of the Commission issued under subsection (c) of section 10 may obtain a review of such order in any United States court of appeals for the circuit in which the violation is alleged to have occurred or where the employer has its principal office, or in the Court of Appeals for the District of Columbia Circuit, by filing in such court within sixty days following the issuance of such order a written petition praying that the order be modified or set aside. A copy of such petition shall be forthwith transmitted by the clerk of the court to the Commission and to the other parties, and thereupon the Commission shall file in the court the record in the proceeding as provided in section 2112 of title 28, United States Code. Upon such filing, the court shall have jurisdiction of the proceeding and of the question determined therein, and shall have power to grant such temporary relief or restraining order as it deems just and proper, and to make and enter upon the pleadings, testimony, and proceedings set forth in such record a decree affirming, modifying, or setting aside in whole or in part, the order of the Commission and enforcing the same to the extent that such order is affirmed or modified. The commencement of proceedings under this subsection shall not, unless ordered by the court, operate as a stay of the order of the Commission. No objection that has not been urged before the Commission shall be considered by the court, unless the failure or neglect to urge such objection shall be excused because of extraordinary circumstances. The findings of the Commission with respect to questions of fact, if supported by substantial evidence on the record considered as a whole, shall be conclusive. If any party shall apply to the court for leave to adduce additional evidence and shall show to the satisfaction of the court that such additional evidence is material and that there were reasonable grounds for the failure to adduce such evidence in the hearing before the Commission, the court may order such additional evidence to be taken before the Commission and to be made a part of the record. The Commission may modify its findings as to the facts, or make new findings, by reason of additional evidence so taken and filed, and it shall file such modified or new findings, which findings with respect to questions of fact, if supported by substantial evidence on the record considered as a whole, shall be conclusive, and its recommendations, if any, for the modification or setting aside of its original order. Upon the filing of the record with it, the jurisdiction of the court shall be exclusive and its judgment and decree shall be final, except that the same shall be subject to review by the Supreme Court of the United States, as provided in section 1254 of title 28, United States Code. Petitions filed under this subsection shall be heard expeditiously.

(b) The Secretary may also obtain review or enforcement of any final order of the Commission by filing a petition for such relief in the United States court of appeals for the circuit in which the alleged violation occurred or in which the employer has its principal office, and the provisions of subsection (a) shall govern such proceedings to the extent applicable. If no petition for review, as provided in subsection (a), is filed within sixty days after service of the Commission's order, the Commission's findings of fact and order shall be conclusive in connection with any petition for enforcement which is filed by the Secretary after the expiration of such sixty-day period. In any such case, as well as in the case of a noncontested citation or notification by the Secretary which has become a final order of the Commission under subsection (a) or (b) of section 10, the clerk of the court, unless otherwise ordered by the court, shall forthwith enter a decree enforcing the order and shall transmit a copy of such decree to the Secretary and the employer named in the petition. In any contempt proceeding brought to enforce a decree of a court of appeals entered pursuant to this subsection or subsection (a), the court of appeals may assess the penalties provided in section 17, in addition to invoking any other available remedies.

(c)(1) No person shall discharge or in any manner discriminate against any employee because such employee has filed any complaint or instituted or caused to be instituted any proceeding under or related to this Act or has testified or is about to testify in any such proceeding or because of the exercise by such employee on behalf of himself or others of any right afforded by this Act.

(2) Any employee who believes that he has been discharged or otherwise discriminated against by any person in violation of this subsection may, within thirty days after such violation occurs, file a complaint with the Secretary alleging such discrimination. Upon receipt of such complaint, the Secretary shall cause such investigation to be made as he deems appropriate. If upon such investigation, the Secretary determines that the provisions of this subsection have been violated, he shall bring an action in any appropriate United States district court against such person. In any such action the United States district courts shall have jurisdiction, for cause shown to restrain violations of paragraph (1) of this subsection and order all appropriate relief including rehiring or reinstatement of the employee to his former position with back pay.

(3) Within 90 days of the receipt of a complaint filed under this subsection the Secretary shall notify the complainant of his determination under paragraph 2 of this subsection.

THE OCCUPATIONAL SAFETY AND HEALTH REVIEW COMMISSION

**SEC. 12.** **(§ 661)** (a) The Occupational Safety and Health Review Commission is hereby established. The Commission shall be composed of three members who shall be appointed by the President, by and with the advice and consent of the Senate, from among persons who by reason of training, education, or experience are qualified to carry out the functions of the Commission under this Act. The President shall designate one of the members of the Commission to serve as Chairman.

(b) The terms of members of the Commission shall be six years except that (1) the members of the Commission first taking office shall serve, as designated by the President at the time of appointment, one for a term of two years, one for a term of four years, and one for a term of six years, and (2) a vacancy caused by the death, resignation, or removal of a member prior to the expiration of the term for which he was appointed shall be filled only for the remainder of such unexpired term. A member of the Commission may be removed by the President for inefficiency, neglect of duty, or malfeasance in office.

* * *

(j) An administrative law judge appointed by the Commission shall hear, and make a determination upon, any proceeding instituted before the Commission and any motion in connection therewith, assigned to such administrative law judge by the Chairman of the Commission, and shall make a report of any such determination which constitutes his final disposition of the proceedings. The report of the administrative law judge shall become the final order of the Commission within thirty days after such report by the administrative law judge unless within such period any Commission member has directed that such report shall be reviewed by the Commission.

* * *

PROCEDURES TO COUNTERACT IMMINENT DANGERS

**SEC. 13.** **(§ 662)** (a) The United States district courts shall have jurisdiction, upon petition of the Secretary, to restrain any conditions or practices in any place of employment which are such that a danger exists which could reasonably be expected to cause death or serious physical harm immediately or before the imminence of such danger can be eliminated through the enforcement procedures otherwise provided by this Act. Any order issued under this section may require such steps to be taken as may be necessary to avoid, correct, or remove such imminent danger and prohibit the employment or presence of any individual in locations or under conditions where such imminent danger exists, except individuals whose presence is necessary to avoid, correct, or remove such imminent danger or to maintain the capacity of a continuous process operation to resume normal operations without a complete cessation of operations, or where a cessation of operations is necessary, to permit such to be accomplished in a safe and orderly manner.

(b) Upon the filing of any such petition the district court shall have jurisdiction to grant such injunctive relief or temporary restraining order pending the outcome of an enforcement proceeding pursuant to this Act. The proceeding shall be as provided by Rule 65 of the Federal Rules, Civil Procedure, except that no temporary restraining order issued without notice shall be effective for a period longer than five days.

(c) Whenever and as soon as an inspector concludes that conditions or practices described in subsection (a) exist in any place of employment, he shall inform the affected employees and employers of the danger and that he is recommending to the Secretary that relief be sought.

(d) If the Secretary arbitrarily or capriciously fails to seek relief under this section, any employee who may be injured by reason of such failure, or the representative of such employees, might bring an action against the Secretary in the United States district court for the district in which the imminent danger is alleged to exist or the employer has its principal office, or for the District of Columbia, for a writ of mandamus to compel the Secretary to seek such an order and for such further relief as may be appropriate.

### REPRESENTATION IN CIVIL LITIGATION

**SEC. 14.** (**§ 663**) Except as provided in section 518(a) of title 28, United States Code, relating to litigation before the Supreme Court, the Solicitor of Labor may appear for and represent the Secretary in any civil litigation brought under this Act but all such litigation shall be subject to the direction and control of the Attorney General.

### CONFIDENTIALITY OF TRADE SECRETS

**SEC. 15.** (**§ 664**) All information reported to or otherwise obtained by the Secretary or his representative in connection with any inspection or proceeding under this Act which contains or which might reveal a trade secret referred to in section 1905 of title 18 of the United States Code shall be considered confidential for the purpose of that section, except that such information may be disclosed to other officers or employees concerned with carrying out this Act or when relevant in any proceeding under this Act. In any such proceeding the Secretary, the Commission, or the court shall issue such orders as may be appropriate to protect the confidentiality of trade secrets.

### VARIATIONS, TOLERANCES, AND EXEMPTIONS

**SEC. 16.** (**§ 655**) The Secretary, on the record, after notice and opportunity for a hearing may provide such reasonable limitations and may make such rules and regulations allowing reasonable variations, tolerances, and exemptions to and from any or all provisions of this Act as he may find necessary and proper to avoid serious impairment of the national defense. Such action shall not be in effect for more than six months without notification to affected employees and an opportunity being afforded for a hearing.

PENALTIES

**SEC. 17.** (**§ 666**) (a) Any employer who willfully or repeatedly violates the requirements of section 654 of this title, any standard, rule, or order promulgated pursuant to section 655 of this title, or regulations prescribed pursuant to this chapter, may be assessed a civil penalty of not more than $70,000 for each violation, but not less than $5,000 for each willful violation.

(b) Any employer who has received a citation for a serious violation of the requirements of section 654 of this title, of any standard, rule, or order promulgated pursuant to section 655 of this title, or of any regulations prescribed pursuant to this chapter, shall be assessed a civil penalty of up to $7,000 for each such violation.

(c) Any employer who has received a citation for a violation of the requirements of section 654 of this title, of any standard, rule, or order promulgated pursuant to section 655 of this title, or of regulations prescribed pursuant to this chapter, and such violation is specifically determined not to be of a serious nature, may be assessed a civil penalty of up to $7,000 for each such violation.

(d) Any employer who fails to correct a violation for which a citation has been issued under section 658(a) of this title within the period permitted for its correction (which period shall not begin to run until the date of the final order of the Commission in the case of any review proceeding under section 659 of this title initiated by the employer in good faith and not solely for delay or avoidance of penalties), may be assessed a civil penalty of not more than $7,000 for each day during which such failure or violation continues.

(e) Any employer who willfully violates any standard, rule, or order promulgated pursuant to section 655 of this title, or of any regulations prescribed pursuant to this chapter, and that violation caused death to any employee, shall, upon conviction, be punished by a fine of not more than $10,000* or by imprisonment for not more than six months, or by both; except that if the conviction is for a violation committed after a first conviction of such person, punishment shall be by a fine of not more than $20,000* or by imprisonment for not more than one year, or by both.

(f) Any person who gives advance notice of any inspection to be conducted under this chapter, without authority from the Secretary or his designees, shall, upon conviction, be punished by a fine of not more than $1,000 or by imprisonment for not more than six months, or by both.

(g) Whoever knowingly makes any false statement, representation, or certification in any application, record, report, plan, or other docu-

---

* 18 U.S.C.A. § 3571 (b) and (c) increase the maximum fines to $250,000 for an individual defendant and $500,000 for an organizational defendant. Individuals acting on behalf of or aiding and abetting organizations to commit criminal offenses are guilty of the same crime as the organization. 18 U.S.C.A. § 2.

ment filed or required to be maintained pursuant to this chapter shall, upon conviction, be punished by a fine of not more than $10,000, or by imprisonment for not more than six months, or by both.

\* \* \*

(i) Any employer who violates any of the posting requirements, as prescribed under the provisions of this Act, shall be assessed a civil penalty of up to $7,000 for each violation.

(j) The Commission shall have authority to assess all civil penalties provided in this section, giving due consideration to the appropriateness of the penalty with respect to the size of the business of the employer being charged, the gravity of the violation, the good faith of the employer, and the history of previous violations.

(k) For purposes of this section, a serious violation shall be deemed to exist in a place of employment if there is a substantial probability that death or serious physical harm could result from a condition which exists, or from one or more practices, means, methods, operations, or processes which have been adopted or are in use, in such place of employment unless the employer did not, and could not with the exercise of reasonable diligence, know of the presence of the violation.

(*l*) Civil penalties owed under this chapter shall be paid to the Secretary for deposit into the Treasury of the United States and shall accrue to the United States and may be recovered in a civil action in the name of the United States brought in the United States district court for the district where the violation is alleged to have occurred or where the employer has its principal office.

SEC. 18. (§ 667). State jurisdiction and plans.

### (a) Assertion of State standards in absence of applicable Federal standards

Nothing in this chapter shall prevent any State agency or court from asserting jurisdiction under State law over any occupational safety or health issue with respect to which no standard is in effect under section 655 of this title.

### (b) Submission of State plan for development and enforcement of State standards to preempt applicable Federal standards

Any State which, at any time, desires to assume responsibility for development and enforcement therein of occupational safety and health standards relating to any occupational safety or health issue with respect to which a Federal standard has been promulgated under section 655 of this title shall submit a State plan for the development of such standards and their enforcement.

### (c) Conditions for approval of plan

The Secretary shall approve the plan submitted by a State under subsection (b) of this section, or any modification thereof, if such plan in his judgment—

**(1)** designates a State agency or agencies as the agency or agencies responsible for administering the plan throughout the State,

**(2)** provides for the development and enforcement of safety and health standards relating to one or more safety or health issues, which standards (and the enforcement of which standards) are or will be at least as effective in providing safe and healthful employment and places of employment as the standards promulgated under section 655 of this title which relate to the same issues, and which standards, when applicable to products which are distributed or used in interstate commerce, are required by compelling local conditions and do not unduly burden interstate commerce,

**(3)** provides for a right of entry and inspection of all workplaces subject to this chapter which is at least as effective as that provided in section 657 of this title, and includes a prohibition on advance notice of inspections,

**(4)** contains satisfactory assurances that such agency or agencies have or will have the legal authority and qualified personnel necessary for the enforcement of such standards,

**(5)** gives satisfactory assurances that such State will devote adequate funds to the administration and enforcement of such standards,

**(6)** contains satisfactory assurances that such State will, to the extent permitted by its law, establish and maintain an effective and comprehensive occupational safety and health program applicable to all employees of public agencies of the State and its political subdivisions, which program is as effective as the standards contained in an approved plan,

**(7)** requires employers in the State to make reports to the Secretary in the same manner and to the same extent as if the plan were not in effect, and

**(8)** provides that the State agency will make such reports to the Secretary in such form and containing such information, as the Secretary shall from time to time require.

(d) Rejection of plan; notice and opportunity for hearing

If the Secretary rejects a plan submitted under subsection (b) of this section, he shall afford the State submitting the plan due notice and opportunity for a hearing before so doing.

(e) Discretion of Secretary to exercise authority over comparable standards subsequent to approval of State plan; duration; retention of jurisdiction by Secretary upon determination of enforcement of plan by State

After the Secretary approves a State plan submitted under subsection (b) of this section, he may, but shall not be required to, exercise his authority under sections 657, 658, 659, 662, and 666 of this title with respect to comparable standards promulgated under section 655 of this title, for the period specified in the next sentence. The Secretary may exercise the authority referred to above until he determines, on the basis of actual operations under the State plan, that the criteria set forth in subsection (c) of this section are being applied, but he shall not make such determination for at least three years after the plan's approval under subsection (c) of this section. Upon making the determination referred to in the preceding sentence, the provisions of sections 654(a)(2), 657 (except for the purpose of carrying out subsection (f) of this section), 658, 659, 662, and 666 of this title, and standards promulgated under section 655 of this title, shall not apply with respect to any occupational safety or health issues covered under the plan, but the Secretary may retain jurisdiction under the above provisions in any proceeding commenced under section 658 or 659 of this title before the date of determination.

(f) Continuing evaluation by Secretary of State enforcement of
approved plan; withdrawal of approval of plan by Secretary;
grounds; procedure; conditions for retention of
jurisdiction by State

The Secretary shall, on the basis of reports submitted by the State agency and his own inspections make a continuing evaluation of the manner in which each State having a plan approved under this section is carrying out such plan. Whenever the Secretary finds, after affording due notice and opportunity for a hearing, that in the administration of the State plan there is a failure to comply substantially with any provision of the State plan (or any assurance contained therein), he shall notify the State agency of his withdrawal of approval of such plan and upon receipt of such notice such plan shall cease to be in effect, but the State may retain jurisdiction in any case commenced before the withdrawal of the plan in order to enforce standards under the plan whenever the issues involved do not relate to the reasons for the withdrawal of the plan.

(g) Judicial review of Secretary's withdrawal of approval or
rejection of plan; jurisdiction; venue; procedure; appropriate
relief; finality of judgment

The State may obtain a review of a decision of the Secretary withdrawing approval of or rejecting its plan by the United States court of appeals for the circuit in which the State is located by filing in such court within thirty days following receipt of notice of such decision a petition to modify or set aside in whole or in part the action of the Secretary. A copy of such petition shall forthwith be served upon the Secretary, and thereupon the Secretary shall certify and file in the court the record upon which the decision complained of was issued as provided in section 2112 of Title 28. Unless the court finds that the Secretary's decision in rejecting a proposed State plan or withdrawing his approval of such a plan is not supported by substantial evidence the court shall affirm the Secretary's decision. The judgment of the court shall be subject to review by the Supreme Court of the United States upon certiorari or certification as provided in section 1254 of Title 28.

(h) Temporary enforcement of State standards

The Secretary may enter into an agreement with a State under which the State will be permitted to continue to enforce one or more occupational health and safety standards in effect in such State until final action is taken by the Secretary with respect to a plan submitted by a State under subsection (b) of this section, or two years from December 29, 1970, whichever is earlier.

---

# WORKER ADJUSTMENT AND RETRAINING NOTIFICATION ACT

29 U.S.C. Secs. 2101–2109 (1988)

## § 2101. Definitions; exclusions from definition of loss of employment

(a) Definitions

As used in this chapter—

(1) the term "employer" means any business enterprise that employs—

(A) 100 or more employees, excluding part-time employees; or

(B) 100 or more employees who in the aggregate work at least 4,000 hours per week (exclusive of hours of overtime);

(2) the term "plant closing" means the permanent or temporary shutdown of a single site of employment, or one or more facilities or operating units within a single site of employment, if the shutdown results in an employment loss at the single site of employment during any 30–day period for 50 or more employees excluding any part-time employees;

(3) the term "mass layoff" means a reduction in force which—

(A) is not the result of a plant closing; and

(B) results in an employment loss at the single site of employment during any 30–day period for—

(i)(I) at least 33 percent of the employees (excluding any part-time employees); and

(II) at least 50 employees (excluding any part-time employees); or

(ii) at least 500 employees (excluding any part-time employees);

(4) the term "representative" means an exclusive representative of employees within the meaning of section 159(a) or 158(f) of this title or section 152 of Title 45;

(5) the term "affected employees" means employees who may reasonably be expected to experience an employment loss as a consequence of a proposed plant closing or mass layoff by their employer;

(6) subject to subsection (b) of this section, the term "employment loss" means (A) an employment termination, other than a discharge for cause, voluntary departure, or retirement, (B) a layoff exceeding 6 months, or (C) a reduction in hours of work of more than 50 percent during each month of any 6–month period;

(7) the term "unit of local government" means any general purpose political subdivision of a State which has the power to levy taxes and spend funds, as well as general corporate and police powers; and

(8) the term "part-time employee" means an employee who is employed for an average of fewer than 20 hours per week or who has been employed for fewer than 6 of the 12 months preceding the date on which notice is required.

(b) Exclusions from definition of employment loss

(1) In the case of a sale of part or all of an employer's business, the seller shall be responsible for providing notice for any plant closing or mass layoff in accordance with section 2102 of this title, up to and including the effective date of the sale. After the effective date of the sale of part or all of an employer's business, the purchaser shall be responsible for providing notice for any plant closing or mass layoff in accordance with section 2102 of this title. Notwithstanding any other provision of this chapter, any person who is an employee of the seller (other than a part-time employee) as of the effective date of the sale shall be considered an employee of the purchaser immediately after the effective date of the sale.

(2) Notwithstanding subsection (a)(6) of this section, an employee may not be considered to have experienced an employment loss if the closing or layoff is the result of the relocation or consolidation of part or all of the employer's business and, prior to the closing or layoff—

(A) the employer offers to transfer the employee to a different site of employment within a reasonable commuting distance with no more than a 6–month break in employment; or

(B) the employer offers to transfer the employee to any other site of employment regardless of distance with no more than a 6–month break in employment, and the employee accepts within 30 days of the offer or of the closing or layoff, whichever is later.

## § 2102. Notice required before plant closings and mass layoffs

(a) Notice to employees, state dislocated worker units, and local governments

An employer shall not order a plant closing or mass layoff until the end of a 60–day period after the employer serves written notice of such an order—

(1) to each representative of the affected employees as of the time of the notice or, if there is no such representative at that time, to each affected employee; and

(2) to the State dislocated worker unit (designated or created under title III of the Job Training Partnership Act [29 U.S.C.A. § 1651 et seq.] ) and the chief elected official of the unit of local government within which such closing or layoff is to occur.

If there is more than one such unit, the unit of local government which the employer shall notify is the unit of local government to which the employer pays the highest taxes for the year preceding the year for which the determination is made.

(b) Reduction of notification period

(1) An employer may order the shutdown of a single site of employment before the conclusion of the 60–day period if as of the time that notice would have been required the employer was actively seeking capital or business which, if obtained, would have enabled the employer to avoid or postpone the shutdown and the employer reasonably and in good faith believed that giving the notice required would have precluded the employer from obtaining the needed capital or business.

(2)(A) An employer may order a plant closing or mass layoff before the conclusion of the 60–day period if the closing or mass layoff is caused by business circumstances that were not reasonably foreseeable as of the time that notice would have been required.

(B) No notice under this chapter shall be required if the plant closing or mass layoff is due to any form of natural disaster, such as a flood, earthquake, or the drought currently ravaging the farmlands of the United States.

(3) An employer relying on this subsection shall give as much notice as is practicable and at that time shall give a brief statement of the basis for reducing the notification period.

(c) Extension of layoff period

A layoff of more than 6 months which, at its outset, was announced to be a layoff of 6 months or less, shall be treated as an employment loss under this chapter unless—

(1) the extension beyond 6 months is caused by business circumstances (including unforeseeable changes in price or cost) not reasonably foreseeable at the time of the initial layoff; and

(2) notice is given at the time it becomes reasonably foreseeable that the extension beyond 6 months will be required.

(d) Determinations with respect to employment loss

For purposes of this section, in determining whether a plant closing or mass layoff has occurred or will occur, employment losses for 2 or more groups at a single site of employment, each of which is less than the minimum number of employees specified in section 2101(a)(2) or (3) of this title but which in the aggregate exceed that minimum number, and which occur within any 90–day period shall be considered to be a plant closing or mass layoff unless the employer demonstrates that the employment losses are the result of separate and distinct actions and causes and are not an attempt by the employer to evade the requirements of this chapter.

### § 2103.  Exemptions

This chapter shall not apply to a plant closing or mass layoff if—

(1) the closing is of a temporary facility or the closing or layoff is the result of the completion of a particular project or undertaking, and the affected employees were hired with the understanding that their employment was limited to the duration of the facility or the project or undertaking; or

(2) the closing or layoff constitutes a strike or constitutes a lockout not intended to evade the requirements of this chapter.  Nothing in this chapter shall require an employer to serve written notice pursuant to section 2102(a) of this title when permanently replacing a person who is deemed to be an economic striker under the National Labor Relations Act [29 U.S.C.A. § 151 et seq.]: Provided, That nothing in this chapter shall be deemed to validate or invalidate any judicial or administrative ruling relating to the hiring of permanent replacements for economic strikers under the National Labor Relations Act.

### § 2104.  Administration and enforcement of requirements

(a) Civil actions against employers

(1) Any employer who orders a plant closing or mass layoff in violation of section 2102 of this title shall be liable to each aggrieved employee who suffers an employment loss as a result of such closing or layoff for—

(A) back pay for each day of violation at a rate of compensation not less than the higher of—

(i) the average regular rate received by such employee during the last 3 years of the employee's employment;  or

(ii) the final regular rate received by such employee;  and

(B) benefits under an employee benefit plan described in section 1002(3) of this title, including the cost of medical expenses incurred during the employment loss which would have been covered under an employee benefit plan if the employment loss had not occurred.

Such liability shall be calculated for the period of the violation, up to a maximum of 60 days, but in no event for more than one-half the number of days the employee was employed by the employer.

(2) The amount for which an employer is liable under paragraph (1) shall be reduced by—

(A) any wages paid by the employer to the employee for the period of the violation;

(B) any voluntary and unconditional payment by the employer to the employee that is not required by any legal obligation; and

(C) any payment by the employer to a third party or trustee (such as premiums for health benefits or payments to a defined contribution pension plan) on behalf of and attributable to the employee for the period of the violation.

In addition, any liability incurred under paragraph (1) with respect to a defined benefit pension plan may be reduced by crediting the employee with service for all purposes under such a plan for the period of the violation.

(3) Any employer who violates the provisions of section 2102 of this title with respect to a unit of local government shall be subject to a civil penalty of not more than $500 for each day of such violation, except that such penalty shall not apply if the employer pays to each aggrieved employee the amount for which the employer is liable to that employee within 3 weeks from the date the employer orders the shutdown or layoff.

(4) If an employer which has violated this chapter proves to the satisfaction of the court that the act or omission that violated this chapter was in good faith and that the employer had reasonable grounds for believing that the act or omission was not a violation of this chapter the court may, in its discretion, reduce the amount of the liability or penalty provided for in this section.

(5) A person seeking to enforce such liability, including a representative of employees or a unit of local government aggrieved under paragraph (1) or (3), may sue either for such person or for other persons similarly situated, or both, in any district court of the United States for any district in which the violation is alleged to have occurred, or in which the employer transacts business.

(6) In any such suit, the court, in its discretion, may allow the prevailing party a reasonable attorney's fee as part of the costs.

(7) For purposes of this subsection, the term, "aggrieved employee" means an employee who has worked for the employer ordering the plant closing or mass layoff and who, as a result of the failure by the employer to comply with section 2102 of this title did not receive timely notice either directly or through his or her representative as required by section 2102 of this title.

(b) Exclusivity of remedies

The remedies provided for in this section shall be the exclusive remedies for any violation of this chapter. Under this chapter, a Federal court shall not have authority to enjoin a plant closing or mass layoff.

## § 2105.  Procedures in addition to other rights of employees

The rights and remedies provided to employees by this chapter are in addition to, and not in lieu of, any other contractual or statutory rights and remedies of the employees, and are not intended to alter or affect such rights and remedies, except that the period of notification required by this chapter shall run concurrently with any period of notification required by contract or by any other statute.

## § 2106.  Procedures encouraged where not required

It is the sense of Congress that an employer who is not required to comply with the notice requirements of section 2102 of this title should, to the extent possible, provide notice to its employees about a proposal to close a plant or permanently reduce its workforce.

## § 2107.  Authority to prescribe regulations

(a) The Secretary of Labor shall prescribe such regulations as may be necessary to carry out this chapter.  Such regulations shall, at a minimum, include interpretative regulations describing the methods by which employers may provide for appropriate service of notice as required by this chapter.

(b) The mailing of notice to an employee's last known address or inclusion of notice in the employee's paycheck will be considered acceptable methods for fulfillment of the employer's obligation to give notice to each affected employee under this chapter.

## § 2108.  Effect on other laws

The giving of notice pursuant to this chapter, if done in good faith compliance with this chapter, shall not constitute a violation of the National Labor Relations Act [29 U.S.C.A. § 151 et seq.] or the Railway Labor Act [45 U.S.C.A. § 151 et seq.].

## § 2109.  Report on employment and international competitiveness

Two years after Aug. 4, 1988, the Comptroller General shall submit to the Committee on Small Business of both the House and Senate, the Committee on Labor and Human Resources, and the Committee on Education and Labor a report containing a detailed and objective analysis of the effect of this chapter on employers (especially small- and medium-sized businesses), the economy (international competitiveness), and employees (in terms of levels and conditions of employment).  The Comptroller General shall assess both costs and benefits, including the effect on productivity, competitiveness, unemployment rates and compensation, and worker retraining and readjustment.

This title is responsible for notifying the plan administrator of such determination within 60 days after the date of the determination and for notifying the plan administrator within 30 days after the date of any final determination under such title or titles that the qualified beneficiary is no longer disabled, and

(4) the administrator shall notify—

(A) in the case of a qualifying event described in paragraph (1), (2), (4), or (6) of section 1163 of this title, any qualified beneficiary with respect to such event, and

(B) in the case of a qualifying event described in paragraph (3) or (5) of section 1163 of this title where the covered employee notifies the administrator under paragraph (3), any qualified beneficiary with respect to such event,

of such beneficiary's rights under this subsection.

(b) Alternative means of compliance with requirement for notification of multiemployer plans by employers

The requirements of subsection (a)(2) of this section shall be considered satisfied in the case of a multiemployer plan in connection with a qualifying event described in paragraph (2) of section 1163 of this title if the plan provides that the determination of the occurrence of such qualifying event will be made by the plan administrator.

(c) Rules relating to notification of qualified beneficiaries by plan administrator

For purposes of subsection (a)(4) of this section, any notification shall be made within 14 days (or, in the case of a group health plan which is a multiemployer plan, such longer period of time as may be provided in the terms of the plan) of the date on which the administrator is notified under paragraph (2) or (3), whichever is applicable, and any such notification to an individual who is a qualified beneficiary as the spouse of the covered employee shall be treated as notification to all other qualified beneficiaries residing with such spouse at the time such notification is made.

———

# EMPLOYEE RETIREMENT INCOME SECURITY ACT OF 1974

## 29 U.S.C. §§ 1001–1461, as amended

[The Employee Retirement Income Security Act of 1974 (ERISA), as amended, is a lengthy, comprehensive and technical statute. As a quick review of the statute shows, a full understanding of ERISA requires familiarity with the Tax Code. We have reproduced enough of ERISA to give you a sense of the law's scope but much less than you would find in a book on the law of employee benefits.—Eds.]

SUBTITLE A—GENERAL PROVISIONS

## § 2  [§ 1001].  Congressional findings and declaration of policy

### (a) Benefit plans as affecting interstate commerce and the Federal taxing power

The Congress finds that the growth in size, scope, and numbers of employee benefit plans in recent years has been rapid and substantial; that the operational scope and economic impact of such plans is increasingly interstate; that the continued well-being and security of millions of employees and their dependents are directly affected by these plans; that they are affected with a national public interest; that they have become an important factor affecting the stability of employment and the successful development of industrial relations; that they have become an important factor in commerce because of the interstate character of their activities, and of the activities of their participants, and the employers, employee organizations, and other entities by which they are established or maintained; that a large volume of the activities of such plans is carried on by means of the mails and instrumentalities of interstate commerce; that owing to the lack of employee information and adequate safeguards concerning their operation, it is desirable in the interests of employees and their beneficiaries, and to provide for the general welfare and the free flow of commerce, that disclosure be made and safeguards be provided with respect to the establishment, operation, and administration of such plans; that they substantially affect the revenues of the United States because they are afforded preferential Federal tax treatment; that despite the enormous growth in such plans many employees with long years of employment are losing anticipated retirement benefits owing to the lack of vesting provisions in such plans; that owing to the inadequacy of current minimum standards, the soundness and stability of plans with respect to adequate funds to pay promised benefits may be endangered; that owing to the termination of plans before requisite funds have been accumulated, employees and their beneficiaries have been deprived of anticipated benefits; and that it is therefore desirable in the interests of employees and their beneficiaries, for the protection of the revenue of the United States, and to provide for the free flow of commerce, that minimum standards be provided assuring the equitable character of such plans and their financial soundness.

### (b) Protection of interstate commerce and beneficiaries by requiring disclosure and reporting, setting standards of conduct, etc., for fiduciaries

It is hereby declared to be the policy of this chapter to protect interstate commerce and the interests of participants in employee benefit plans and their beneficiaries, by requiring the disclosure and reporting to participants and beneficiaries of financial and other information with respect thereto, by establishing standards of conduct, responsibility, and obligation for fiduciaries of employee benefit plans, and by providing for appropriate remedies, sanctions, and ready access to the Federal courts.

**(c) Protection of interstate commerce, the Federal taxing power, and beneficiaries by vesting of accrued benefits, setting minimum standards of funding, requiring termination insurance**

It is hereby further declared to be the policy of this chapter to protect interstate commerce, the Federal taxing power, and the interests of participants in private pension plans and their beneficiaries by improving the equitable character and the soundness of such plans by requiring them to vest the accrued benefits of employees with significant periods of service, to meet minimum standards of funding, and by requiring plan termination insurance.

**§ 1001a.  Additional Congressional findings and declaration of policy**

**(a) Effects of multiemployer pension plans**

The Congress finds that—

**(1)** multiemployer pension plans have a substantial impact on interstate commerce and are affected with a national public interest;

**(2)** multiemployer pension plans have accounted for a substantial portion of the increase in private pension plan coverage over the past three decades;

**(3)** the continued well-being and security of millions of employees, retirees, and their dependents are directly affected by multiemployer pension plans; and

**(4)(A)** withdrawals of contributing employers from a multiemployer pension plan frequently result in substantially increased funding obligations for employers who continue to contribute to the plan, adversely affecting the plan, its participants and beneficiaries, and labor-management relations, and

**(B)** in a declining industry, the incidence of employer withdrawals is higher and the adverse effects described in subparagraph (A) are exacerbated.

**(b) Modification of multiemployer plan termination insurance provisions and replacement of program**

The Congress further finds that—

**(1)** it is desirable to modify the current multiemployer plan termination insurance provisions in order to increase the likelihood of protecting plan participants against benefit losses; and

**(2)** it is desirable to replace the termination insurance program for multiemployer pension plans with an insolvency-based benefit protection program that will enhance the financial soundness of such plans, place primary emphasis on plan continuation, and contain program costs within reasonable limits.

### (c) Policy

It is hereby declared to be the policy of this Act—

**(1)** to foster and facilitate interstate commerce,

**(2)** to alleviate certain problems which tend to discourage the maintenance and growth of multiemployer pension plans,

**(3)** to provide reasonable protection for the interests of participants and beneficiaries of financially distressed multiemployer pension plans, and

**(4)** to provide a financially self-sufficient program for the guarantee of employee benefits under multiemployer plans.

## § 1001b. Additional Congressional findings and declaration of policy; single-employer plan termination insurance system

### (a) Findings

The Congress finds that—

**(1)** single-employer defined benefit pension plans have a substantial impact on interstate commerce and are affected with a national interest;

**(2)** the continued well-being and retirement income security of millions of workers, retirees, and their dependents are directly affected by such plans;

**(3)** the existence of a sound termination insurance system is fundamental to the retirement income security of participants and beneficiaries of such plans; and

**(4)** the current termination insurance system in some instances encourages employers to terminate pension plans, evade their obligations to pay benefits, and shift unfunded pension liabilities onto the termination insurance system and the other premium-payers.

### (b) Additional findings

The Congress further finds that modification of the current termination insurance system and an increase in the insurance premium for single-employer defined benefit pension plans—

**(1)** is desirable to increase the likelihood that full benefits will be paid to participants and beneficiaries of such plans;

**(2)** is desirable to provide for the transfer of liabilities to the termination insurance system only in cases of severe hardship;

**(3)** is necessary to maintain the premium costs of such system at a reasonable level; and

**(4)** is necessary to finance properly current funding deficiencies and future obligations of the single-employer pension plan termination insurance system.

### (c) Declaration of policy

It is hereby declared to be the policy of this title—

**(1)** to foster and facilitate interstate commerce;

**(2)** to encourage the maintenance and growth of single-employer defined benefit pension plans;

**(3)** to increase the likelihood that participants and beneficiaries under single-employer defined benefit pension plans will receive their full benefits;

**(4)** to provide for the transfer of unfunded pension liabilities onto the single-employer pension plan termination insurance system only in cases of severe hardship;

**(5)** to maintain the premium costs of such system at a reasonable level; and

**(6)** to assure the prudent financing of current funding deficiencies and future obligations of the single-employer pension plan termination insurance system by increasing termination insurance premiums.

## § 3 [§ 1002]. Definitions

For purposes of this subchapter:

**(1)** The terms "employee welfare benefit plan" and "welfare plan" mean any plan, fund, or program which was heretofore or is hereafter established or maintained by an employer or by an employee organization, or by both, to the extent that such plan, fund, or program was established or is maintained for the purpose of providing for its participants or their beneficiaries, through the purchase of insurance or otherwise, (A) medical, surgical, or hospital care or benefits, or benefits in the event of sickness, accident, disability, death or unemployment, or vacation benefits, apprenticeship or other training programs, or day care centers, scholarship funds, or prepaid legal services, or (B) any benefit described in section 186(c) of this title (other than pensions on retirement or death, and insurance to provide such pensions).

**(2)(A)** Except as provided in subparagraph (B), the terms "employee pension benefit plan" and "pension plan" mean any plan, fund, or program which was heretofore or is hereafter established or maintained by an employer or by an employee organization, or by both, to the extent that by its express terms or as a result of surrounding circumstances such plan, fund, or program—

**(i)** provides retirement income to employees, or

**(ii)** results in a deferral of income by employees for periods extending to the termination of covered employment or beyond, regardless of the method of calculating the contributions made to the plan, the method of calculating the benefits under the plan or the method of distributing benefits from the plan.

**(B)** The Secretary may by regulation prescribe rules consistent with the standards and purposes of this chapter providing one or more exempt categories under which—

(i) severance pay arrangements, and

(ii) supplemental retirement income payments, under which the pension benefits of retirees or their beneficiaries are supplemented to take into account some portion or all of the increases in the cost of living (as determined by the Secretary of Labor) since retirement,

shall, for purposes of this subchapter, be treated as welfare plans rather than pension plans. * * *

**(3)** The term "employee benefit plan" or "plan" means an employee welfare benefit plan or an employee pension benefit plan or a plan which is both an employee welfare benefit plan and an employee pension benefit plan.

**(4)** The term "employee organization" means any labor union or any organization of any kind, or any agency or employee representation committee, association, group, or plan, in which employees participate and which exists for the purpose, in whole or in part, of dealing with employers concerning an employee benefit plan, or other matters incidental to employment relationships; or any employees' beneficiary association organized for the purpose in whole or in part, of establishing such a plan.

* * *

**(19)** The term "nonforfeitable" when used with respect to a pension benefit or right means a claim obtained by a participant or his beneficiary to that part of an immediate or deferred benefit under a pension plan which arises from the participant's service, which is unconditional, and which is legally enforceable against the plan.

* * *

**(24)** The term "normal retirement age" means the earlier of—

**(A)** the time a plan participant attains normal retirement age under the plan, or

**(B)** the latest of—

(i) the time a plan participant attains age 65,

(ii) in the case of a plan participant who commences participation in the plan within 5 years before attaining normal retirement age under the plan, the 5th anniversary of the time the plan participant commences participation in the plan, or

(iii) in the case of a plan participant not described in clause (ii), the 10th anniversary of the time the plan participant commences participation in the plan.

\* \* \*

(34) The term "individual account plan" or "defined contribution plan" means a pension plan which provides for an individual account for each participant and for benefits based solely upon the amount contributed to the participant's account, and any income, expenses, gains and losses, and any forfeitures of accounts of other participants which may be allocated to such participant's account.

(35) The term "defined benefit plan" means a pension plan other than an individual account plan; except that a pension plan which is not an individual account plan and which provides a benefit derived from employer contributions which is based partly on the balance of the separate account of a participant—

(A) \* \* \* shall be treated as an individual account plan \* \* \*

(37)(A) The term "multiemployer plan" means a plan—

(i) to which more than one employer is required to contribute,

(ii) which is maintained pursuant to one or more collective bargaining agreements between one or more employee organizations and more than one employer, and

(iii) which satisfies such other requirements as the Secretary may prescribe by regulation.

(B) For purposes of this paragraph, all trades or businesses (whether or not incorporated) which are under common control within the meaning of section 1301(b)(1) of this title are considered a single employer.

\* \* \*

## § 4 [§ 1003]. Coverage

(a) Except as provided in subsection (b) of this section and in sections 201, 301 and 401 of this title, this subchapter shall apply to any employee benefit plan if it is established or maintained—

(1) by any employer engaged in commerce or in any industry or activity affecting commerce; or

(2) by any employee organization or organizations representing employees engaged in commerce or in any industry or activity affecting commerce; or

(3) by both.

(b) The provisions of this subchapter shall not apply to any employee benefit plan if—

(1) such plan is a governmental plan \* \* \*;

(2) such plan is a church plan \* \* \*;

(3) such plan is maintained solely for the purpose of complying with applicable workmen's compensation laws or unemployment compensation or disability insurance laws;

(4) such plan is maintained outside of the United States primarily for the benefit of persons substantially all of whom are nonresident aliens; or

(5) such plan is an excess benefit plan * * * and is unfunded.

SUBTITLE B—REGULATORY PROVISIONS

*Part 1—Reporting and Disclosure [omitted]*

*Part 2—Participation and Vesting*

### § 201 [§ 1051]. Coverage

This part [Secs. 201–211] shall apply to any employee benefit plan described in section 4(a) of this title (and not exempted under section 4(b) of this title) other than—

(1) an employee welfare benefit plan;

(2) a plan which is unfunded and is maintained by an employer primarily for the purpose of providing deferred compensation for a select group of management or highly compensated employees;

\* \* \*

(4) a plan which is established and maintained by a labor organization described in section 501(c)(5) of Title 26 and which does not at any time after September 2, 1974, provide for employer contributions;

\* \* \*

(8) [a]ny plan, fund or program under which an employer, all of whose stock is directly or indirectly owned by employees, former employees or their beneficiaries, proposes through an unfunded arrangement to compensate retired employees for benefits which were forfeited by such employees under a pension plan maintained by a former employer prior to the date such pension plan became subject to this chapter.

### § 202 [§ 1052]. Minimum participation standards

(a)(1)(A) No pension plan may require, as a condition of participation in the plan, that an employee complete a period of service with the employer or employers maintaining the plan extending beyond the later of the following dates—

(i) the date on which the employee attains the age of 21; or

(ii) the date on which he completes 1 year of service.

(B)(i) In the case of any plan which provides that after not more than 3 years of service each participant has a right to 100 percent of his accrued benefit under the plan which is nonforfeitable at the time such benefit accrues, clause (ii) of subparagraph (A) shall be applied by substituting "2 years of service" for "1 year of service".

\* \* \*

**(2)** No pension plan may exclude from participation (on the basis of age) employees who have attained a specified age, unless—

**(A)** the plan is a—

**(i)** defined benefit plan, or

**(ii)** target benefit plan (as defined under regulations prescribed by the Secretary of the Treasury), and

**(B)** such employees begin employment with the employer after they have attained a specified age which is not more than 5 years before the normal retirement age under the plan.

\* \* \*

**(5)(A)** In the case of each individual who is absent from work for any period—

**(i)** by reason of the pregnancy of the individual,

**(ii)** by reason of the birth of a child of the individual,

**(iii)** by reason of the placement of a child with the individual in connection with the adoption of such child by such individual, or

**(iv)** for purposes of caring for such child for a period beginning immediately following such birth or placement,

the plan shall treat as hours of service, solely for purposes of determining under this subsection whether a 1-year break in service (as defined in section 1053(b)(3)(A) of this title) has occurred, the hours described in subparagraph (B).

**(B)** The hours described in this subparagraph are—

**(i)** the hours of service which otherwise would normally have been credited to such individual but for such absence, or

**(ii)** in any case in which the plan is unable to determine the hours described in clause (i), 8 hours of service per day of such absence,

except that the total number of hours treated as hours of service under this subparagraph by reason of any such pregnancy or placement shall not exceed 501 hours.

\* \* \*

## § 1053. Minimum vesting standards

### (a) Nonforfeitability requirements

Each pension plan shall provide that an employee's right to his normal retirement benefit is nonforfeitable upon the attainment of normal retirement age and in addition shall satisfy the requirements of paragraphs (1) and (2) of this subsection.

**(1)** A plan satisfies the requirements of this paragraph if an employee's rights in his accrued benefit derived from his own contributions are nonforfeitable.

**(2)** A plan satisfies the requirements of this paragraph if it satisfies the requirements of subparagraph (A), (B), or (C).

**(A)** A plan satisfies the requirements of this subparagraph if an employee who has at least 5 years of service has a nonforfeitable right to 100 percent of his accrued benefit derived from employer contributions.

**(B)** A plan satisfies the requirements of this subparagraph if an employee who has completed at least 5 years of service has a nonforfeitable right to a percentage of his accrued benefit derived from employer contributions which percentage is not less than the percentage determined under the following table:

| Years of service: | Nonforfeitable percentage |
|---|---|
| 5 | 25 |
| 6 | 30 |
| 7 | 35 |
| 8 | 40 |
| 9 | 45 |
| 10 | 50 |
| 11 | 60 |
| 12 | 70 |
| 13 | 80 |
| 14 | 90 |
| 15 or more | 100. |

**(C)(i)** A plan satisfies the requirements of this subparagraph if a participant who is not separated from the service, who has completed at least 5 years of service, and with respect to whom the sum of his age and years of service equals or exceeds 45, has a nonforfeitable right to a percentage of his accrued benefit derived from employer contributions determined under the following table:

| If years of service equal or exceed— | and sum of age and service equals or exceeds— | then the nonforfeitable percentage is— |
|---|---|---|
| 5 | 45 | 50 |
| 6 | 47 | 60 |
| 7 | 49 | 70 |
| 8 | 51 | 80 |
| 9 | 53 | 90 |
| 10 | 55 | 100. |

(ii) Notwithstanding clause (i), a plan shall not be treated as satisfying the requirements of this subparagraph unless any participant who has completed at least 10 years of service has a nonforfeitable right to not less than 50 percent of his accrued benefit derived from employer contributions and to not less than an additional 10 percent for each additional year of service thereafter.

### Amendment of subsec. (a)(2)

*Pub.L. 99–514, Title XI, § 1113(e)(1), (e), Oct. 22, 1986, 100 Stat. 2447, 2448, provided that, applicable to plan years beginning after December 31, 1988 \* \* \*, subsec. (a)(2) of this section is amended to read as follows:*

*"(2) A plan satisfies the requirements of this paragraph if it satisfies the following requirements of subparagraph (A), (B), or (C).*

*"(A) A plan satisfies the requirements of this subparagraph if an employee who has completed at least 5 years of service has a nonforfeitable right to 100 percent of the employee's accrued benefit derived from employer contributions.*

*"(B) A plan satisfies the requirements of this subparagraph if an employee has a nonforfeitable right to a percentage of the employee's accrued benefit derived from employer contributions determined under the following table:*

| *"Years of service:* | *The nonforfeitable percentage is:* |
|---|---|
| *3* | *20* |
| *4* | *40* |
| *5* | *60* |
| *6* | *80* |
| *7 or more* | *100.* |

*"(C) A plan satisfies the requirements of this subparagraph if—*

*'(i) the plan is a multiemployer plan (within the meaning of section 3(37)), and*

*"(ii) under the plan—*

*"(I) an employee who is covered pursuant to a collective bargaining agreement described in section 414(f)(1)(B) and who has completed at least 10 years of service has a nonforfeitable right to 100 percent of the employee's accrued benefit derived from employer contributions, and*

*"(II) the requirements of subparagraph (A) or (B) are met with respect to employees not described in subclause (I)."*

### (c) Plan amendments altering vesting schedule

(1)(A) A plan amendment changing any vesting schedule under the plan shall be treated as not satisfying the requirements of subsection (a)(2) of this section if the nonforfeitable percentage of the accrued benefit derived from employer contributions (determined as of the later of the date such amendment is adopted, or the date such amendment becomes effective) of any employee who is a participant in the plan is less than such nonforfeitable percentage computed under the plan without regard to such amendment.

**(B)** A plan amendment changing any vesting schedule under the plan shall be treated as not satisfying the requirements of subsection (a)(2) of this section unless each participant having not less than 5 years of service is permitted to elect, within a reasonable period after adoption of such amendment, to have his nonforfeitable percentage computed under the plan without regard to such amendment. [After Dec. 31, 1988, substitute "3 years" for "five years"—Eds.]

\* \* \*

### (d) Nonforfeitable benefits after lesser period and in greater amounts than required

A pension plan may allow for nonforfeitable benefits after a lesser period and in greater amounts than are required by this part.

\* \* \*

### § 206 [§ 1056]. Form and payment of benefits

#### (a) Commencement date for payment of benefits

Each pension plan shall provide that unless the participant otherwise elects, the payment of benefits under the plan to the participant shall begin not later than the 60th day after the latest of the close of the plan year in which—

**(1)** the date on which the participant attains the earlier of age 65 or the normal retirement age specified under the plan,

**(2)** occurs the 10th anniversary of the year in which the participant commenced participation in the plan, or

**(3)** the participant terminates his service with the employer.

In the case of a plan which provides for the payment of an early retirement benefit, such plan shall provide that a participant who satisfied the service requirements for such early retirement benefit, but separated from the service (with any nonforfeitable right to an accrued benefit) before satisfying the age requirement for such early retirement benefit, is entitled upon satisfaction of such age requirement to receive a benefit not less than the benefit to which he would be entitled at the normal retirement age, actuarially reduced under regulations prescribed by the Secretary of the Treasury.

\* \* \*

### § 208   [§ 1058].   Mergers and consolidations of plans or transfers of plan assets

A pension plan may not merge or consolidate with, or transfer its assets or liabilities to, any other plan after September 2, 1974, unless each participant in the plan would (if the plan then terminated) receive a benefit immediately after the merger, consolidation, or transfer which is equal to or greater than the benefit he would have been entitled to receive immediately before the merger, consolidation, or transfer (if the plan had then terminated).  The preceding sentence shall not apply to any transaction to the extent that participants either before or after the transaction are covered under a multiemployer plan to which subchapter III of this chapter applies.

### § 210   [§ 1060].   Multiple employer plans

#### (a) Plan maintained by more than one employer

Notwithstanding any other provision of this part or part 3, the following provisions of this subsection shall apply to a plan maintained by more than one employer:

(1) Section 202 of this title shall be applied as if all employees of each of the employers were employed by a single employer.

(2) Sections 203 and 204 of this title shall be applied as if all such employers constituted a single employer, except that the application of any rules with respect to breaks in service shall be made under regulations prescribed by the Secretary.

(3) The minimum funding standard provided by section 302 of this title shall be determined as if all participants in the plan were employed by a single employer.

#### (b) Maintenance of plan of predecessor employer

For purposes of this part and part 3—

(1) in any case in which the employer maintains a plan of a predecessor employer, service for such predecessor shall be treated as service for the employer, and

(2) in any case in which the employer maintains a plan which is not the plan maintained by a predecessor employer, service for such predecessor shall, to the extent provided in regulations prescribed by the Secretary of the Treasury, be treated as service for the employer.

\* \* \*

*Part 3—Funding*

### § 301   [§ 1081].   Coverage

#### (a) Plans excepted from applicability of this part

This part [secs. 301–306] shall apply to any employee pension benefit plan described in section 4(a) of this title, (and not exempted under section 4(b) of this title), other than—

**(1)** an employee welfare benefit plan;

\* \* \*

**(3)** a plan which is unfunded and is maintained by an employer primarily for the purpose of providing deferred compensation for a select group of management or highly compensated employees;

\* \* \*

**(10)** [a]ny plan, fund or program under which an employer, all of whose stock is directly or indirectly owned by employees, former employees or their beneficiaries, proposes through an unfunded arrangement to compensate retired employees for benefits which were forfeited by such employees under a pension plan maintained by a former employer prior to the date such pension plan became subject to this chapter.

\* \* \*

## § 303 [§ 1083]. Variance from minimum funding standard

### (a) Waiver of requirements in event of business hardship

If an employer, or in the case of a multiemployer plan, 10 percent or more of the number of employers contributing to or under the plan are unable to satisfy the minimum funding standard for a plan year without temporary substantial business hardship (substantial business hardship in the case of a multiemployer plan) and if application of the standard would be adverse to the interests of plan participants in the aggregate, the Secretary of the Treasury may waive the requirements of section 1082(a) of this title for such year \* \* \*. The Secretary of the Treasury shall not waive the minimum funding standard with respect to a plan for more than 3 of any 15 (5 of any 15 in the case of a multiemployer plan) consecutive plan years. \* \* \*

### (b) Matters considered in determining business hardship

For purposes of this part, the factors taken into account in determining temporary substantial business hardship (substantial business hardship in the case of a multiemployer plan) shall include (but shall not be limited to) whether—

**(1)** the employer is operating at an economic loss,

**(2)** there is substantial unemployment or underemployment in the trade or business and in the industry concerned.

**(3)** the sales and profits of the industry concerned are depressed or declining, and

**(4)** it is reasonable to expect that the plan will be continued only if the waiver is granted.

\* \* \*

*Part 4—Fiduciary Responsibility*

## § 401  [§ 1101].  Coverage

(a) This part shall apply to any employee benefit plan described in section 4(a) of this title (and not exempted under section 4(b) of this title), other than—

(1) a plan which is unfunded and is maintained by an employer primarily for the purpose of providing deferred compensation for a select group of management or highly compensated employees; or

(2) any agreement described in section 736 of Title 26, which provides payments to a retired partner or deceased partner or a deceased partner's successor in interest.

\* \* \*

## § 402  [§ 1102].  Establishment of plan

### (a) Named fiduciaries

(1) Every employee benefit plan shall be established and maintained pursuant to a written instrument. Such instrument shall provide for one or more named fiduciaries who jointly or severally shall have authority to control and manage the operation and administration of the plan.

\* \* \*

### (b) Requisite features of plan

Every employee benefit plan shall—

(1) provide a procedure for establishing and carrying out a funding policy and method consistent with the objectives of the plan and the requirements of this subchapter,

(2) describe any procedure under the plan for the allocation of responsibilities for the operation and administration of the plan (including any procedure described in section 405(c)(1)),

(3) provide a procedure for amending such plan, and for identifying the persons who have authority to amend the plan, and

(4) specify the basis on which payments are made to and from the plan.

\* \* \*

### (b) Exceptions

The requirements of subsection (a) of this section shall not apply—
\* \* \*

(6) [to a]ny plan, fund or program under which an employer, all of whose stock is directly or indirectly owned by employees, former employees or their beneficiaries, proposes through an unfunded arrangement to compensate retired employees for benefits which were forfeited by such employees under a pension plan maintained

by a former employer prior to the date such pension plan became subject to this chapter.

\* \* \*

### (c) Assets of plan not to inure to benefit of employer; allowable purposes of holding plan assets

(1) Except as [otherwise] provided, the assets of a plan shall never inure to the benefit of any employer and shall be held for the exclusive purposes of providing benefits to participants in the plan and their beneficiaries and defraying reasonable expenses of administering the plan.

\* \* \*

### § 404 [§ 1104]. Fiduciary duties

### (a) Prudent man standard of care

(1) Subject to sections 403(c) and (d), 4042, and 4044 of this title, a fiduciary shall discharge his duties with respect to a plan solely in the interest of the participants and beneficiaries and—

(A) for the exclusive purpose of:

(i) providing benefits to participants and their beneficiaries; and

(ii) defraying reasonable expenses of administering the plan;

(B) with the care, skill, prudence, and diligence under the circumstances then prevailing that a prudent man acting in a like capacity and familiar with such matters would use in the conduct of an enterprise of a like character and with like aims;

(C) by diversifying the investments of the plan so as to minimize the risk of large losses, unless under the circumstances it is clearly prudent not to do so; and

(D) in accordance with the documents and instruments governing the plan insofar as such documents and instruments are consistent with the provisions of this subchapter or subchapter IV of this chapter.

(2) In the case of an eligible individual account plan (as defined in section 407(d)(3) of this title), the diversification requirement of paragraph (1)(C) and the prudence requirement (only to the extent that it requires diversification) of paragraph (1)(B) is not violated by acquisition or holding of qualifying employer real property or qualifying employer securities (as defined in section 407(d)(4) and (5) of this title).

\* \* \*

### § 406 [§ 1106]. Prohibited transactions

### (a) Transactions between plan and party in interest

Except as provided in section 408 of this title:

**(1)** A fiduciary with respect to a plan shall not cause the plan to engage in a transaction, if he knows or should know that such transaction constitutes a direct or indirect—

**(A)** sale or exchange, or leasing, of any property between the plan and a party in interest;

**(B)** lending of money or other extension of credit between the plan and a party in interest;

**(C)** furnishing of goods, services, or facilities between the plan and a party in interest;

**(D)** transfer to, or use by or for the benefit of, a party in interest, of any assets of the plan; or

**(E)** acquisition, on behalf of the plan, of any employer security or employer real property in violation of section 407(a) of this title.

(2) No fiduciary who has authority or discretion to control or manage the assets of a plan shall permit the plan to hold any employer security or employer real property if he knows or should know that holding such security or real property violates section 407(a) of this title.

### (b) Transactions between plan and fiduciary

A fiduciary with respect to a plan shall not—

**(1)** deal with the assets of the plan in his own interest or for his own account,

**(2)** in his individual or in any other capacity act in any transaction involving the plan on behalf of a party (or represent a party) whose interests are adverse to the interests of the plan or the interests of its participants or beneficiaries, or

**(3)** receive any consideration for his own personal account from any party dealing with such plan in connection with a transaction involving the assets of the plan.

### (c) Transfer of real or personal property to plan by party in interest

A transfer of real or personal property by a party in interest to a plan shall be treated as a sale or exchange if the property is subject to a mortgage or similar lien which the plan assumes or if it is subject to a mortgage or similar lien which a party-in-interest placed on the property within the 10–year period ending on the date of the transfer.

## § 407 [§ 1107]. Limitation with respect to acquisition and holding of employer securities and employer real property by certain plans

### (a) Percentage limitation

Except as otherwise provided in this section and section 414 of this title:

**(1)** A plan may not acquire or hold—

(**A**) any employer security which is not a qualifying employer security, or

(**B**) any employer real property which is not qualifying employer real property.

**(2)** A plan may not acquire any qualifying employer security or qualifying employer real property, if immediately after such acquisition the aggregate fair market value of employer securities and employer real property held by the plan exceeds 10 percent of the fair market value of the assets of the plan.

\* \* \*

### (d) Definitions

For purposes of this section—

\* \* \*

**(6)** The term "employee stock ownership plan" means an individual account plan—

(**A**) which is a stock bonus plan which is qualified, or a stock bonus plan and money purchase both of which are qualified, under section 401 of Title 26, and which is designed to invest primarily in qualifying employee securities, and

(**B**) which meets such other requirements as the Secretary of the Treasury may prescribe by regulation.

\* \* \*

### § 408 [§ 1108]. Exemptions from prohibited transactions

\* \* \*

### (b) Enumeration of transactions exempted
### from section 406 prohibitions

The prohibitions provided in section 406 of this title shall not apply to any of the following transactions:

**(1)** Any loans made by the plan to parties in interest who are participants or beneficiaries of the plan if such loans (A) are available to all such participants and beneficiaries on a reasonably equivalent basis, (B) are not made available to highly compensated employees, officers, or shareholders in an amount greater than the amount made available to other employees, (C) are made in accordance with specific provisions regarding such loans set forth in the plan, (D) bear a reasonable rate of interest and (E) are adequately secured.

**(2)** Contracting or making reasonable arrangements with a party in interest for office space, or legal, accounting, or other services necessary for the establishment or operation of the plan, if no more than reasonable compensation is paid therefor.

**(3)** A loan to an employee stock ownership plan (as defined in section 407(d)(6) of this title), if—

    **(A)** such loan is primarily for the benefit of participants and beneficiaries of the plan, and

    **(B)** such loan is at an interest rate which is not in excess of a reasonable rate.

If the plan gives collateral to a party in interest for such loan, such collateral may consist only of qualifying employer securities (as defined in section 407(d)(5) of this title).

* * *

### (c) Fiduciary benefits and compensation not prohibited

Nothing in section 406 of this title shall be construed to prohibit any fiduciary from—

    **(1)** receiving any benefit to which he may be entitled as a participant or beneficiary in the plan, so long as the benefit is computed and paid on a basis which is consistent with the terms of the plan as applied to all other participants and beneficiaries;

    **(2)** receiving any reasonable compensation for services rendered, or for the reimbursement of expenses properly and actually incurred, in the performance of his duties with the plan; except that no person so serving who already receives full-time pay from an employer or an association of employers, whose employees are participants in the plan, or from an employee organization whose members are participants in such plan shall receive compensation from such plan, except for reimbursement of expenses properly and actually incurred; or

    (3) serving as a fiduciary in addition to being an officer, employee, agent, or other representative of a party in interest.

### (d) Owner-employees; family members; shareholder employees

Section 407(b) of this title and subsections (a), (c), and (e) of this section shall not apply to any transaction in which a plan, directly or indirectly—

    **(1)** lends any part of the corpus or income of the plan to;

    **(2)** pays any compensation for personal services rendered to the plan to; or

    **(3)** acquires for the plan any property from or sells any property to;

any person who is with respect to the plan an owner-employee (as defined in section 401(c)(3) of Title 26), a member of the family (as defined in section 267(c)(4) of Title 26) of any such owner-employee, or a corporation controlled by any such owner-employee through the ownership, directly or indirectly, of 50 percent or more of the total combined voting power of all classes of stock entitled to vote or 50 percent or more of the total value of shares of all classes of stock of the corporation. For purposes of this subsection a shareholder employee (as defined in section 1379 of Title 26 as in effect on the day before the date of the enactment of the Subchapter S Revision Act of 1982) and a participant or beneficiary of an individual retirement account, individual retirement annuity, or an individual retirement bond (as defined in section 408 or 409 of Title 26) and an employer or association of employers which establishes such an account or annuity under section 408(c) of Title 26 shall be deemed to be an owner-employee.

\* \* \*

## § 410  [§ 1110.]  Exculpatory provisions; insurance

(a) Except as [otherwise] provided \* \* \*, any provision in an agreement or instrument which purports to relieve a fiduciary from responsibility or liability for any responsibility, obligation, or duty under this part shall be void as against public policy.

(b) Nothing in this [part] shall preclude—

(1) a plan from purchasing insurance for its fiduciaries or for itself to cover liability or losses occurring by reason of the act or omission of a fiduciary, if such insurance permits recourse by the insurer against the fiduciary in the case of a breach of a fiduciary obligation by such fiduciary;

(2) a fiduciary from purchasing insurance to cover liability under this part from and for his own account; or

(3) an employer or an employee organization from purchasing insurance to cover potential liability of one or more persons who serve in a fiduciary capacity with regard to an employee benefit plan.

*Part 5—Administration and Enforcement*

## § 502  [§ 1132].  Civil enforcement

### (a) Persons empowered to bring a civil action

A civil action may be brought—

(1) by a participant or beneficiary—

(A) for the relief provided for in subsection (c) of this section, or

(B) to recover benefits due to him under the terms of his plan, to enforce his rights under the terms of the plan, or to clarify his rights to future benefits under the terms of the plan;

(2) by the Secretary, or by a participant, beneficiary or fiduciary for appropriate relief under section 1109 of this title;

(3) by a participant, beneficiary, or fiduciary (A) to enjoin any act or practice which violates any provision of this subchapter or the

terms of the plan, or (B) to obtain other appropriate equitable relief (i) to redress such violations or (ii) to enforce any provisions of this subchapter or the terms of the plan;

**(4)** by the Secretary, or by a participant, or beneficiary for appropriate relief in the case of a violation of 1025(c) of this title;

**(5)** except as otherwise provided in subsection (b) of this section, by the Secretary (A) to enjoin any act or practice which violates any provision of this subchapter, or (B) to obtain other appropriate equitable relief (i) to redress such violation or (ii) to enforce any provision of this subchapter;

**(6)** by the Secretary to collect any civil penalty under subsection (i) of this section.

\* \* \*

### (d) Status of employee benefit plan as entity

**(1)** An employee benefit plan may sue or be sued under this subchapter as an entity. Service of summons, subpena, or other legal process of a court upon a trustee or an administrator of an employee benefit plan in his capacity as such shall constitute service upon the employee benefit plan. In a case where a plan has not designated in the summary plan description of the plan an individual as agent for the service of legal process, service upon the Secretary shall constitute such service. The Secretary, not later than 15 days after receipt of service under the preceding sentence, shall notify the administrator or any trustee of the plan of receipt of such service.

**(2)** Any money judgment under this subchapter against an employee benefit plan shall be enforceable only against the plan as an entity and shall not be enforceable against any other person unless liability against such person is established in his individual capacity under this subchapter.

\* \* \*

### § 510 [§ 1140]. Interference with protected rights

It shall be unlawful for any person to discharge, fine, suspend, expel, discipline, or discriminate against a participant or beneficiary for exercising any right to which he is entitled under the provisions of an employee benefit plan, this subchapter, section 1201 of this title, or the Welfare and Pension Plans Disclosure Act [29 U.S.C.A. § 301 et seq.], or for the purpose of interfering with the attainment of any right to which such participant may become entitled under the plan, this subchapter, or the Welfare and Pension Plans Disclosure Act. It shall be unlawful for any person to discharge, fine, suspend, expel, or discriminate against any person because he has given information or has testified or is about to testify in any inquiry or proceeding relating to this chapter or the Welfare and Pension Plans Disclosure Act. The provisions of section 502 of this title shall be applicable in the enforcement of this section.

## § 514 [§ 1144]. Other laws

### (a) Supersedure; effective date

Except as provided in subsection (b) of this section, the provisions of this title and Title IV of this chapter shall supersede any and all State laws insofar as they may now or hereafter relate to any employee benefit plan described in section 4(a) of this title and not exempt under section 4(b) of this title.  * * *

### (b) Construction and application

\* \* \*

**(2)(A)** Except as provided in subparagraph (B), nothing in this subchapter shall be construed to exempt or relieve any person from any law of any State which regulates insurance, banking, or securities.

**(B)** Neither an employee benefit plan described in section 4(a) of this title, which is not exempt under section 4(b) of this title (other than a plan established primarily for the purpose of providing death benefits), nor any trust established under such a plan, shall be deemed to be an insurance company or other insurer, bank, trust company, or investment company or to be engaged in the business of insurance or banking for purposes of any law of any State purporting to regulate insurance companies, insurance contracts, banks, trust companies, or investment companies.

\* \* \*

### (d) Alteration, amendment, modification, invalidation, impairment, or supersedure of any law of United States prohibited

Nothing in this subchapter shall be construed to alter, amend, modify, invalidate, impair, or supersede any law of the United States (except as provided in sections 111 and 507(b) of this title) or any rule or regulation issued under any such law.

*Part 6—Continuation Coverage Under Group Health Plans*

## § 601 [§ 1161]. Plans must provide continuation coverage to certain individuals

### (a) In general

The plan sponsor of each group health plan shall provide, in accordance with this part, that each qualified beneficiary who would lose coverage under the plan as a result of a qualifying event is entitled, under the plan, to elect, within the election period, continuation coverage under the plan.

### (b) Exception for certain plans

Subsection (a) of this section shall not apply to any group health plan for any calendar year if all employers maintaining such plan normally employed fewer than 20 employees on a typical business day during the preceding calendar year.   * * *

## § 602    [§ 1162].    Continuation coverage

For purposes of section 1161 of this title the term "continuation coverage" means coverage under the plan which meets the following requirements:

### (1) Type of benefit coverage

The coverage must consist of coverage which, as of the time the coverage is being provided, is identical to the coverage provided under the plan to similarly situated beneficiaries under the plan with respect to whom a qualifying event has not occurred. If coverage is modified under the plan for any group of similarly situated beneficiaries, such coverage shall also be modified in the same manner for all individuals who are qualified beneficiaries under the plan pursuant to this part in connection with such group.

### (2) Period of coverage

The coverage must extend for at least the period beginning on the date of the qualifying event and ending not earlier than the earliest of the following:

#### (A) Maximum required period

**(i) General rule for terminations and reduced hours.**   * * *, the date which is 18 months after the date of the qualifying event.

* * *

### (3) Premium requirements

The plan may require payment of a premium for any period of continuation coverage, except that such premium—

**(A)** shall not exceed 102 percent of the applicable premium for such period, and

**(B)** may, at the election of the payor, be made in monthly installments.   * * *

### (4) No requirement of insurability

The coverage may not be conditioned upon, or discriminate on the basis of lack of, evidence of insurability.

### (5) Conversion option

In the case of a qualified beneficiary whose period of continuation coverage expires under paragraph (2)(A), the plan must, during the 180–day period ending on such expiration date, provide to the qualified beneficiary the option of enrollment under a conversion health plan otherwise generally available under the plan.

* * *

TITLE IV—PLAN TERMINATION INSURANCE

\* \* \*

## § 4002 [§ 1302]. Pension Benefit Guaranty Corporation

### (a) Establishment within Department of Labor

There is established within the Department of Labor a body corporate to be known as the Pension Benefit Guaranty Corporation. \* \* \* The purposes of this subchapter, which are to be carried out by the corporation, are—

(1) to encourage the continuation and maintenance of voluntary private pension plans for the benefit of their participants,

(2) to provide for the timely and uninterrupted payment of pension benefits to participants and beneficiaries under plans to which this subchapter applies, and

(3) to maintain premiums established by the corporation under section 4006 of this title at the lowest level consistent with carrying out its obligations under this subchapter.

\* \* \*

## § 4006 [§ 1306]. Premium Rates

### (a) Schedules for Premium Rates and Bases for Application; Establishment, Coverage, etc.

(1) The corporation shall prescribe such schedules of premium rates and bases for the application of those rates as may be necessary to provide sufficient revenue to the fund for the corporation to carry out its functions under this subchapter. The premium rates charged by the corporation for any period shall be uniform for all plans, other than multiemployer plans, insured by the corporation with respect to basic benefits guaranteed by it under section 4022 of this title, and shall be uniform for all multiemployer plans with respect to basic benefits guaranteed by it under section 4022a of this title.

\* \* \*

### (c) Rates for plans for basic benefits

(1) Except as provided in subsection (a)(3) of this section, and subject to paragraph (2), the rate for all plans for basic benefits guaranteed under this subchapter with respect to plan years ending after September 2, 1974, is—

(A) in the case of each plan which was not a multiemployer plan in a plan year—

\* \* \*

(iii) with respect to each plan year beginning after December 31, 1985, and before January 1, 1988, an amount equal to

$8.50 for each individual who was a participant in such plan during the plan year, and

**(B)** in the case of each plan which was a multiemployer plan in a plan year, an amount equal to 50 cents for each individual who was a participant in such plan during the plan year.

\* \* \*

## § 4021 [§ 1321]. Coverage

### (a) Plans covered

Except as provided in subsection (b) of this section, this section applies to any plan (including a successor plan) which, for a plan year—

**(1)** is an employee pension benefit plan (as defined in paragraph (2) of section 3 of this title) established or maintained—

**(A)** by an employer engaged in commerce or in any industry or activity affecting commerce, or

**(B)** by any employee organization, or organization representing employees, engaged in commerce or in any industry or activity affecting commerce, or

**(C)** by both,

which has, in practice, met the requirements of part I of subchapter D of chapter 1 of Title 26 (as in effect for the preceding 5 plan years of the plan) applicable to plans described in paragraph (2) for the preceding 5 plan years; \* \* \*

For purposes of this subchapter, a successor plan is considered to be a continuation of a predecessor plan. For this purpose, unless otherwise specifically indicated in this subchapter, a successor plan is a plan which covers a group of employees which includes substantially the same employees as a previously established plan, and provides substantially the same benefits as that plan provided.

### (b) Plans not covered

This section does not apply to any plan—

**(1)** which is an individual account plan, as defined in paragraph (34) of section 3 of this title,

**(2)** established and maintained for its employees by the Government of the United States, by the government of any State or political subdivision thereof, or by any agency or instrumentality of any of the foregoing \* \* \*

**(3)** which is a church plan \* \* \*

\* \* \*

**(5)** which has not at any time after September 2, 1974, provided for employer contributions;

\* \* \*

**(11)** maintained solely for the purpose of complying with applicable workmen's compensation laws or unemployment compensation or disability insurance laws

\* \* \*

## § 4022 [§ 1322]. Single-employer plan benefits guaranteed

### (a) Nonforfeitable benefits

Subject to the limitations contained in subsection (b) of this section, the corporation shall guarantee, in accordance with this section, the payment of all nonforfeitable benefits (other than benefits becoming nonforfeitable solely on account of the termination of a plan) under a single-employer plan which terminates at a time when this title applies to it.

### (b) Exceptions

\* \* \*

## § 4041 [§ 1341]. Termination of single-employer plans

### (a) General rules governing single-employer plan termination

#### (1) Exclusive means of plan termination

Except in the case of a termination for which proceedings are otherwise instituted by the corporation as provided in section 4042 of this title, a single-employer plan may be terminated only in a standard termination under subsection (b) of this section or a distress termination under subsection (c) of this section.

#### (2) 60–day notice of intent to terminate

Not less than 60 days before the proposed termination date of a standard termination under subsection (b) of this section or a distress termination under subsection (c) of this section, the plan administrator shall provide to each affected party (other than the corporation in the case of a standard termination) a written notice of intent to terminate stating that such termination is intended and the proposed termination date. The written notice shall include any related additional information required in regulations of the corporation.

#### (3) Adherence to collective bargaining agreements

The corporation shall not proceed with a termination of a plan under this section if the termination would violate the terms and conditions of an existing collective bargaining agreement. Nothing in the preceding sentence shall be construed as limiting the authority of the corporation to institute proceedings to involuntarily terminate a plan under section 4042 of this title.

## (b) Standard termination of single-employer plans

## (1) General requirements

A single-employer plan may terminate under a standard termination only if—

(A) the plan administrator provides the 60–day advance notice of intent to terminate to affected parties required under subsection (a)(2) of this section,

(B) the requirements of subparagraphs (A) and (B) of paragraph (2) are met,

(C) the corporation does not issue a notice of noncompliance under subparagraph (C) of paragraph (2), and

(D) when the final distribution of assets occurs, the plan is sufficient for benefit liabilities (determined as of the termination date).

## (c)(2) Termination requirements

\* \* \*

## (B) Determination by corporation of necessary distress criteria

\* \* \* The requirements of this subparagraph are met if each person who is (as of the termination date) a contributing sponsor of such plan or a member of such sponsor's controlled group meets the requirements of any of the following clauses:

## (i) Liquidation in bankruptcy or insolvency proceedings \* \* \*

## (ii) Reorganization in bankruptcy or insolvency proceedings

The requirements of this clause are met by a person if—\* \* \*

(IV) the bankruptcy court (or such other appropriate court) determines that, unless the plan is terminated, such person will be unable to pay all its debts pursuant to a plan of reorganization and will be unable to continue in business outside the chapter 11 reorganization process and approves the termination.

## (iii) Termination required to enable payment of debts while staying in business or to avoid unreasonably burdensome pension costs caused by declining workforce

The requirements of this clause are met by a person if such person demonstrates to the satisfaction of the corporation that—

   **(I)** unless a distress termination occurs, such person will be unable to pay such person's debts when due and will be unable to continue in business, or

   **(II)** the costs of providing pension coverage have become unreasonably burdensome to such person, solely as a result of a decline of such person's workforce covered as participants under all single-employer plans of which such person is a contributing sponsor.

\* \* \*

### § 4042 [§ 1342]. Termination by corporation

#### (a) Authority to institute proceedings to terminate plan

The corporation may institute proceedings under this section to terminate a plan whenever it determines that—

   **(1)** the plan has not met the minimum funding standard \* \* \*

   **(2)** the plan will be unable to pay benefits when due,

   **(3)** the reportable event described in section 4043(b)(7) of this title has occurred, or

   **(4)** the possible long-run loss of the corporation with respect to the plan may reasonably be expected to increase unreasonably if the plan is not terminated.

The corporation shall as soon as practicable institute proceedings under this section to terminate a single-employer plan whenever the corporation determines that the plan does not have assets available to pay benefits which are currently due under the terms of the plan.  The corporation may prescribe a simplified procedure to follow in terminating small plans as long as that procedure includes substantial safeguards for the rights of the participants and beneficiaries under the plans, and for the employers who maintain such plans (including the requirement for a court decree under subsection (c) of this section).  Notwithstanding any other provision of this title, the corporation is authorized to pool assets of terminated plans for purposes of administration, investment, payment of liabilities of all such terminated plans, and such other purposes as it determines to be appropriate in the administration of this Subchapter.

\* \* \*

### § 4043 [§ 1343]. Reportable events

\* \* \*

#### (b) Enumeration of reportable events

For purposes of this section a reportable event occurs—

(1) when the Secretary of the Treasury issues notice that a plan has ceased to be a plan described in section 4021(a)(2) of this title, or when the Secretary of Labor determines the plan is not in compliance with subchapter I of this chapter;

(2) when an amendment of the plan is adopted if, under the amendment, the benefit payable with respect to any participant may be decreased;

(3) when the number of active participants is less than 80 percent of the number of such participants at the beginning of the plan year, or is less than 75 percent of the number of such participants at the beginning of the previous plan year;

(4) when the Secretary of the Treasury determines that there has been a termination or partial termination of the plan within the meaning of section 411(d)(3) of Title 26, but the occurrence of such a termination or partial termination does not, by itself, constitute or require a termination of a plan under this subchapter;

(5) when the plan fails to meet the minimum funding standards * * *;

(6) when the plan is unable to pay benefits thereunder when due;

(7) when there is a distribution under the plan to a participant who is a substantial owner as defined in section 4022(b)(6) of this title if—

    (A) such distribution has a value of $10,000 or more;

    (B) such distribution is not made by reason of the death of the participant;  and

    (C) immediately after the distribution, the plan has nonforfeitable benefits which are not funded;

(8) when a plan merges, consolidates, or transfers its assets under section 208 of this title * * *;  or

(9) when any other event occurs which the corporation determines may be indicative of a need to terminate the plan.

For purposes of paragraph (7), all distributions to a participant within any 24–month period are treated as a single distribution.

* * *

SUBTITLE D—LIABILITY

## § 4062 [§ 1362]. * * *

### (f) Treatment of substantial cessation of operations

If an employer ceases operations at a facility in any location and, as a result of such cessation of operations, more than 20 percent of the total number of his employees who are participants under a plan established and maintained by him are separated from employment, the employer shall be treated with respect to that plan as if he were a substantial employer under a plan under which more than one employer makes contributions and the provisions of sections 4063, 4064, and 4065 of this title shall apply. [These sections detail the extent of withdrawal liability.—Eds.]

## § 4069 [§ 1369]. Treatment of transactions to evade liability; corporate reorganization

\* \* \*

### (b) Effect of corporate reorganization

For purposes of this subtitle, the following rules apply in the case of certain corporate reorganizations:

#### (1) Change of identity, form, etc.

If a person ceases to exist by reason of a reorganization which involves a mere change in identity, form, or place of organization, however effected, a successor corporation resulting from such reorganization shall be treated as the person to whom this subtitle applies.

#### (2) Liquidation into parent corporation

If a person ceases to exist by reason of liquidation into a parent corporation, the parent corporation shall be treated as the person to whom this subtitle applies.

#### (3) Merger, consolidation, or division

If a person ceases to exist by reason of a merger, consolidation, or division, the successor corporation or corporations shall be treated as the person to whom this subtitle applies.

\* \* \*

## § 4201 [§ 1381]. Withdrawal liability established; criteria and definitions

(a) If an employer withdraws from a multiemployer plan in a complete withdrawal or a partial withdrawal, then the employer is liable to the plan in the amount determined under this part to be the withdrawal liability.

\* \* \*

# CONSOLIDATED OMNIBUS BUDGET RECONCILIATION ACT OF 1985

29 U.S.C. §§ 1161–1168

Enacting Part 6 of ERISA

Continuation Coverage Under Group Health Plans

## § 601 [§ 1161]. Plans must provide continuation coverage to certain individuals

**(a) In general.** The plan sponsor of each group health plan shall provide, in accordance with this part, that each qualified beneficiary who would lose coverage under the plan as a result of a qualifying event is entitled, under the plan, to elect, within the election period, continuation coverage under the plan.

**(b) Exception for certain plans.** Subsection (a) shall not apply to any group health plan for any calendar year if all employers maintaining such plan normally employed fewer than 20 employees on a typical business day during the preceding calendar year.

## § 602 [§ 1162]. Continuation coverage

For purposes of section 601, the term "continuation coverage" means coverage under the plan which meets the following requirements:

**(1) Type of benefit coverage.** The coverage must consist of coverage which, as of the time the coverage is being provided, is identical to the coverage provided under the plan to similarly situated beneficiaries under the plan with respect to whom a qualifying event has not occurred. If coverage is modified under the plan for any group of similarly situated beneficiaries, such coverage shall also be modified in the same manner for all individuals who are qualified beneficiaries under the plan pursuant to this part in connection with such group.

**(2) Period of coverage.** The coverage must extend for at least the period beginning on the date of the qualifying event and ending not earlier than the earliest of the following:

**(A) Maximum required period.**

**(i) General rule for terminations and reduced hours.** In the case of a qualifying event described in section 603(2), except as provided in clause (ii), the date which is 18 months after the date of the qualifying event.

**(ii) Special rule for multiple qualifying events.** If a qualifying event (other than a qualifying event described in section 603(6)) occurs during the 18 months after the date of a qualifying event described in section 603(2), the date which is 36 months after the date of the qualifying event described in section 603(2).

**(iii) Special rule for certain bankruptcy proceedings.** In the case of a qualifying event described in section 603(6) (relating to bankruptcy proceedings), the date of the death of the covered employee or qualified beneficiary (described in section 607(3)(C)(iii)), or in the case of the surviving spouse or dependent children of the covered employee, 36 months after the date of the death of the covered employee.

**(iv) General rule for other qualifying events.** In the case of a qualifying event not described in section 603(2) or 603(6), the date which is 36 months after the date of the qualifying event.

**(v) Qualifying event involving medicare entitlement.** In the case of an event described in section 603(4) (without regard to whether such event is a qualifying event), the period of coverage for qualified beneficiaries other than the covered employee for such event or any subsequent qualifying event shall not terminate before the close of the 36-month period beginning on the date the covered employee becomes entitled to benefits under title XVIII of the Social Security Act.

In the case of an individual who is determined, under title II or XVI of the Social Security Act, to have been disabled at the time of a qualifying event described in section 603(2), any reference in clause (i) or (ii) to 18 months with respect to such event is deemed a reference to 29 months, but only if the qualified beneficiary has provided notice of such determination under section 606(3) before the end of such 18 months.

**(B) End of plan.** The date on which the employer ceases to provide any group health plan to any employee.

**(C) Failure to pay premium.** The date on which coverage ceases under the plan by reason of a failure to make timely payment of any premium required under the plan with respect to the qualified beneficiary. The payment of any premium (other than any payment referred to in the last sentence of paragraph (3)) shall be considered to be timely if made within 30 days after the date due or within such longer period as applies to or under the plan.

**(D) Group health plan coverage or medicare entitlement.** The date on which the qualified beneficiary first becomes, after the date of the election—

(i) covered under any other group health plan (as an employee or otherwise) which does not contain any exclusion or limitation with respect to any preexisting condition of such beneficiary, or

(ii) in the case of a qualified beneficiary other than a qualified beneficiary described in section 607(3)(C), entitled to benefits under title XVIII of the Social Security Act.

**(E) Termination of extended coverage for disability.** In the case of a qualified beneficiary who is disabled at the time of a qualifying event described in section 603(2), the month that begins more than 30 days after the date of the final determination under title II or XVI of the Social Security Act that the qualified beneficiary is no longer disabled.

**(3) Premium requirements.** The plan may require payment of a premium for any period of continuation coverage, except that such premium—

(A) shall not exceed 102 percent of the applicable premium for such period, and

(B) may, at the election of the payor, be made in monthly installments.

In no event may the plan require the payment of any premium before the day which is 45 days after the day on which the qualified beneficiary made the initial election for continuation coverage. In the case of an individual described in the last sentence of paragraph (2)(A), any reference in subparagraph (A) of this paragraph to "102 percent" is deemed a reference to "150 percent" for any month after the 18th month of continuation coverage described in clause (i) or (ii) of paragraph (2)(A).

**(4) No requirement of insurability.** The coverage may not be conditioned upon, or discriminate on the basis of lack of, evidence of insurability.

**(5) Conversion option.** In the case of a qualified beneficiary whose period of continuation coverage expires under paragraph (2)(A), the plan must, during the 180–day period ending on such expiration date, provide to the qualified beneficiary the option of enrollment under a conversion health plan otherwise generally available under the plan.

## § 603 [§ 1163]. Qualifying event

For purposes of this part, the term "qualifying event" means, with respect to any covered employee, any of the following events which, but for the continuation coverage required under this part, would result in the loss of coverage of a qualified beneficiary:

(1) The death of the covered employee.

(2) The termination (other than by reason of such employee's gross misconduct), or reduction of hours, of the covered employee's employment.

(3) The divorce or legal separation of the covered employee from the employee's spouse.

(4) The covered employee becoming entitled to benefits under title XVIII of the Social Security Act.

(5) A dependent child ceasing to be a dependent child under the generally applicable requirements of the plan.

(6) A proceeding in a case under Title 11, United States Code, commencing on or after July 1, 1986, with respect to the employer from whose employment the covered employee retired at any time.

In the case of an event described in paragraph (6), a loss of coverage includes a substantial elimination of coverage with respect to a qualified beneficiary described in section 607(3)(C) within one year before or after the date of commencement of the proceeding.

## § 604 [§ 1164]. Applicable premium

For purposes of this part—

**(1) In general.** The term "applicable premium" means, with respect to any period of continuation coverage of qualified beneficiaries, the cost to the plan for such period of the coverage for similarly situated beneficiaries with respect to whom a qualifying event has not occurred (without regard to whether such cost is paid by the employer or employee).

**(2) Special rule for self-insured plans.** To the extent that a plan is a self-insured plan—

**(A) In general.** Except as provided in subparagraph (B), the applicable premium for any period of continuation coverage of qualified beneficiaries shall be equal to a reasonable estimate of the cost of providing coverage for such period for similarly situated beneficiaries which—

(i) is determined on an actuarial basis, and

(ii) takes into account such factors as the Secretary may prescribe in regulations.

**(B) Determination on basis of past cost.** If an administrator elects to have this subparagraph apply, the applicable premium for any period of continuation coverage of qualified beneficiaries shall be equal to—

(i) the cost to the plan for similarly situated beneficiaries for the same period occurring during the preceding determination period under paragraph (3), adjusted by

(ii) the percentage increase or decrease in the implicit price deflator of the gross national product (calculated by the Department of Commerce and published in the Survey of Current Business) for the 12–month period ending on the last day of the sixth month of such preceding determination period.

**(C) Subparagraph (B) not to apply where significant change.** An administrator may not elect to have subparagraph (B) apply in any case in which there is any significant difference, between the determination period and the preceding determination period, in coverage under, or in employees covered by, the plan. The determination under the preceding sentence for any determination period shall be made at the same time as the determination under paragraph (3).

**(3) Determination period.** The determination of any applicable premium shall be made for a period of 12 months and shall be made before the beginning of such period.

## § 605   [§ 1165].   Election

For purposes of this part—

**(1) Election period.** The term "election period" means the period which—

    (A) begins not later than the date on which coverage terminates under the plan by reason of a qualifying event,

    (B) is of at least 60 days' duration, and

    (C) ends not earlier than 60 days after the later of—

        (i) the date described in subparagraph (A), or

        (ii) in the case of any qualified beneficiary who receives notice under section 606(4), the date of such notice.

**(2) Effect of election on other beneficiaries.** Except as otherwise specified in an election, any election of continuation coverage by a qualified beneficiary described in subparagraph (A)(i) or (B) of section 607(3) shall be deemed to include an election of continuation coverage on behalf of any other qualified beneficiary who would lose coverage under the plan by reason of the qualifying event. If there is a choice among types of coverage under the plan, each qualified beneficiary is entitled to make a separate selection among such types of coverage.

## § 606   [§ 1166].   Notice requirements

**(a) In general.** In accordance with regulations prescribed by the Secretary—

    (1) the group health plan shall provide, at the time of commencement of coverage under the plan, written notice to each covered employee and spouse of the employee (if any) of the rights provided under this subsection [should read "part"],

    (2) the employer of an employee under a plan must notify the administrator of a qualifying event described in paragraph (1), (2), (4), or (6) of section 603 within 30 days (or, in the case of a group health plan which is a multiemployer plan, such longer period of time as may be provided in the terms of the plan) of the date of the qualifying event,

(3) each covered employee or qualified beneficiary is responsible for notifying the administrator of the occurrence of any qualifying event described in paragraph (3) or (5) of section 603 within 60 days after the qualifying event and each qualified beneficiary who is determined, under title II or XVI of the Social Security Act, to have been disabled at the time of a qualifying event described in section 603(2) is responsible for notifying the plan administrator of such determination within 60 days after the date of the determination and for notifying the plan administrator within 30 days after the date of any final determination under such title or titles that the qualified beneficiary is no longer disabled, and

(4) the administrator shall notify—

(A) in the case of a qualifying event described in paragraph (1), (2), (4), or (6) of section 603, any qualified beneficiary with respect to such event, and

(B) in the case of a qualifying event described in paragraph (3) or (5) of section 603 where the covered employee notifies the administrator under paragraph (3), any qualified beneficiary with respect to such event,

of such beneficiary's rights under this subsection [part].

**(b) Alternative means of compliance with requirement for notification of multiemployer plans by employers.** The requirements of subsection (a)(2) of this section shall be considered satisfied in the case of a multiemployer plan in connection with a qualifying event described in paragraph (2) of section 603 if the plan provides that the determination of the occurrence of such qualifying event will be made by the plan administrator.

**(c) Rules relating to notification of qualified beneficiaries by plan administrator.** For purposes of subsection (a)(4) of this section, any notification shall be made within 14 days (or, in the case of a group health plan which is a multiemployer plan, such longer period of time as may be provided in the terms of the plan) of the date on which the administrator is notified under paragraph (2) or (3), whichever is applicable, and any such notification to an individual who is a qualified beneficiary as the spouse of the covered employee shall be treated as notification to all other qualified beneficiaries residing with such spouse at the time such notification is made.

## § 607 [§ 1167]. Definitions and special rules

For purposes of this part—

**(1) Group health plan.** The term "group health plan" means an employee welfare benefit plan providing medical care (as defined in section 213(d) of the Internal Revenue Code of 1986) to participants or beneficiaries directly or through insurance, reimbursement, or otherwise.

**(2) Covered employee.** The term "covered employee" means an individual who is (or was) provided coverage under a group health plan by virtue of the performance of services by the individual for 1 or more persons maintaining the plan (including as an employee defined in section 401(c)(1) of the Internal Revenue Code of 1986).

**(3) Qualified beneficiary.**

**(A) In general.** The term "qualified beneficiary" means, with respect to a covered employee under a group health plan, any other individual who, on the day before the qualifying event for that employee, is a beneficiary under the plan—

(i) as the spouse of the covered employee, or

(ii) as the dependent child of the employee.

**(B) Special rule for terminations and reduced employment.** In the case of a qualifying event described in section 603(2), the term "qualified beneficiary" includes the covered employee.

**(C) Special rule for retirees and widows.** In the case of a qualifying event described in section 603(6), the term "qualified beneficiary" includes a covered employee who had retired on or before the date of substantial elimination of coverage and any other individual who, on the day before such qualifying event, is a beneficiary under the plan—

(i) as the spouse of the covered employee,

(ii) as the dependent child of the employee, or

(iii) as the surviving spouse of the covered employee.

**(4) Employer.** Subsection (n) (relating to leased employees) and subsection (t) (relating to application of controlled group rules to certain employee benefits) of section 414 of the Internal Revenue Code of 1986 shall apply for purposes of this part in the same manner and to the same extent as such subsections apply for purposes of section 106 of such Code. Any regulations prescribed by the Secretary pursuant to the preceding sentence shall be consistent and coextensive with any regulations prescribed for similar purposes by the Secretary of the Treasury (or such Secretary's delegate) under such subsections.

**(5) Optional extension of required periods.** A group health plan shall not be treated as failing to meet the requirements of this part solely because the plan provides both—

(A) that the period of extended coverage referred to in section 602(2) commences with the date of the loss of coverage, and

(B) that the applicable notice period provided under section 606(a)(2) commences with the date of the loss of coverage.

## § 608 [§ 1168]. Regulations

The Secretary may prescribe regulations to carry out the provisions of this part.

———

# FAMILY AND MEDICAL LEAVE ACT

29 U.S.C. Secs. 2601–2654

## § 2601.  Findings and purposes

(a) Findings

Congress finds that—

(1) the number of single-parent households and two-parent households in which the single parent or both parents work is increasing significantly;

(2) it is important for the development of children and the family unit that fathers and mothers be able to participate in early childrearing and the care of family members who have serious health conditions;

(3) the lack of employment policies to accommodate working parents can force individuals to choose between job security and parenting;

(4) there is inadequate job security for employees who have serious health conditions that prevent them from working for temporary periods;

(5) due to the nature of the roles of men and women in our society, the primary responsibility for family caretaking often falls on women, and such responsibility affects the working lives of women more than it affects the working lives of men; and

(6) employment standards that apply to one gender only have serious potential for encouraging employers to discriminate against employees and applicants for employment who are of that gender.

(b) Purposes

It is the purpose of this Act—

(1) to balance the demands of the workplace with the needs of families, to promote the stability and economic security of families, and to promote national interests in preserving family integrity;

(2) to entitle employees to take reasonable leave for medical reasons, for the birth or adoption of a child, and for the care of a child, spouse, or parent who has a serious health condition;

(3) to accomplish the purposes described in paragraphs (1) and (2) in a manner that accommodates the legitimate interests of employers;

(4) to accomplish the purposes described in paragraphs (1) and (2) in a manner that, consistent with the Equal Protection Clause of the Fourteenth Amendment, minimizes the potential for employment discrimination on the basis of sex by ensuring generally that leave is available for eligible medical reasons (including maternity-related disability) and for compelling family reasons, on a gender-neutral basis; and

(5) to promote the goal of equal employment opportunity for women and men, pursuant to such clause.

### Sec. 101 [§ 2611]. Definitions

As used in this subchapter:

(1) Commerce. The terms "commerce" and "industry or activity affecting commerce" mean any activity, business, or industry in commerce or in which a labor dispute would hinder or obstruct commerce or the free flow of commerce, and include "commerce" and any "industry affecting commerce", as defined in paragraphs (1) and (3) of section 142 of this title.

(2) Eligible employee.

(A) In general

The term "eligible employee" means an employee who has been employed—

(i) for at least 12 months by the employer with respect to whom leave is requested under section 2612 of this title; and

(ii) for at least 1,250 hours of service with such employer during the previous 12–month period.

(B) Exclusions

The term "eligible employee" does not include—

(i) any Federal officer or employee covered under subchapter V of chapter 63 of Title 5; or

(ii) any employee of an employer who is employed at a worksite at which such employer employs less than 50 employees if the total number of employees employed by that employer within 75 miles of that worksite is less than 50.

(C) Determination. For purposes of determining whether an employee meets the hours of service requirement specified in subparagraph (A)(ii), the legal standards established under section 207 of this title shall apply.

(3) Employ; employee; State. The terms "employ", "employee", and "State" have the same meanings given such terms in subsections (c), (e), and (g) of section 203 of this title.

(4) Employer

(A) In general

The term "employer"—

(i) means any person engaged in commerce or in any industry or activity affecting commerce who employs 50 or more employees for each working day during each of 20 or more calendar workweeks in the current or preceding calendar year;

(ii) includes—

(I) any person who acts, directly or indirectly, in the interest of an employer to any of the employees of such employer; and

(II) any successor in interest of an employer; and

(iii) includes any "public agency", as defined in section 203(x) of this title.

(B) Public agency

For purposes of subparagraph (A)(iii), a public agency shall be considered to be a person engaged in commerce or in an industry or activity affecting commerce.

(5) Employment benefits. The term "employment benefits" means all benefits provided or made available to employees by an employer, including group life insurance, health insurance, disability insurance, sick leave, annual leave, educational benefits, and pensions, regardless of whether such benefits are provided by a practice or written policy of an employer or through an "employee benefit plan", as defined in section 1002(3) of this title.

(6) Health care provider. The term "health care provider" means—

(A) a doctor of medicine or osteopathy who is authorized to practice medicine or surgery (as appropriate) by the State in which the doctor practices; or

(B) any other person determined by the Secretary to be capable of providing health care services.

(7) Parent. The term "parent" means the biological parent of an employee or an individual who stood in loco parentis to an employee when the employee was a son or daughter.

(8) Person. The term "person" has the same meaning given such term in section 203(a) of this title.

(9) Reduced leave schedule. The term "reduced leave schedule" means a leave schedule that reduces the usual number of hours per workweek, or hours per workday, of an employee.

(10) Secretary. The term "Secretary" means the Secretary of Labor.

(11) Serious health condition. The term "serious health condition" means an illness, injury, impairment, or physical or mental condition that involves—

(A) inpatient care in a hospital, hospice, or residential medical care facility; or

(B) continuing treatment by a health care provider.

(12) Son or daughter. The term "son or daughter" means a biological, adopted, or foster child, a stepchild, a legal ward, or a child of a person standing in loco parentis, who is—

(A) under 18 years of age; or

(B) 18 years of age or older and incapable of self-care because of a mental or physical disability.

(13) Spouse. The term "spouse" means a husband or wife, as the case may be.

## Sec. 102 [§ 2612]. Leave requirement

(a) In general

(1) Entitlement to leave. Subject to section 2613 of this title, an eligible employee shall be entitled to a total of 12 workweeks of leave during any 12–month period for one or more of the following:

(A) Because of the birth of a son or daughter of the employee and in order to care for such son or daughter.

(B) Because of the placement of a son or daughter with the employee for adoption or foster care.

(C) In order to care for the spouse, or a son, daughter, or parent, of the employee, if such spouse, son, daughter, or parent has a serious health condition.

(D) Because of a serious health condition that makes the employee unable to perform the functions of the position of such employee.

(2) Expiration of entitlement. The entitlement to leave under subparagraphs (A) and (B) of paragraph (1) for a birth or placement of a son or daughter shall expire at the end of the 12–month period beginning on the date of such birth or placement.

(b) Leave taken intermittently or on a reduced leave schedule

(1) In general. Leave under subparagraph (A) or (B) of subsection (a)(1) of this section shall not be taken by an employee intermittently or on a reduced leave schedule unless the employee and the employer of the employee agree otherwise. Subject to paragraph (2), subsection (e)(2) of this section, and section 2613(b)(5) of this title, leave under subparagraph (C) or (D) of subsection (a)(1) of this section may be taken intermittently or on a reduced leave schedule when medically necessary. The taking of leave intermittently or on a reduced leave schedule pursuant to this paragraph shall not result in a reduction in the total amount of leave to which the employee is entitled under subsection (a) of this section beyond the amount of leave actually taken.

(2) Alternative position. If an employee requests intermittent leave, or leave on a reduced leave schedule, under subparagraph (C) or (D) of subsection (a)(1) of this section, that is foreseeable based on planned medical treatment, the employer may require such employee to transfer temporarily to an available alternative position offered by the employer for which the employee is qualified and that—

(A) has equivalent pay and benefits; and

(B) better accommodates recurring periods of leave than the regular employment position of the employee.

(c) Unpaid leave permitted.  Except as provided in subsection (d) of this section, leave granted under subsection (a) of this section may consist of unpaid leave.  Where an employee is otherwise exempt under regulations issued by the Secretary pursuant to section 213(a)(1) of this title, the compliance of an employer with this subchapter by providing unpaid leave shall not affect the exempt status of the employee under such section.

(d) Relationship to paid leave

(1) Unpaid leave.  If an employer provides paid leave for fewer than 12 workweeks, the additional weeks of leave necessary to attain the 12 workweeks of leave required under this subchapter may be provided without compensation.

(2) Substitution of paid leave

(A) In general.  An eligible employee may elect, or an employer may require the employee, to substitute any of the accrued paid vacation leave, personal leave, or family leave of the employee for leave provided under subparagraph (A), (B), or (C) of subsection (a)(1) of this section for any part of the 12–week period of such leave under such subsection.

(B) Serious health condition.  An eligible employee may elect, or an employer may require the employee, to substitute any of the accrued paid vacation leave, personal leave, or medical or sick leave of the employee for leave provided under subparagraph (C) or (D) of subsection (a)(1) of this section for any part of the 12–week period of such leave under such subsection, except that nothing in this subchapter shall require an employer to provide paid sick leave or paid medical leave in any situation in which such employer would not normally provide any such paid leave.

(e) Foreseeable leave

(1) Requirement of notice.  In any case in which the necessity for leave under subparagraph (A) or (B) of subsection (a)(1) of this section is foreseeable based on an expected birth or placement, the employee shall provide the employer with not less than 30 days' notice, before the date the leave is to begin, of the employee's intention to take leave under such subparagraph, except that if the date of the birth or placement requires leave to begin in less than 30 days, the employee shall provide such notice as is practicable.

(2) Duties of employee.  In any case in which the necessity for leave under subparagraph (C) or (D) of subsection (a)(1) of this section is foreseeable based on planned medical treatment, the employee—

(A) shall make a reasonable effort to schedule the treatment so as not to disrupt unduly the operations of the employer, subject to the approval of the health care provider of the employee or the health care provider of the son, daughter, spouse, or parent of the employee, as appropriate;  and

(B) shall provide the employer with not less than 30 days' notice, before the date the leave is to begin, of the employee's intention to take leave under such subparagraph, except that if the date of the treatment requires leave to begin in less than 30 days, the employee shall provide such notice as is practicable.

(f) Spouses employed by the same employer. In any case in which a husband and wife entitled to leave under subsection (a) of this section are employed by the same employer, the aggregate number of workweeks of leave to which both may be entitled may be limited to 12 workweeks during any 12–month period, if such leave is taken—

(1) under subparagraph (A) or (B) of subsection (a)(1) of this section; or

(2) to care for a sick parent under subparagraph (C) of such subsection.

### Sec. 103   [§ 2613].   Certification

(a) In general.   An employer may require that a request for leave under subparagraph (C) or (D) of section 2612(a)(1) of this title be supported by a certification issued by the health care provider of the eligible employee or of the son, daughter, spouse, or parent of the employee, as appropriate.   The employee shall provide, in a timely manner, a copy of such certification to the employer. . . .

(c) Second opinion

(1) In general.   In any case in which the employer has reason to doubt the validity of the certification provided under subsection (a) of this section for leave under subparagraph (C) or (D) of section 2612(a)(1) of this title, the employer may require, at the expense of the employer, that the eligible employee obtain the opinion of a second health care provider designated or approved by the employer concerning any information certified under subsection (b) of this section for such leave.

(2) Limitation.   A health care provider designated or approved under paragraph (1) shall not be employed on a regular basis by the employer.

(d) Resolution of conflicting opinions

(1) In general.   In any case in which the second opinion described in subsection (c) of this section differs from the opinion in the original certification provided under subsection (a) of this section, the employer may require, at the expense of the employer, that the employee obtain the opinion of a third health care provider designated or approved jointly by the employer and the employee concerning the information certified under subsection (b) of this section.

(2) Finality.   The opinion of the third health care provider concerning the information certified under subsection (b) of this section shall be considered to be final and shall be binding on the employer and the employee.

(e) Subsequent recertification. The employer may require that the eligible employee obtain subsequent recertifications on a reasonable basis.

§ 2614. Employment and benefits protection

**Sec. 104 [§ 2614]. Employment and benefits protection**

(a) Restoration to position

(1) In general. Except as provided in subsection (b) of this section, any eligible employee who takes leave under section 2612 of this title for the intended purpose of the leave shall be entitled, on return from such leave—

(A) to be restored by the employer to the position of employment held by the employee when the leave commenced; or

(B) to be restored to an equivalent position with equivalent employment benefits, pay, and other terms and conditions of employment.

(2) Loss of benefits. The taking of leave under section 2612 of this title shall not result in the loss of any employment benefit accrued prior to the date on which the leave commenced.

(3) Limitations. Nothing in this section shall be construed to entitle any restored employee to—

(A) the accrual of any seniority or employment benefits during any period of leave; or

(B) any right, benefit, or position of employment other than any right, benefit, or position to which the employee would have been entitled had the employee not taken the leave.

(4) Certification. As a condition of restoration under paragraph (1) for an employee who has taken leave under section 2612(a)(1)(D) of this title, the employer may have a uniformly applied practice or policy that requires each such employee to receive certification from the health care provider of the employee that the employee is able to resume work, except that nothing in this paragraph shall supersede a valid State or local law or a collective bargaining agreement that governs the return to work of such employees.

(5) Construction. Nothing in this subsection shall be construed to prohibit an employer from requiring an employee on leave under section 2612 of this title to report periodically to the employer on the status and intention of the employee to return to work.

(b) Exemption concerning certain highly compensated employees

(1) Denial of restoration. An employer may deny restoration under subsection (a) of this section to any eligible employee described in paragraph (2) if—

(A) such denial is necessary to prevent substantial and grievous economic injury to the operations of the employer;

(B) the employer notifies the employee of the intent of the employer to deny restoration on such basis at the time the employer determines that such injury would occur; and

(C) in any case in which the leave has commenced, the employee elects not to return to employment after receiving such notice.

(2) Affected employees. An eligible employee described in paragraph (1) is a salaried eligible employee who is among the highest paid 10 percent of the employees employed by the employer within 75 miles of the facility at which the employee is employed.

(c) Maintenance of health benefits

(1) Coverage. Except as provided in paragraph (2), during any period that an eligible employee takes leave under section 2612 of this title, the employer shall maintain coverage under any "group health plan" (as defined in section 5000(b)(1) of Title 26) for the duration of such leave at the level and under the conditions coverage would have been provided if the employee had continued in employment continuously for the duration of such leave.

(2) Failure to return from leave. The employer may recover the premium that the employer paid for maintaining coverage for the employee under such group health plan during any period of unpaid leave under section 2612 of this title if—

(A) the employee fails to return from leave under section 2612 of this title after the period of leave to which the employee is entitled has expired; and

(B) the employee fails to return to work for a reason other than—

(i) the continuation, recurrence, or onset of a serious health condition that entitles the employee to leave under subparagraph (C) or (D) of section 2612(a)(1) of this title; or

(ii) other circumstances beyond the control of the employee.

(3) Certification

(A) Issuance. An employer may require that a claim that an employee is unable to return to work because of the continuation, recurrence, or onset of the serious health condition described in paragraph (2)(B)(i) be supported by—

(i) a certification issued by the health care provider of the son, daughter, spouse, or parent of the employee, as appropriate, in the case of an employee unable to return to work because of a condition specified in section 2612(a)(1)(C) of this title; or

(ii) a certification issued by the health care provider of the eligible employee, in the case of an employee unable to return to work because of a condition specified in section 2612(a)(1)(D) of this title.

(B) Copy. The employee shall provide, in a timely manner, a copy of such certification to the employer.

(C) Sufficiency of certification

(i) Leave due to serious health condition of employee.  The certification described in subparagraph (A)(ii) shall be sufficient if the certification states that a serious health condition prevented the employee from being able to perform the functions of the position of the employee on the date that the leave of the employee expired.

(ii) Leave due to serious health condition of family member.  The certification described in subparagraph (A)(i) shall be sufficient if the certification states that the employee is needed to care for the son, daughter, spouse, or parent who has a serious health condition on the date that the leave of the employee expired.

## Sec. 105  [§ 2615].  Prohibited acts

(a) Interference with rights

(1) Exercise of rights.  It shall be unlawful for any employer to interfere with, restrain, or deny the exercise of or the attempt to exercise, any right provided under this subchapter.

(2) Discrimination.  It shall be unlawful for any employer to discharge or in any other manner discriminate against any individual for opposing any practice made unlawful by this subchapter.

(b) Interference with proceedings or inquiries.  It shall be unlawful for any person to discharge or in any other manner discriminate against any individual because such individual—

(1) has filed any charge, or has instituted or caused to be instituted any proceeding, under or related to this subchapter;

(2) has given, or is about to give, any information in connection with any inquiry or proceeding relating to any right provided under this subchapter;  or

(3) has testified, or is about to testify, in any inquiry or proceeding relating to any right provided under this subchapter.

## Sec. 106  [§ 2616].  Investigative authority

(a) In general.  To ensure compliance with the provisions of this subchapter, or any regulation or order issued under this subchapter, the Secretary shall have, subject to subsection (c) of this section, the investigative authority provided under section 211(a) of this title....

## Sec. 107  [§ 2617].  Enforcement

(a) Civil action by employees

(1) Liability.  Any employer who violates section 2615 of this title shall be liable to any eligible employee affected—

(A) for damages equal to—

(i) the amount of—

(I) any wages, salary, employment benefits, or other compensation denied or lost to such employee by reason of the violation;  or

(II) in a case in which wages, salary, employment benefits, or other compensation have not been denied or lost to the employee, any actual monetary losses sustained by the employee as a direct result of the violation, such as the cost of providing care, up to a sum equal to 12 weeks of wages or salary for the employee;

(ii) the interest on the amount described in clause (i) calculated at the prevailing rate; and

(iii) an additional amount as liquidated damages equal to the sum of the amount described in clause (i) and the interest described in clause (ii), except that if an employer who has violated section 2615 of this title proves to the satisfaction of the court that the act or omission which violated section 2615 of this title was in good faith and that the employer had reasonable grounds for believing that the act or omission was not a violation of section 2615 of this title, such court may, in the discretion of the court, reduce the amount of the liability to the amount and interest determined under clauses (i) and (ii), respectively; and

(B) for such equitable relief as may be appropriate, including employment, reinstatement, and promotion.

(2) Right of action. An action to recover the damages or equitable relief prescribed in paragraph (1) may be maintained against any employer (including a public agency) in any Federal or State court of competent jurisdiction by any one or more employees for and in behalf of—

(A) the employees; or

(B) the employees and other employees similarly situated.

(3) Fees and costs. The court in such an action shall, in addition to any judgment awarded to the plaintiff, allow a reasonable attorney's fee, reasonable expert witness fees, and other costs of the action to be paid by the defendant.

(4) Limitations. The right provided by paragraph (2) to bring an action by or on behalf of any employee shall terminate—

(A) on the filing of a complaint by the Secretary in an action under subsection (d) of this section in which restraint is sought of any further delay in the payment of the amount described in paragraph (1)(A) to such employee by an employer responsible under paragraph (1) for the payment; or

(B) on the filing of a complaint by the Secretary in an action under subsection (b) of this section in which a recovery is sought of the damages described in paragraph (1)(A) owing to an eligible employee by an employer liable under paragraph (1),

unless the action described in subparagraph (A) or (B) is dismissed without prejudice on motion of the Secretary.

(b) Action by the Secretary

(1) Administrative action. The Secretary shall receive, investigate, and attempt to resolve complaints of violations of section 2615 of this

title in the same manner that the Secretary receives, investigates, and attempts to resolve complaints of violations of sections 206 and 207 of this title.

(2) Civil action. The Secretary may bring an action in any court of competent jurisdiction to recover the damages described in subsection (a)(1)(A) of this section.

(3) Sums recovered. Any sums recovered by the Secretary pursuant to paragraph (2) shall be held in a special deposit account and shall be paid, on order of the Secretary, directly to each employee affected. Any such sums not paid to an employee because of inability to do so within a period of 3 years shall be deposited into the Treasury of the United States as miscellaneous receipts.

(c) Limitation

(1) In general. Except as provided in paragraph (2), an action may be brought under this section not later than 2 years after the date of the last event constituting the alleged violation for which the action is brought.

(2) Willful violation. In the case of such action brought for a willful violation of section 2615 of this title, such action may be brought within 3 years of the date of the last event constituting the alleged violation for which such action is brought.

(3) Commencement. In determining when an action is commenced by the Secretary under this section for the purposes of this subsection, it shall be considered to be commenced on the date when the complaint is filed.

(d) Action for injunction by Secretary. The district courts of the United States shall have jurisdiction, for cause shown, in an action brought by the Secretary—

(1) to restrain violations of section 2615 of this title, including the restraint of any withholding of payment of wages, salary, employment benefits, or other compensation, plus interest, found by the court to be due to eligible employees; or

(2) to award such other equitable relief as may be appropriate, including employment, reinstatement, and promotion....

### Sec. 109 [§ 2619]. Notice

(a) In general. Each employer shall post and keep posted, in conspicuous places on the premises of the employer where notices to employees and applicants for employment are customarily posted, a notice, to be prepared or approved by the Secretary, setting forth excerpts from, or summaries of, the pertinent provisions of this subchapter and information pertaining to the filing of a charge.

(b) Penalty. Any employer that willfully violates this section may be assessed a civil money penalty not to exceed $100 for each separate offense.

# STATE LAWS

## MODEL EMPLOYMENT TERMINATION ACT

National Conference of Commissioners on
Uniform State Laws 1991

*[Editor's Note: Brackets indicate possible deletions or alternatives
for particular state legislatures to consider.]*

### § 1. Definitions.

In this [Act]:

(1) "Employee" means an individual who works for hire, including
an individual employed in a supervisory, managerial, or confidential
position, but not an independent contractor.

(2) "Employer" means a person [, excluding this State, a political
subdivision, a municipal corporation, or any other governmental subdivision, agency, or instrumentality,] that has employed [five] or more
employees for each working day in each of 20 or more calendar weeks in
the two-year period next preceding a termination or an employer's filing
of a complaint pursuant to Section 5(c), excluding a parent, spouse, child,
or other member of the employer's immediate family or of the immediate
family of an individual having a controlling interest in the employer.

(3) "Fringe benefit" means vacation leave, sick leave, medical insurance plan, disability insurance plan, life insurance plan, pension benefit
plan, or other benefit of economic value, to the extent the leave, plan, or
benefit is paid for by the employer.

(4) "Good cause" means (i) a reasonable basis related to an individual employee for termination of the employee's employment in view of
relevant factors and circumstances, which may include the employee's
duties, responsibilities, conduct on the job or otherwise, job performance,
and employment record, or (ii) the exercise of business judgment in good
faith by the employer, including setting its economic or institutional
goals and determining methods to achieve those goals, organizing or
reorganizing operations, discontinuing, consolidating, or divesting operations or positions or parts of operations or positions, determining the
size of its work force and the nature of the positions filled by its work
force, and determining and changing standards of performance for
positions.

(5) "Good faith" means honesty in fact.

(6) "Pay," as a noun, means hourly wages or periodic salary, including tips, regularly paid and nondiscretionary commissions and bonuses, and regularly paid overtime, but not fringe benefits.

(7) "Person" means an individual, corporation, business trust, estate, trust, partnership, association, joint venture, or any other legal or commercial entity [, excluding government or a governmental subdivision, agency, or instrumentality].

(8) "Termination" means:

(i) a dismissal, including that resulting from the elimination of a position, of an employee by an employer;

(ii) a layoff or suspension of an employee by an employer for more than two consecutive months; or

(iii) a quitting of employment or a retirement by an employee induced by an act or omission of the employer, after notice to the employer of the act or omission without appropriate relief by the employer, so intolerable that under the circumstances a reasonable individual would quit or retire.

## § 2.  Scope.

(a) This [Act] applies only to a termination that occurs after the effective date of this [Act].

(b) This [Act] does not apply to a termination at the expiration of an express oral or written agreement of employment for a specified duration, which was valid, subsisting, and in effect on the [effective] date of this [Act].

(c) Except as provided in subsection (e), this [Act] displaces and extinguishes all common-law rights and claims of a terminated employee against the employer, its officers, directors, and employees, which are based on the termination or on acts taken or statements made that are reasonably necessary to initiate or effect the termination if the employee's termination requires good cause under Section 3(a), is subject to an agreement for severance pay under Section 4(c), or is permitted by the expiration of an agreement for a specified duration under Section 4(d).

(d) An employee whose termination is not subject to Section 3(a) or 4(d) and who is not a party to an agreement under Section 4(c) retains all common-law rights and claims.

(e) This [Act] does not displace or extinguish rights or claims of a terminated employee against an employer arising under state or federal statutes or administrative rules or regulations having the force of law [or local ordinances valid under state law], a collective-bargaining agreement between an employer and a labor organization, or an express oral or written agreement relating to employment which does not violate this [Act].  Those rights and claims may not be asserted under this [Act], except as otherwise provided in this [Act].  The existence or adjudication of those rights or claims does not limit the employee's rights or claims under this [Act], except as stated in Section 7(d).

## § 3.  Prohibited Terminations.

(a) Unless otherwise provided in an agreement for severance pay under Section 4(c) or for a specified duration under Section 4(d), an employer may not terminate the employment of an employee without good cause.

(b) Subsection (a) applies only to an employee who has been employed by the same employer for a total period of one year or more and has worked for the employer for a least 520 hours during 26 weeks next preceding the termination.  A layoff or other break in service is not counted in determining whether an employee's period of employment totals one year, but the employee is considered to be employed during paid vacations and other authorized leaves.  If an employee is rehired after a break in service exceeding one year, not counting absences due to labor disputes or authorized leaves, the employee is considered to be newly hired.  The 26-week period for purposes of this subsection does not include any week during which the employee was absent because of layoffs of one year or less, paid vacations, authorized leaves, or labor disputes.

## § 4.  Agreements between Employer and Employee.

(a) A right of an employee under this [Act] may not be waived by agreement except as provided in this section.

(b) By express written agreement, an employer and an employee may provide that the employee's failure to meet specified business-related standards of performance or the employee's commission or omission of specified business related acts will constitute good cause for termination in proceedings under this [Act].  Those standards or prohibitions are effective only if they have been consistently enforced and they have not been applied to a particular employee in a disparate manner without justification.  If the agreement authorizes changes by the employer in the standards or prohibitions, the changes must be clearly communicated to the employee.

(c) By express written agreement, an employer and an employee may mutually waive the requirement of good cause for termination, if the employer agrees that upon the termination of the employee for any reason other than willful misconduct of the employee, the employer will provide severance pay in an amount equal to at least one month's pay for each period of employment totaling one year, up to a maximum total payment equal to 30 months' pay at the employee's rate of pay in effect immediately before the termination.  The employer shall make the payment in a lump sum or in a series of monthly installments, none of which may be less than one month's pay plus interest on the principal balance.  The lump-sum payment must be made or payment of the monthly installments must begin within 30 days after the employee's termination.  An agreement under this subsection constitutes a waiver by the employer and the employee of the right to civil trial, including jury trial, concerning disputes over the nature of the termination and the employee's entitlement to severance pay, and constitutes a stipulation by the parties that those disputes will be subject to the procedures and remedies of this [Act].

(d) The requirement of good cause for termination does not apply to the termination of an employee at the expiration of an express oral or written agreement of employment for a specified duration related to the completion of a specified task, project, undertaking, or assignment. If the employment continues after the expiration of the agreement, Section 3 applies to its termination unless the parties enter into a new express oral or written agreement under this subsection. The period of employment under an agreement described in this subsection counts toward the minimum periods of employment required by Section 3(b).

(e) An employer may provide substantive and procedural rights in addition to those provided by this [Act], either to one or more specific employees by express oral or written agreement, or to employees generally by a written personnel policy or statement, and may provide that those rights are enforceable under the procedures of this [Act].

(f) An employing person and an employee not otherwise subject to this [Act] may become subject to its provisions to the extent provided by express written agreement, in which case the employing person is deemed to be an employer.

(g) An agreement between an employer and an employee subject to this [Act] imposes a duty of good faith in its formation, performance, and enforcement.

(h) By express written agreement, and employer and employee may settle at any time a claim arising under this [Act].

(i) By express written agreement before or after a dispute or claim arises under this [Act], an employer and an employee may agree to private arbitration or other alternative dispute-resolution procedure for resolving the dispute or claim.

(j) By express written agreement after a dispute or claim arises under this [Act], an employer and an employee may agree to judicial resolution of the dispute or claim.

(k) The substantive provisions of this [Act] apply under an agreement authorized by subsections (i) and (j).

## § 5.  Procedure and Limitations.

(a) An employee whose employment is terminated may file a complaint and demand for arbitration under this [Act] with the [Commission; Department; Service] not later than 180 days after the effective date of the termination, the date of the breach of an agreement for severance pay under Section 4(c), or the date the employee learns or should have learned of the facts forming the basis of the claim, whichever is latest. The time for filing is suspended while the employee is pursuing the employer's internal remedies and has not been notified in writing by the employer that the internal procedures have been concluded. Resort to an employer's internal procedures is not a condition for filing a complaint under this [Act].

(b) Except when an employee quits, an employer, within 10 business days after a termination, shall mail or deliver to the terminated employee a written statement of the reasons for the termination and a copy of this [Act] or a summary approved by the [Commission; Department; Service].

(c) An employer may file a complaint and demand for arbitration under this [Act] with the [Commission; Department; Service] to determine whether there is good cause for the termination of a named employee. At least 15 business days before filing, the employer shall mail or deliver to the employee a written statement of the employer's intention to file and the factors alleged to constitute good cause for a termination.

(d) The [Commission; Department; Service] shall promptly mail or deliver to the respondent a copy of the complaint and demand for arbitration. Within 21 days after receipt of a complaint, the respondent must file an answer with the [Commission; Department; Service] and mail a copy of the answer to the complainant. The answer of a respondent employer must include a copy of the statement of the reasons for the termination furnished the employee.

[ (e) When a complaint is filed, a complainant employee or employer shall pay a filing fee to the [Commission; Department; Service] in [the amount of $___] [an amount not exceeding the maximum filing fee for a civil action in the courts of general jurisdiction of this State]. The [Commission; Department; Service] may waive or defer payment of the filing fee upon a showing of the complainant employee's indigency.]

## § 6. Arbitration; Selection and Powers of Arbitrator; Hearings; Burden of Proof.

(a) Except as otherwise provided in this [Act], the [Uniform Arbitration Act] [_____ arbitration act of this State] applies to proceedings under this [Act] as if the parties had agreed to arbitrate under that statute. The [commission; Department; Service] shall adopt procedural rules to regulate arbitration under this [Act]. The [Administrative Procedure Act and other] statutes of this State applicable to the procedures of state agencies do not apply to arbitration under this [Act].

(b) The [Commission; Department; Service] shall adopt rules specifying the qualifications, method of selection, and appointment of arbitrators. An arbitrator serving under this [Act] exercises the authority of the state.

(c) Subject to rules adopted by the [Commission; Department; Service], all forms of discovery [provided by applicable state statute, rule, or regulation] are available in the discretion of the arbitrator, who shall ensure there is no undue delay, expense, or inconvenience. Upon request, the employer shall provide the complainant or respondent employee a complete copy of the employee's personnel file.

(d) A party may be represented in arbitration by an attorney or other person authorized under the laws of this State to represent an individual in arbitration.

(e) A complainant employee has the burden of proving that a termination was without good cause or that an employer breached an agreement for severance pay under Section 4(c). A complainant employer has the burden of proving that there is good cause for a termination. In all arbitrations, the employer shall present its case first unless the employee alleges that a quitting or retirement was a termination within the meaning of Section 1(8)(iii).

(f) If an employee establishes that a termination was motivated in part by impermissible grounds, the employer, to avoid liability, must establish by a preponderance of the evidence that it would have terminated the employment even in the absence of the impermissible grounds.

## § 7. Awards.

(a) Within 30 days after the close of an arbitration hearing or at a later time agreeable to the parties, the arbitrator shall mail or deliver to the parties a written award sustaining or dismissing the complaint, in whole or in part, and specifying appropriate remedies, if any.

(b) An arbitrator may make one or more of the following awards for a termination in violation of this [Act]:

(1) reinstatement to the position of employment the employee held when employment was terminated or, if that is impractical, to a comparable position;

(2) full or partial backpay and reimbursement for lost fringe benefits, with interest, reduced by interim earnings from employment elsewhere, benefits received, and amounts that could have been received with reasonable diligence;

(3) if reinstatement is not awarded, a lump-sum severance payment at the employee's rate of pay in effect before the termination, for a period not exceeding [36 months] after the date of the award, together with the value of fringe benefits lost during that period, reduced by likely earnings and benefits from employment elsewhere, and taking into account such equitable considerations as the employee's length of service with the employer and the reasons for the termination; and

(4) reasonable attorney's fees and costs.

(c) An arbitrator may make either or both of the following awards for a violation of an agreement for severance pay under Section 4(c):

(1) enforcement of the severance pay and other applicable provisions of the agreement, with interest; and

(2) reasonable attorney's fees and costs.

(d) An arbitrator may not make an award except as provided in subsections (b) and (c). The arbitrator may not award damages for pain and suffering, emotional distress, defamation, fraud, or other injury under the common law; punitive damages; compensatory damages; or any other monetary award. In making a monetary award under this section, the arbitrator shall reduce the award by the amount of any monetary award to the employee in another forum for the same conduct of the employer. In making an award, the arbitrator is subject to the rules of issue, fact, and judgment preclusion applicable in courts of record in this State.

(e) If an arbitrator dismisses an employee's complaint and finds it frivolous, unreasonable, or without foundation, the arbitrator may award reasonable attorney's fees and costs to the prevailing employer.

(f) An arbitrator may sustain an employer's complaint and make an award declaring that there is good cause for the termination of a named employee. If the arbitrator dismisses the employer's complaint, the arbitrator may award reasonable attorney's fees and costs to the prevailing employee.

## § 8. Judicial Review and Enforcement.

(a) Either party to an arbitration may seek vacation, modification, or enforcement of the arbitrator's award in the [court of general jurisdiction] for the [county] in which the termination occurred or in which the employee resides.

(b) An application for vacation or modification must be filed within [90] days after issuance of the arbitrator's award. An application for enforcement may be filed at any time after issuance of the arbitrator's award.

(c) The court may vacate or modify an arbitrator's award only if the court finds that:

(1) the award was procured by corruption, fraud, or other improper means;

(2) there was evident partiality by the arbitrator or misconduct prejudicing the rights of a party;

(3) the arbitrator exceeded the powers of an arbitrator;

(4) the arbitrator committed a prejudicial error of law; or

(5) another ground exists for vacating the award under the [Uniform Arbitration Act] [_____ arbitration act of this State].

(d) In an application for vacation, modification, or enforcement of an arbitrator's award, the court may award a prevailing employee reasonable attorney's fees and costs. In an application by an employee for vacation of an arbitrator's award, the court may award a prevailing employer reasonable attorney's fees and costs if the court finds the employee's application is frivolous, unreasonable, or without foundation.

## § 9.  Posting.

An employer shall post a copy of this [Act] or a summary approved by the [Commission; Department; Service] in a prominent place in the work area.  An employer who violates this section is subject to a civil penalty not exceeding [$___].  The [Attorney General] may bring a civil action, on behalf of this State, to impose and collect any civil penalty arising under this section.

## § 10.  Retaliation Prohibited and Civil Action Created.

An employer or other employing person may not directly or indirectly take adverse action in retaliation against an individual for filing a complaint, giving testimony, or otherwise lawfully participating in proceedings under this [Act], whether or not the individual is an employee having rights under this [Act].  An employer or other employing person who violates this section is liable to the individual subjected to the adverse action in retaliation for damage caused by the action, punitive damages when appropriate, and reasonable attorney's fees.  A separate civil action may be brought to enforce this liability.  The employer is also subject to applicable procedures and remedies provided by Sections 5 through 8.

## § 11.  Severability Clause.

If any provision of this [Act] or its application to any person or circumstance is held invalid, the invalidity does not affect other provisions or applications of this [Act] which can be given effect, without the invalid provision or application, and to this end the provisions of this [Act] are severable.

## § 12.  Effective Date.

This [Act] takes effect _____.

## § 13.  Repeals.

The following acts and parts of acts are repealed:

(1) . . . .

(2) . . . .

(3) . . . .

## § 14.  Savings and Transitional Provisions.

This [Act] does not apply to a termination of an employee within six months after the effective date of this [Act] based upon the employee's refusal to enter into an agreement meeting the minimum standards of Section 4(c), which the employer, in the exercise of good faith business judgment, may impose as a condition of continued employment.

# CONSCIENTIOUS EMPLOYEE PROTECTION ACT

## 34:19—Secs. 1–8
## New Jersey, 1986.

**34:19–2.** Definitions

As used in this act:

a. "Employer" means any individual, partnership, association, corporation or any person or group of persons acting directly or indirectly on behalf of or in the interest of an employer with the employer's consent and shall include all branches of State Government, or the several counties and municipalities thereof, or any other political subdivision of the State, or a school district, or any special district, or any authority, commission, or board or any other agency or instrumentality thereof.

b. "Employee" means any individual who performs services for and under the control and direction of an employer for wages or other remuneration.

c. "Public body" means:

(1) the United States Congress, and State legislature, or any popularly-elected local governmental body, or any member or employee thereof;

(2) any federal, State, or local judiciary, or any member or employee thereof, or any grand or petit jury;

(3) any federal, State, or local regulatory, administrative, or public agency or authority, or instrumentality thereof;

(4) any federal, State, or local law enforcement agency, prosecutorial office, or police or peace officer;

(5) any federal, State or local department of an executive branch of government; or

(6) any division, board, bureau, office, committee or commission of any of the public bodies described in the above paragraphs of this subsection.

d. "Supervisor" means any individual with an employer's organization who has the authority to direct and control the work performance of the affected employee, who has authority to take corrective action regarding the violation of the law, rule or regulation of which the employee complains, or who has been designated by the employer on the notice required under section 7 of this act.[1]

e. "Retaliatory action" means the discharge, suspension or demotion of an employee, or other adverse employment action taken against an employee in the terms and conditions of employment.

**34:19–3.** Employer retaliatory action; protected employee actions

An employer shall not take any retaliatory action against an employee because the employee does any of the following:

a. Discloses, or threatens to disclose to a supervisor or to a public body an activity, policy or practice of the employer that the employee reasonably believes is in violation of a law, or a rule or regulation promulgated pursuant to law;

b. Provides information to, or testifies before, any public body conducting an investigation, hearing or inquiry into any violation of law, or a rule or regulation promulgated pursuant to law by the employer; or

c. Objects to, or refuses to participate in any activity, policy or practice which the employee reasonably believes:

(1) is in violation of a law, or a rule or regulation promulgated pursuant to law;

(2) is fraudulent or criminal; or

(3) is incompatible with a clear mandate of public policy concerning the public health, safety or welfare.

**34:19–4.** Disclosure to public body; requirement of notice and opportunity to correct

The protection against retaliatory action provided by this act pertaining to disclosure to a public body shall not apply to an employee who makes a disclosure to a public body unless the employee has brought the activity, policy or practice in violation of a law, or a rule or regulation promulgated pursuant to law to the attention of a supervisor of the employee by written notice and has afforded the employer a reasonable opportunity to correct the activity, policy or practice. Disclosure shall not be required where the employee is reasonably certain that the activity, policy or practice is known to one or more supervisors of the employer or where the employee reasonably fears physical harm as a result of the disclosure provided, however, that the situation is emergency in nature.

**34:19–5.** Violations; civil action

Upon a violation of any of the provisions of this act, an aggrieved employee or former employee may institute a civil action in a court of competent jurisdiction, within one year, for relief which may include, and which the court may order, the following:

a. An injunction to restrain continued violation of this act;

b. The reinstatement of the employee to the same position held before the retaliatory action, or to an equivalent position;

c. The reinstatement of full fringe benefits and seniority rights;

d. The compensation for lost wages, benefits and other remuneration;

e.  The payment by the employer of reasonable costs, and attorney's fees;

f.  Punitive damages;  or

g.  An assessment of a civil fine of not more than $1,000.00 for the first violation of the act and not more than $5,000.00 for each subsequent violation, which shall be paid to the State Treasurer for deposit in the General Fund.

**34:19–6.**  Award of attorney's fees and costs to employer;  action without basis in law or fact

A court, upon notice of motion in accordance with the Rules Governing the Courts of the State of New Jersey, may also order that reasonable attorneys' fees and court costs be awarded to an employer if the court determines that an action brought by an employee under this act was without basis in law or in fact.  However, an employee shall not be assessed attorneys' fees under this section if, after exercising reasonable and diligent efforts after filing a suit, the employee files a voluntary dismissal concerning the employer, within a reasonable time after determining that the employer would not be found to be liable for damages.

**34:19–7.**  Informing employees of protections and obligations under act;  name of person designated to receive notices

An employer shall conspicuously display notices of its employees' protections and obligations under this act, and use other appropriate means to keep its employees so informed.  Each notice posted pursuant to this section shall include the name of the person or persons the employer has designated to receive written notifications pursuant to section 4 of this act.[1]

**34:19–8.**  Effect of act on rights, privileges, or remedies of employees under other laws, regulations, or agreements

Nothing in this act shall be deemed to diminish the rights, privileges, or remedies of any employee under any other federal or State law or regulation or under any collective bargaining agreement or employment contract;  except that the institution of an action in accordance with this act shall be deemed a waiver of the rights and remedies available under any other contract, collective bargaining agreement, State law, rule or regulation or under the common law.

----

# AN ACT CONCERNING DRUG TESTING IN THE WORKPLACE

### P.A. 87–551

### Connecticut, 1987.

**Section 1.**  For the purposes of this act:

(1) "Employee" means any individual currently employed or formerly employed by an employer and includes any individual in a managerial position;

(2) "Employer" means any individual, corporation, partnership or unincorporated association, excluding the state or any political subdivision thereof.

**Sec. 2.** No employer may determine an employee's eligibility for promotion, additional compensation, transfer, termination, disciplinary or other adverse personnel action solely on the basis of a positive urinalysis drug test result unless (1) the employer has given the employee a urinalysis drug test, utilizing a reliable methodology, which produced a positive result, (2) such positive test result was confirmed by a second urinalysis drug test which was separate and independent from the initial test, utilizing a reliable methodology, and (3) such positive test result was confirmed by a third urinalysis drug test which was separate and independent from the initial test, utilizing a gas chromatography and mass spectrometry methodology or a methodology which has been determined by the commissioner of health services to be as reliable or more reliable than the gas chromatography and mass spectrometry methodology.

**Sec. 3.** No employer may require a prospective employee to submit to a urinalysis drug test as part of the application procedure for employment with such employer unless (1) the prospective employee is informed in writing at the time of application of the employer's intent to conduct such a drug test, (2) such test is conducted in accordance with the requirements of subdivisions (1) to (3), inclusive, of section 2 of this act and (3) the prospective employee is given a copy of any positive urinalysis drug test result. The results of any such test shall be confidential and shall not be disclosed by the employer or its employees to any person other than any such employee to whom such disclosure is necessary.

**Sec. 4.** No employer or employer representative, agent or designee engaged in a urinalysis drug testing program shall directly observe an employee or prospective employee in the process of producing the urine specimen.

**Sec. 5.** Any results of urinalysis drug tests conducted by or on behalf of an employer shall be maintained along with other employee medical records and shall be subject to the privacy protections provided for in * * * the general statutes. Such results shall be inadmissible in any criminal proceeding.

**Sec. 6.** No employer may require an employee to submit to a urinalysis drug test unless the employer has reasonable suspicion that the employee is under the influence of drugs or alcohol which adversely affects or could adversely affect such employee's job performance.

**Sec. 7.** Notwithstanding the provisions of section 6 of this act, an employer may require an employee to submit to a urinalysis drug test on a random basis if (1) such test is authorized under federal law, (2) the employee serves in an occupation which has been designated as a high-risk or safety-sensitive occupation pursuant to regulations adopted by the commissioner of labor * * * or (3) the urinalysis is conducted as part of an employee assistance program sponsored or authorized by the employer in which the employee voluntarily participates.

**Sec. 8.**   Nothing in this act shall prevent an employer from conducting medical screenings, with the express written consent of the employees, to monitor exposure to toxic or other unhealthy substances in the workplace or in the performance of their job responsibilities. Any such screenings or tests shall be limited to the specific substances expressly identified in the employee consent form.

**Sec. 9.**   Nothing in this act shall restrict an employer's ability to prohibit the use of intoxicating substances during work hours, or restrict an employer's ability to discipline an employee for being under the influence of intoxicating substances during work hours.

**Sec. 10.**    Nothing in this act shall restrict or prevent a urinalysis drug test program conducted under the supervision of the division of special revenue within the department of revenue services relative to jai alai players, jai alai court judges, jockeys, harness drivers or stewards participating in activities upon which pari-mutuel wagering is authorized under * * * the general statutes.

**Sec. 11.**   (a) Any aggrieved person may enforce the provisions of this act by means of a civil action. Any employer, laboratory or medical facility that violates any provision of this act or who aids in the violation of any provision of this act shall be liable to the person aggrieved for special and general damages, together with attorney's fees and costs.

(b) Any employer, laboratory or medical facility that commits, or proposes to commit, an act in violation of any provision of this act may be enjoined therefrom by any court of competent jurisdiction. An action for injunctive relief under this subsection may be brought by any aggrieved person, by the attorney general or by any person or entity which will fairly and adequately represent the interests of the protected class.

**Sec. 12.**   No provision of any collective bargaining agreement may contravene or supersede any provision of this act so as to infringe the privacy rights of any employee.

––––––

# STATE EMPLOYMENT RELATIONS ACT

### Secs. 111.80–94
### Wisconsin, 1966, as amended.

**Sec. 111.80.  Declaration of policy.**  The public policy of the state as to labor relations and collective bargaining in state employment, in the furtherance of which this subchapter is enacted, is as follows:

(1) It recognizes that there are three major interests involved: that of the public, that of the state employee and that of the state as an employer. These three interests are to a considerable extent interrelated. It is the policy of this state to protect and promote each of these interests with due regard to the situation and to the rights of the others.

(2) Orderly and constructive employment relations for state employee and the efficient administration of state government are promotive of all these interests. They are largely dependent upon the maintenance of fair, friendly and mutually satisfactory employee-management relations in state employment, and the availability of suitable machinery for fair and peaceful adjustment of whatever controversies may arise. It is recognized that whatever may be the rights of disputants with respect to each other in any controversy regarding state employment relations, neither party has any right to engage in acts or practices which jeopardize the public safety and interest and interferes with the effective conduct of public business.

(3) Where permitted under this subchapter, negotiations of terms and conditions of state employment should result from voluntary agreement between the state and its agents as an employer, and its employees. For that purpose a state employee may, if he desires, associate with others in organizing and in bargaining collectively through representatives of his own choosing without intimidation or coercion from any source.

(4) It is the policy of this state, in order to preserve and promote the interests of the public, the state employee and the state as an employer alike, to encourage the practices and procedures of collective bargaining in state employment subject to the requirements of the public service and related laws, rules and policies governing state employment, by establishing standards of fair conduct in state employment relations and by providing a convenient, expeditious and impartial tribunal in which these interests may have their respective rights determined.

**Sec. 111.81. Definitions** * * * (7) "Employee" includes: (a) Any state employee in the classified service of the state, * * * except limited term employees, seasonal employees, project employees, supervisors, management employees and individuals who are privy to confidential matters affecting the employer-employee relationships, as well as all employees of the commission.

(b) Program, project or teaching assistants employed by the University of Wisconsin system, except supervisors, management employees and individuals who are privy to confidential matters affecting the employer-employee relationship.

(8) "Employer" means the state of Wisconsin.

(9) "Fair-share agreement" means an agreement between the employer and a labor organization representing employees or supervisors specified in Sec. 111.825(5) under which all of the employees or supervisors in a collective bargaining unit are required to pay their proportion-

ate share of the cost of the collective bargaining process and contract administration measured by the amount of dues uniformly required of all members.

* * *

(11) "Labor dispute" means any controversy with respect to the subjects of bargaining provided in this subchapter.

(12) "Labor organization" means any employee organization whose purpose is to represent state employees in collective bargaining with the state, or its agents, on matters pertaining to terms and conditions of employment; but the term shall not include any organization:

(a) Which advocates the overthrow of the constitutional form of government in the United States; or

(b) Which discriminates with regard to the terms or conditions of membership because of race, color, creed, sex, age, sexual orientation or national origin.

(12m) "Maintenance of membership agreement" means an agreement between the employer and a labor organization representing employees or supervisors specified in Sec. 111.825(5) which requires that all of the employees or supervisors whose dues are being deducted from earnings under Sec. 20.921(1) or 111.84(1)(f) at the time the agreement takes effect shall continue to have dues deducted for the duration of the agreement and that dues shall be deducted from the earnings of all employees or supervisors who are hired on or after the effective date of the agreement.

(13) "Management" includes those personnel engaged predominantly in executive and managerial functions, including such officials as division administrators, bureau directors, institutional heads and employees exercising similar functions and responsibilities as determined by the commission.

* * *

(15) "Professional employee" means: (a) Any employee in the classified service who is engaged in work:

1. Predominately intellectual and varied in character as opposed to routine mental, manual, mechanical or physical work;

2. Involving the consistent exercise of discretion and judgment in its performance;

3. Of such character that the output produced or the result accomplished cannot be standardized in relation to a given period of time;

4. Requiring knowledge of an advanced type in a field of science or learning customarily acquired by a prolonged course of specialized intellectual instruction and study in an institution of higher learning or a hospital, as distinguished from a general academic education or from an apprenticeship or from training in the performance of routine mental, manual or physical process; or

(b) Any employee in the classified service who:

1.   Has completed the courses of specialized intellectual instruction and study described in paragraph (a)4; and

2.   Is performing related work under the supervision of a professional person to qualify himself to become a professional employee as defined in paragraph (a).

(15m) "Program assistant" or "project assistant" means a graduate student enrolled in the University of Wisconsin system who is assigned to conduct research, training, administrative responsibilities or other academic or academic support projects or programs, except regular preparation of instructional materials for courses or manual or clerical assignments, under the supervision of a member of the faculty or academic staff, as defined in Sec. 36.05(1) or (8), primarily for the benefit of the university, faculty or academic staff supervisor or a granting agency. "Project assistant" or "program assistant" does not include a graduate student who does work which is primarily for the benefit of the student's own learning and research and which is independent or self-directed.

(16) "Referendum" means a proceeding conducted by the commission in which employees, or supervisors specified in Sec. 111.825(5), in a collective bargaining unit may cast a secret ballot on the question of directing the labor organization and the employer to enter into a fair-share or maintenance of membership agreement or to terminate such an agreement.

(17) "Representative" includes any person chosen by an employee to represent him.

(18) "Strike" includes any strike or other concerted stoppage of work by employees, and any concerted slowdown or other concerted interruption of operations or services by employees, or any concerted refusal to work or perform their usual duties as employees of the state.

(19) "Supervisor" means any individual whose principal work is different from that of his subordinates and who has authority, in the interest of employer, to hire, transfer, suspend, layoff, recall, promote, discharge, assign, reward or discipline employees, or to adjust their grievances, or to authoritatively recommend such action, if his exercise of such authority is not of a merely routine or clerical nature, but requires the use of independent judgment.

(19m) "Teaching assistant" means a graduate student enrolled in the University of Wisconsin system who is regularly assigned teaching and related responsibilities, other than manual or clerical responsibilities, under the supervision of a member of the faculty as defined in Sec. 36.05(8).

* * *

**Sec. 111.82.  Rights of state employees.**  State employees shall have the right of self-organization and the right to form, join or assist labor organizations, to bargain collectively through representatives of their own choosing under this subchapter, and to engage in lawful, concerted activities for the purpose of collective bargaining or other mutual aid or protection. Such employees shall also have the right to refrain from any or all of such activities.

**Sec. 111.825. Collective bargaining units.** (1) It is the legislative intent that in order to foster meaningful collective bargaining, units must be structured in such a way as to avoid excessive fragmentation whenever possible. In accordance with this policy, collective bargaining units for employees in the classified service of the state are structured on a statewide basis with one collective bargaining unit for each of the following:

1. Clerical and related.

2. Blue collar and nonbuilding trades.

3. Building trades crafts.

4. Security and public safety.

5. Technical.

6. Professional:

a. Fiscal and staff services.

b. Research, statistics and analysis.

c. Legal.

d. Patient treatment.

e. Patient care.

f. Social services.

g. Education.

h. Engineering.

i. Science.

(2) Collective bargaining units for employees in the unclassified service of the state shall be structured with one collective bargaining unit for each of the following groups:

(a) The program, project and teaching assistants of the University of Wisconsin–Madison and the University of Wisconsin-Extension.

(b) The program, project and teaching assistants of the University of Wisconsin–Milwaukee.

(c) The program, project and teaching assistants of the Universities of Wisconsin–Eau Claire, Green Bay, La Crosse, Oshkosh, Parkside, Platteville, River Falls, Stevens Point, Stout, Superior and Whitewater.

(3) The commission shall assign employees to the appropriate collective bargaining units set forth in subsections (1) and (2).

(4) Any labor organization may petition for recognition as the exclusive representative of a collective bargaining unit specified in sub-

section (1) or (2) in accordance with the election procedures set forth in Sec. 111.83, provided the petition is accompanied by a 30 percent showing of interest in the form of signed authorization cards. Each additional labor organization seeking to appear on the ballot shall file petitions within 60 days of the date of filing of the original petition and prove, through signed authorization cards, that at least 10 percent of the employees in the collective bargaining unit want it to be their representative.

(5) Although supervisors are not considered employees for purposes of this subchapter, the commission may consider a petition for a state-wide collective bargaining unit of professional supervisory employees in the classified service, but the representative of supervisors may not be affiliated with any labor organization representing employees assigned to the collective bargaining units set forth in subsections (1) and (2). The certified representative for supervisors may not bargain with respect to any matter other than wages and fringe benefits as defined in Sec. 111.91(1).

**Sec. 111.83. Representatives and elections.** (1) Except as provided in subsection (5), a representative chosen for the purposes of collective bargaining by a majority of the employees voting in a collective bargaining unit shall be the exclusive representative of all of the employees in such unit for the purposes of collective bargaining. * * *

**Sec. 111.84. Unfair labor practices.** (1) It is an unfair labor practice for an employer individually or in concert with others:

(a) To interfere with, restrain or coerce state employes in the exercise of their rights guaranteed in Sec. 111.82.

(b) To initiate, create, dominate or interfere with the formation or administration of any labor or employe organization or contribute financial support to it. However, it is not an unfair labor practice for the employer to reimburse state employes at their prevailing wage rate for the time spent during the employe's regularly scheduled hours conferring with the employer's officers or agents and for attendance at commission or court hearings necessary for the administration of this subchapter. Professional supervisory or craft personnel may maintain membership in professional or craft organizations; however, as members of such organizations they shall be prohibited from those activities related to collective bargaining in which the organizations may engage.

(c) To encourage or discourage membership in any labor organization by discrimination in regard to hiring, tenure or other terms or conditions of employment. This paragraph does not apply to fair-share or maintenance of membership agreements.

(d) To refuse to bargain collectively on matters set forth in Sec. 111.91 with a representative of a majority of its employees in an appropriate collective bargaining unit. Where the employer has a good faith doubt as to whether a labor organization claiming the support of a majority of its employees in appropriate collective bargaining unit does in fact have that support, it may file with the commission a petition requesting an election as to that claim. It is not deemed to have refused to bargain until an election has been held and the results thereof certified to it by the commission. A violation of this paragraph includes, but is not limited to, the refusal to execute a collective bargaining agreement previously orally agreed upon.

(e) To violate any collective bargaining agreement previously agreed upon by the parties with respect to wages, hours and conditions of employment affecting state employes, including an agreement to arbitrate or to accept the terms of an arbitration award, where previously the parties have agreed to accept such award as final and binding upon them.

(f) To deduct labor organization dues from an employe's earnings, unless the employer has been presented with an individual order therefor, signed by the employee personally, and terminable by at least the end of any year of its life or earlier by the employee giving at least 30 but not more than 120 days' written notice of such termination to the employer and to the representative labor organization, except if there is a fair-share or maintenance of membership agreement in effect. The employer shall give notice to the labor organization of receipt of such termination.

(2) It is an unfair practice for an employe individually or in concert with others:

(a) To coerce or intimidate an employe in the enjoyment of his legal rights, including those guaranteed in Sec. 111.82.

(b) To coerce, intimidate or induce any officer or agent of the employer to interfere with any of its employes in the enjoyment of their legal rights, including those guaranteed in Sec. 111.82 or to engage in any practice with regard to its employes which would constitute an unfair labor practice if undertaken by him on his own initiative.

(c) To refuse to bargain collectively on matters set forth in Sec. 111.91(1) with the duly authorized officer or agent of the employer which is the recognized or certified exclusive collective bargaining representative of employees specified in Sec. 111.81(7)(a) in an appropriate collective bargaining unit or with the certified exclusive collective bargaining representative of employees specified in Sec. 111.81(7)(b) in an appropriate collective bargaining unit. Such refusal to bargain shall include, but not be limited to, the refusal to execute a collective bargaining agreement previously orally agreed upon.

(d) To violate the provisions of any written agreement with respect to terms and conditions of employment affecting employes, including an agreement to arbitrate or to accept the terms of an arbitration award, where previously the parties have agreed to accept such awards as final and binding upon them.

(e) To engage in, induce or encourage any employes to engage in a strike, or a concerted refusal to work or perform their usual duties as employes.

(f) To coerce or intimidate a supervisory employe, officer or agent of the employer, working at the same trade or profession as its employes, to induce him to become a member of or act in concert with the labor organization of which the employe is a member.

(3) It is an unfair labor practice for any person to do or cause to be done on behalf of or in the interest of employers or employes, or in connection with or to influence the outcome of any controversy as to employment relations, any act prohibited by subs. (1) and (2).

(4) Any controversy concerning unfair labor practices may be submitted to the commission as provided in Sec. 111.07, except that the commission shall fix hearing on complaints involving alleged violations of sub. (2)(e) within three days after filing of such complaints, and notice shall be given to each party interested by service on him personally, or by telegram, advising him of the nature of the complaint and of the date, time and place of hearing thereon. The commission may in its discretion appoint a substitute tribunal to hear unfair labor practice charges by either appointing a three-member panel or submitting a seven-member panel to the parties and allowing each to strike two names. Such panel shall report its finding to the commission for appropriate action.

**Sec. 111.85. Fair-share and maintenance of membership agreements.** (1)(a) No fair-share or maintenance of membership agreement may become effective unless authorized by referendum. The commission shall order a referendum whenever it receives a petition supported by proof that at least 30 percent of the employees or supervisor specified in Sec. 111.825(5) in a collective bargaining unit desire that a fair-share or maintenance of membership agreement be entered into between the employer and a labor organization. A petition may specify that a referendum is requested on a maintenance of membership agreement only, in which case the ballot shall be limited to that question.

(b) For a fair-share agreement to be authorized, at least two-thirds of the eligible employees or supervisors voting in a referendum shall vote in favor of the agreement. For a maintenance of membership agreement to be authorized, at least a majority of the eligible employees or supervisors voting in a referendum shall vote in favor of the agreement. In a referendum on a fair-share agreement, if less than two-thirds but more than one-half of the eligible employees or supervisors vote in favor of the agreement, a maintenance of membership agreement is authorized.

(c) If a fair-share or maintenance of membership agreement is authorized in a referendum, the employer shall enter into such an agreement with the labor organization named on the ballot in the referendum. Each fair-share or maintenance of membership agreement shall contain a provision requiring the employer to deduct the amount of dues as certified by the labor organization from the earnings of the employees or supervisors affected by the agreement and to pay the amount so deducted to the labor organization. Unless the parties agree to an earlier date, the agreement shall take effect 60 days after certification by the commission that the referendum vote authorized the agreement. The employer shall be held harmless against any claims, demands, suits and other forms of liability made by the employees or supervisors or local labor organizations which may arise for actions taken by the employer in compliance with this section. All such lawful claims, demands, suits and other forms of liability are the responsibility of the labor organization entering into the agreement.

(d) Under each fair-share or maintenance of membership agreement, an employee or supervisor who has religious convictions against dues payments to a labor organization based on teachings or tenets of a church or religious body of which he or she is a member shall, on request to the labor organization, have his or her dues paid to a charity mutually agreed upon by the employee or supervisor and the labor organization. Any dispute concerning this paragraph may be submitted to the commission for adjudication.

(2)(a) Once authorized, a fair-share or maintenance of membership agreement shall continue in effect subject to the right of the employer or labor organization concerned to petition the commission to conduct a new referendum. Such petition must be supported by proof that at least 30 percent of the employees or supervisors in the collective bargaining unit desire that the fair-share or maintenance of membership agreement be discontinued. Upon so finding, the commission shall conduct a new referendum. If the continuance of the fair-share or maintenance of membership agreement is approved in the referendum by at least the percentage of eligible voting employees or supervisors required for its initial authorization, it shall be continued in effect, subject to the right of employer or labor organization to later initiate a further vote following the procedure described in this subsection. If the continuation of the agreement is not supported in any referendum, it is deemed terminated at the termination of the collective bargaining agreement, or one year from the date of certification of the result of the referendum, whichever is earlier.

(b) The commission shall declare any fair-share or maintenance of membership agreement suspended upon such conditions and for such time as the commission decides whenever it finds that the labor organization involved has refused on the basis of race, color, sexual orientation or creed to receive as a member of any employee or supervisor in the collective bargaining unit involved, and the agreement shall be made subject to the findings and orders of the commission. Any of the parties to the agreement, or any employee or supervisor covered thereby, may come before the commission, as provided in Sec. 111.07, and petition the commission to make such a finding.

* * *

**Sec. 111.86. Grievance arbitration.** Parties to the dispute pertaining to the interpretation of a collective bargaining agreement may agree in writing to have the commission or any other appointing agency serve as arbitrator or may designate any other competent, impartial and disinterested persons to so serve. Such arbitration proceedings shall be governed by Ch. 788.

**Sec. 111.87. Mediation.** The commission may appoint any competent, impartial, disinterested person to act as mediator in any labor dispute either upon its own initiative or upon the request of one of the parties to the dispute. It is the function of such mediator to bring the parties together voluntarily under such favorable auspices as will tend to effectuate settlement of the dispute, but neither the mediator nor the commission shall have any power of compulsion in mediation proceedings.

**Sec. 111.88. Fact finding.** (1) If a dispute has not been settled after a reasonable period of negotiation and after the settlement procedures, if any, established by the parties have been exhausted, the representative, which has been certified by the commission after an election, or, in the case of a representative of employees specified in Sec. 111.81(7)(a), has been duly recognized by the employer, as the exclusive representative of employes in an appropriate collective bargaining unit, and the employer, its officers and agents, after a reasonable period of negotiation, are deadlocked with respect to any dispute existing between them arising in the collective bargaining process, the parties jointly, may petition the commission in writing, to initiate fact finding under this section, and to make recommendations to resolve the deadlock.

(2) Upon receipt of a petition to initiate fact-finding, the commission shall make an investigation with or without a formal hearing, to determine whether a deadlock exists. After its investigation, the commission shall certify the results thereof. If the commission decides that fact-finding should be initiated, it shall appoint a qualified, disinterested person or three-member panel, when jointly requested by the parties, to function as a fact finder.

(3) The fact finder may establish dates and place of hearings and shall conduct the hearings under rules established by the commission. Upon request, the commission shall issue subpoenas for hearings conducted by the fact finder. The fact finder may administer oaths. Upon completion of the hearing, the fact finder shall make written findings of fact and recommendations for solution of the dispute and shall cause the same to be served on the parties and the commission. In making such findings and recommendations, the fact finder shall take into consideration among other pertinent factors the principles vital to the public interest in efficient and economical governmental administration. Cost of fact-finding proceedings shall be divided equally between the parties. At the time the fact finder submits a statement of his costs to the parties, he shall submit a copy thereof to the commission at its Madison office.

(4) Nothing herein shall be construed as prohibiting any fact finder from endeavoring to mediate the dispute at any time prior to the issuance of his recommendations.

(5) Within 30 days of the receipt of the fact finder's recommendations or within such time period as is mutually agreed upon by the parties, each party shall advise each other, in writing, as to his acceptance or rejection, in whole or in part, of the fact finder's recommendations and, at the same time, send a copy of such notification to the commission at its Madison office. Failure to comply with this subsection, by the state employer or employe representative constitutes a violation of Sec. 111.84(1)(d) or (2)(c).

**Sec. 111.89. Strike prohibited.** (1) Upon establishing that a strike is in progress, the employer may either seek an injunction or file an unfair labor practice charge with the commission under Sec. 111.84(2)(e) or both. In this regard it shall be the responsibility of the department of employment relations to decide whether to seek an injunction or file an unfair labor practice charge. The existence of an administrative remedy shall not constitute grounds for denial of injunctive relief.

(2) The occurrence of a strike and the participation therein by a state employe do not affect the rights of the employer, in law or in equity, to deal with the strike, including:

(a) The right to impose discipline, including discharge, or suspension without pay, of any employe participating therein;

(b) The right to cancel the reinstatement eligibility of any employe engaging therein; and

(c) The right of the employer to request the imposition of fines, either against the labor organization or the employe engaging therein, or to sue for damages because of such strike activity.

**Sec. 111.90. Management rights.** Nothing in this subchapter shall interfere with the right of the employer, in accordance with this subchapter to:

(1) Carry out the statutory mandate and goals assigned to the agency utilizing personnel, methods and means in the most appropriate and efficient manner possible.

(2) Manage the employes of the agency; hire, promote, transfer, assign or retain employes in positions within the agency; and in that regard to establish reasonable work rules.

(3) Suspend, demote, discharge or take other appropriate disciplinary action against the employe for just cause; or to lay off employes in the event of lack of work or funds or under conditions where continuation of such work would be inefficient and nonproductive.

**Sec. 111.91. Subjects of bargaining.** (1)(a) Except as provided in paragraphs (b) to (e), matters subject to collective bargaining to the point of impasse are wage rates, as related to general salary scheduled adjustments consistent with subsection (2), and salary adjustments upon temporary assignment of employes to duties of a higher classification or downward reallocations of an employe's position; fringe benefits; hours and conditions of employment.

(b) The employer shall not be required to bargain on management rights under Sec. 111.90, except that procedures for the adjustment or settlement of grievances or disputes arising out of any type of disciplinary action referred to in Sec. 111.90(3) shall be a subject of bargaining.

(c) The employer shall be prohibited from bargaining on matters contained in sub. (2), except as provided under sub. (3).

(d) Demands relating to retirement and group insurance shall be submitted to the employer at least one year prior to commencement of negotiations.

(e) The employer shall not be required to bargain on matters related to employee occupancy of houses or other lodging provided by the state.

(2) Except as provided in sub. (3), the employer is prohibited from bargaining on:

(a) The mission and goals of state agencies as set forth in the statutes.

(b) Policies, practices and procedures of the civil service merit system relating to:

1.  Original appointments and promotions specifically including recruitment, examinations, certification, appointments, and policies with respect to probationary periods.

2.  The job evaluation system specifically including position classification, position qualification standards, establishment and abolition of classifications, assignment and reassignment of classifications to salary ranges, and allocation and reallocation of positions to classifications, and the determination of an incumbent's status resulting from position reallocations.

(c) Disciplinary actions and position abandonments governed by Sec. 230.34(1)(a), (am) and (ar), except as provided in those paragraphs.

(d) Amendments to this subchapter.

(3) The employer may bargain and reach agreement with a labor organization which is certified or recognized to represent a collective bargaining unit composed of classified employees to provide for an impartial hearing officer to hear appeals on differences arising under actions taken by the employer under sub. (2)(b)1 and 2. The hearing officer shall make a decision accompanied by findings of fact and conclusions of law. The decision shall be reviewed by the personnel commission under Sec. 230.45(1)(f) on the record and either affirmed, modified or reversed, and the personnel commission's action is subject to review under Ch. 227. This subsection does not empower the hearing officer to expand the basis of adjudication beyond the test of "arbitrary

and capricious" action, nor does this subsection diminish the authority of the personnel commission under Sec. 230.45.

\* \* \*

**Sec. 111.92. Agreements.** (1) Tentative agreements reached between the department of employment relations, acting for the executive branch, and any certified labor organization shall, after official ratification by the labor organization, be submitted to the joint committee on employment relations, which shall hold a public hearing before determining its approval or disapproval. If the committee approves the tentative agreement, it shall introduce in a bill or companion bills, to be put on the calendar, or referred to the appropriate scheduling committee of each house, that portion of the tentative agreement which requires legislative action for implementation, such as salary and wage adjustments, changes in fringe benefits, and any proposed amendments, deletions or additions to existing law. Such bill or companion bills shall not be subject to Secs. 13.093(1), 13.50(6)(a) and (b) and 16.47(2). The committee may, however, submit suitable portions of the tentative agreement to appropriate legislative committees for advisory recommendations on the proposed terms. The committee shall accompany the introduction of such proposed legislation with a message that informs the legislature of the committee's concurrence with the matters under consideration and which recommends the passage of such legislation without change. If the joint committee on employment relations does not approve the tentative agreement, it shall be returned to the parties for renegotiation. If the legislature does not adopt without change that portion of the tentative agreement introduced by the joint committee on employment relations, the tentative agreement shall be returned to the parties for negotiation.

(2) No portion of any tentative agreement shall become effective separately.

(3) Agreements shall coincide with the fiscal year or biennium.

(4) It is the declared intention under this subchapter that the negotiation of collective bargaining agreements and their approval by the parties should coincide with the overall fiscal planning and processes of the state.

(5) Notwithstanding any other provision of the statutes, all compensation adjustments for state employees shall be effective on the beginning date of the pay period nearest the statutory or administrative date.

\* \* \*

# FIRST AMENDMENT RIGHTS OF EMPLOYEES

### Secs. 31-51q.

### Connecticut, 1983.

Any employer, including the state and any instrumentality or political subdivision thereof, who subjects any employee to discipline or discharge on account of the exercise by such employee of rights guaranteed by the First Amendment to the U.S. Constitution or Sec. 3, 4 or 14 of Article 1 of the Constitution of the State, provided such activity does not substantially or materially interfere with the employee's bona fide job performance or the working relationship between the employee and the employer, shall be liable to such employee for damages caused by such discipline or discharge, including punitive damages, and for reasonable attorney's fees as part of the costs of any such action for damages. If the court determines that such action for damages was brought without substantial justification, the court may award costs and reasonable attorney's fees to the employer.

———

# FORMS AND DOCUMENTS

---

## EEOC CHARGE

(PLEASE PRINT OR TYPE)

| APPROVED BY OMB<br><br>3046—0011<br>Expires 12/31/83 | CHARGE OF DISCRIMINATION<br><br>IMPORTANT: This form is affected by the Privacy Act of 1974; see Privacy Act Statement on reverse before completing it. | CHARGE NUMBER(S) (AGENCY USE ONLY)<br>☐ EEOC |
|---|---|---|

Equal Employment Opportunity Commission

| NAME (Indicate Mr., Ms. or Mrs.) | HOME TELEPHONE NUMBER (Include area code) |
|---|---|
| STREET ADDRESS | |
| CITY, STATE, AND ZIP CODE | COUNTY |

NAMED IS THE EMPLOYER, LABOR ORGANIZATION, EMPLOYMENT AGENCY, APPRENTICESHIP COMMITTEE, STATE OR LOCAL GOVERNMENT AGENCY WHO DISCRIMINATED AGAINST ME. (If more than one list below).

| NAME | TELEPHONE NUMBER (Include area code) |
|---|---|
| STREET ADDRESS          CITY, STATE, AND ZIP CODE | |

| NAME | TELEPHONE NUMBER (Include area code) |
|---|---|
| STREET ADDRESS          CITY, STATE, AND ZIP CODE | |

CAUSE OF DISCRIMINATION BASED ON MY (Check appropriate box(es))

☐ RACE    ☐ COLOR    ☐ SEX    ☐ RELIGION    ☐ NATIONAL ORIGIN    ☐ OTHER (Specify)

DATE MOST RECENT OR CONTINUING DISCRIMINATION TOOK PLACE (*Month, day, and year*)

THE PARTICULARS ARE:

[E5935]

# FROM NLRB CHARGE TO COURT ENFORCEMENT

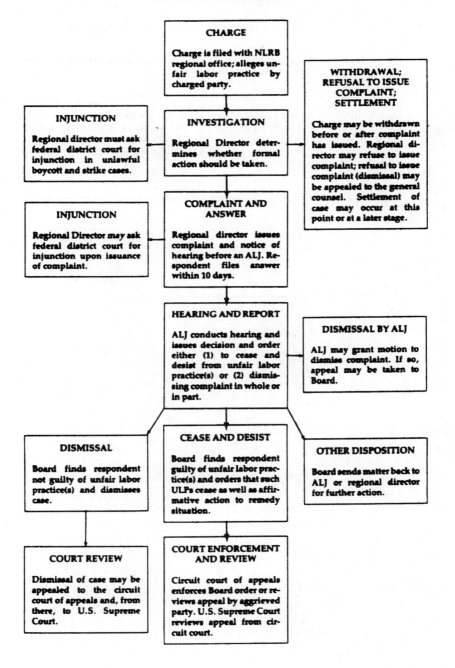

**CHARGE**

Charge is filed with NLRB regional office; alleges unfair labor practice by charged party.

**WITHDRAWAL; REFUSAL TO ISSUE COMPLAINT; SETTLEMENT**

Charge may be withdrawn before or after complaint has issued. Regional director may refuse to issue complaint; refusal to issue complaint (dismissal) may be appealed to the general counsel. Settlement of case may occur at this point or at a later stage.

**INJUNCTION**

Regional director must ask federal district court for injunction in unlawful boycott and strike cases.

**INVESTIGATION**

Regional Director determines whether formal action should be taken.

**INJUNCTION**

Regional Director may ask federal district court for injunction upon issuance of complaint.

**COMPLAINT AND ANSWER**

Regional director issues complaint and notice of hearing before an ALJ. Respondent files answer within 10 days.

**HEARING AND REPORT**

ALJ conducts hearing and issues decision and order either (1) to cease and desist from unfair labor practice(s) or (2) dismissing complaint in whole or in part.

**DISMISSAL BY ALJ**

ALJ may grant motion to dismiss complaint. If so, appeal may be taken to Board.

**DISMISSAL**

Board finds respondent not guilty of unfair labor practice(s) and dismisses case.

**CEASE AND DESIST**

Board finds respondent guilty of unfair labor practice(s) and orders that such ULPs cease as well as affirmative action to remedy situation.

**OTHER DISPOSITION**

Board sends matter back to ALJ or regional director for further action.

**COURT REVIEW**

Dismissal of case may be appealed to the circuit court of appeals and, from there, to U.S. Supreme Court.

**COURT ENFORCEMENT AND REVIEW**

Circuit court of appeals enforces Board order or reviews appeal by aggrieved party. U.S. Supreme Court reviews appeal from circuit court.

## SAMPLE AUTHORIZATION CARD

Date of signing _____

I, _____ , now employed by
                (print your name here)

_____ (name of company)
have voluntarily accepted membership in the United Factory Workers
Union (AFL-CIO) and designate said Union as my collective bargaining
agent in all matters pertaining to wages, hours and other conditions of
employment. I hereby further subscribe to the dues deduction provisions
printed on the reverse side of this card.

Signed _____

_____
(Signer's home address)

_____
(Phone No.)

# NLRB PETITION FOR ELECTION

FORM NLRB-502
(11 64)

UNITED STATES OF AMERICA
NATIONAL LABOR RELATIONS BOARD

## PETITION

| DO NOT WRITE IN THIS SPACE |
| --- |
| CASE NO |
| DATE FILED |

INSTRUCTIONS—Submit an original and four (4) copies of this Petition to the N.L.R.B. Regional Office in the Region in which the employer concerned is located.
If more space is required for any one item attach additional sheets, numbering item accordingly.

The Petitioner alleges that the following circumstances exist and requests that the National Labor Relations Board proceed under its proper authority pursuant to Section 9 of the National Labor Relations Act.

1. Purpose of this Petition (If box RC, RM or RD is checked and a charge under Section 8(b)(7) of the Act has been filed involving the Employer named herein, the statement following the description of the type of petition shall not be deemed made.)
(Check one)

☒ RC—CERTIFICATION OF REPRESENTATIVE—A substantial number of employees wish to be represented for purposes of collective bargaining by Petitioner and Petitioner desires to be certified as representative of the employees.

☐ RM—REPRESENTATION (EMPLOYER PETITION)—One or more individuals or labor organizations have presented a claim to Petitioner to be recognized as the representative of employees of Petitioner.

☐ RD—DECERTIFICATION—A substantial number of employees assert that the certified or currently recognized bargaining representative is no longer their representative.

☐ UD—WITHDRAWAL OF UNION SHOP AUTHORITY—Thirty percent (30%) or more of employees in a bargaining unit covered by an agreement between their employer and a labor organization desire that such authority be rescinded.

☐ UC—UNIT CLARIFICATION—A labor organization is currently recognized by employer, but petitioner seeks clarification of placement of certain employees:
(Check one) ☐ In unit not previously certified
☐ In unit previously certified in Case No. _____

☐ AC—AMENDMENT OF CERTIFICATION—Petitioner seeks amendment of certification issued in Case No. _____
Attach statement describing the specific amendment sought.

| 2. NAME OF EMPLOYER<br>Enderby Industries, Inc. | EMPLOYER REPRESENTATIVE TO CONTACT<br>M. Crickboom | PHONE NO<br>426-7000 |
| --- | --- | --- |

3. ADDRESS(ES) OF ESTABLISHMENT(S) INVOLVED (Street and number, city, State, and ZIP Code)
Brown's Pond Industrial Park, U.S. Highway 81

| 4a. TYPE OF ESTABLISHMENT (Factory, mine, wholesaler, etc.)<br>Factory | 4b. IDENTIFY PRINCIPAL PRODUCT OR SERVICE<br>Rubber and Plastic Products |
| --- | --- |

5. Unit Involved in (In UC position, describe PRESENT bargaining unit and attach description of proposed clarification.)

Included   All production and maintenance employees, including technicians, in the employer's Rubber Division.

Excluded   All supervisors (including leadmen), professionals, and guards as defined in the Act.

| 6a. NUMBER OF EMPLOYEES IN UNIT |
| --- |
| PRESENT   120 |
| PROPOSED (BY UC/AC) |

6b. IS THIS PETITION SUPPORTED BY 30% OR MORE OF THE EMPLOYEES

☒ YES    ☐ NO

* Not applicable in RM, UC, and AC

(If you have checked box RC in 1 above, check and complete EITHER item 7a or 7b, whichever is applicable)

7a. ☒ Request for recognition as Bargaining Representative was made on February 18, 1995 and Employer
(Month, day, year)

declined recognition on or about March 1, 1995 (If no reply received, so state)
(Month, day, year)

7b. ☐ Petitioner is currently recognized as Bargaining Representative and desires certification under the act.

8. Recognized or Certified Bargaining Agent (If there is none, so state)

| NAME | AFFILIATION |
| --- | --- |
| ADDRESS | DATE OF RECOGNITION OR CERTIFICATION |

| 9. DATE OF EXPIRATION OF CURRENT CONTRACT, IF ANY (Show month, day, and year)<br><br>None | 10. IF YOU HAVE CHECKED BOX UD IN 1 ABOVE, SHOW HERE THE DATE OF EXECUTION OF AGREEMENT GRANTING UNION SHOP (Month, day, and year) |
| --- | --- |

| 11a. IS THERE NOW A STRIKE OR PICKETING AT THE EMPLOYER'S ESTABLISHMENT(S) INVOLVED?<br>YES ...... NO  X | 11b. IF SO, APPROXIMATELY HOW MANY EMPLOYEES ARE PARTICIPATING? |
| --- | --- |

11c. THE EMPLOYER HAS BEEN PICKETED BY OR ON BEHALF OF ......................................................... A
(Insert name)

LABOR ORGANIZATION, OF ...................................................... SINCE ..................
(Insert address)                                         (Month, day, year)

12. ORGANIZATIONS OR INDIVIDUALS OTHER THAN PETITIONER (AND OTHER THAN THOSE NAMED IN ITEMS 8 AND 11c) WHICH HAVE CLAIMED RECOGNITION AS REPRESENTATIVES AND OTHER ORGANIZATIONS AND INDIVIDUALS KNOWN TO HAVE A REPRESENTATIVE INTEREST IN ANY EMPLOYEES IN THE UNIT DESCRIBED IN ITEM 5 ABOVE. (IF NONE, SO STATE.)

| NAME | AFFILIATION | ADDRESS | DATE OF CLAIM (Required only if Petition is filed by Employer) |
| --- | --- | --- | --- |
|  |  |  |  |
|  |  |  |  |

I declare that I have read the above petition and that the statements therein are true to the best of my knowledge and belief.

United Factory Workers of America
(Petitioner and affiliation, if any)

By /s/ Ruth Blair                                                   ☐ Regional Organizer
(Signature of representative or person filing petition)              (Title, if any)

Address 17 Union Square, New York, New York                          (212)498-8600
(Street and number, city, State and ZIP Code)                        (Telephone number)

WILLFULLY FALSE STATEMENT ON THIS PETITION CAN BE PUNISHED BY FINE AND IMPRISONMENT (U.S. CODE, TITLE 18, SECTION 1001)

[E5936]

# NLRB CHARGE AGAINST EMPLOYER

## (Ptolemy Discharge)

FORM NLRB–501
·2-67·

### UNITED STATES OF AMERICA
### NATIONAL LABOR RELATIONS BOARD

### CHARGE AGAINST EMPLOYER

| INSTRUCTIONS: File an original and 4 copies of this charge with NLRB regional director for the region in which the alleged unfair labor practice occurred or is occurring. | DO NOT WRITE IN THIS SPACE |
|---|---|
| | Case No. |
| | Date Filed |

### 1. EMPLOYER AGAINST WHOM CHARGE IS BROUGHT

| a. Name of Employer<br>Mercy Hospital | b. Number of Workers Employed<br>250 | |
|---|---|---|
| c. Address of Establishment (Street and number, city, State, and ZIP code)<br>Comfort Drive<br>Center City | d. Employer Representative to Contact | e. Phone No. |
| f. Type of Establishment (Factory, mine, wholesaler, etc.)<br>Hospital | g. Identify Principal Product or Service<br>Health Care | |

h. The above-named employer has engaged in and is engaging in unfair labor practices within the meaning of section 8(a), subsections (1) and (3) _____ of the National Labor Relations Act,
_____ (List subsections)

and these unfair labor practices are unfair labor practices affecting commerce within the meaning of the Act.

2. Basis of the Charge (Be specific as to facts, names, addresses, plants involved, dates, places, etc.)

On or about September 15, 19 , the above named employer, by its officers, employees or agents, discriminated against H. Ptolemy by discharging Ptolemy in order to discourage union activity.

By this and other acts the above named employer has interfered with the Section 7 rights of its employees.

By the above and other acts, the above-named employer has interfered with, restrained, and coerced employees in the exercise of the rights guaranteed in Section 7 of the Act.

3. Full Name of Party Filing Charge (If labor organization, give full name, including local name and number)
Unified Medical Care Association

| 4a. Address (Street and number, city, State, and ZIP code)<br>12 Random Road<br>Eugene, Oregon | 4b. Telephone No.<br>(503) 259-7040 |
|---|---|

5. Full Name of National or International Labor Organization of Which It Is an Affiliate or Constituent Unit (To be filled in when charge is filed by a labor organization)

### 6. DECLARATION

I declare that I have read the above charge and that the statements therein are true to the best of my knowledge and belief.

By _____*E. Walker*_____      International Representative
(Signature of representative or person filing charge)      (Title, if any)

Address _____    _____    9/11/
                                            (Telephone number)        (Date)

WILLFULLY FALSE STATEMENTS ON THIS CHARGE CAN BE PUNISHED BY FINE AND IMPRISONMENT (U.S. CODE, TITLE 18 SECTION 1001)

[E5937]

# OSHA COMPLAINT

U.S. DEPARTMENT OF LABOR

OCCUPATIONAL SAFETY AND HEALTH ADMINISTRATION

????????
OMB No. 044RI449

| For Official Use Only | | |
|---|---|---|
| Area | Date Received | Time |
| Region | Received By | |

### COMPLAINT

This form is provided for the assistance of any complainant and is not intended to constitute the exclusive means by which a complaint may be registered with the U.S. Department of Labor.

The undersigned *(check one)*

☐ Employee  ☐ Representative of employees  ☐ Other *(specify)* ————
believes that a violation at the following place of employment of an occupational safety or health standard exists which is a job safety or health hazard.

Does this hazard(s) immediately threaten death or serious physical harm?  ☐ Yes  ☐ No

Employer's Name ——————————————————————————
(Street ———————————————————— Telephone ——————

Address    (
(City ——————————— State ————— Zip Code ————

1. Kind of business ——————————————————
2. Specify the particular building or worksite where the alleged violation is located, including address. ————

3. Specify the name and phone number of employer's agent(s) in charge.

4. Describe briefly the hazard which exists there including the approximate number of employees exposed to or threatened by such hazard.

*(Continue on reverse side if necessary)*

Sec. 8(f)(1) of the Williams-Steiger Occupational Safety and Health Act, 29 U.S.C. 651, provides as follows: Any employees or representative of employees who believe that a violation of a safety or health standard exists that threatens physical harm, or that an imminent danger exists, may request an inspection by giving notice to the Secretary or his authorized representative of such violation or danger. Any such notice shall be reduced to writing, shall set forth with reasonable particularity the grounds for the notice, and shall be signed by the employees or representative of employees, and a copy shall be provided the employer or his agent no later than at the time of inspection, except that, upon request of the person giving such notice, his name and the names of individual employees referred to therein shall not appear in such copy or on any record published, released, or made available pursuant to subsection (g) of this section. If upon receipt of such notification the Secretary determines there are reasonable grounds to believe that such violation or danger exists, he shall make a special inspection in accordance with the provisions of this section as soon as practicable, to determine if such violation or danger exists. If the Secretary determines there are no reasonable grounds to believe that a violation or danger exists he shall notify the employees or representative of the employees in writing of such determination.

[E5938]    Form OSHA-7
Rev. Jan. 1972

5. List by number and/or name the particular standard *(or standards)* issued by the Department of Labor which you claim has been violated, if known.

_____

_____

_____

6. (a) To your knowledge has this violation been considered previously by any Government agency? _____

_____

(b) If so, please state the name of the agency _____

(c) and, the approximate date it was so considered. _____

7. (a) Is this complaint, or a complaint alleging a similar violation, being filed with any other Government agency?

_____

(b) If so, give the name and address of each. _____

8. (a) To your knowledge, has this violation been the subject of any union/management grievance or have you *(or anyone you know)* otherwise called it to the attention of, or discussed it with, the employer or any representative thereof? _____

_____

(b) If so, please give the results thereof, including any efforts by management to correct the violation. _____

_____

9. Please indicate your desire:

☐ I do not want my name revealed to the employer.
☐ My name may be revealed to the employer.

*Continue Item 4 here, if additional space is needed.*

_____

_____

_____

_____

_____

**COMPLAINANT'S NAME**

— — — — — — — — — — — — — — — — — — — — — —

*Signature* _____ *Date* _____

*Typed or Printed Name* _____

      *(Street* _____ *Telephone* _____

*Address*   *(*

      *(City* _____ *State* _____ *Zip Code* _____

*If you are a representative of employees,*
*state the name of your organization* _____

[E5939]

†